"Edmund Chia has provided a marvelous service for the teaching of interreligious dialogue at practically every level of theological education. Only someone who, like Dr. Chia, has spent his life in actual interfaith dialogue could lay out the issues so clearly and simply, but with real profundity. This is a wonderfully conceived book, very learned and yet very accessible at the same time. It is truly what it sets out to be: a *summa* of interreligious dialogue. Teachers will find it teachable. Students will find it readable. Everyone will find it valuable."

    —Stephen Bevans, SVD
        Professor Emeritus of Mission and Culture
        Catholic Theological Union

"This is an original and comprehensive introduction to the encounter between world Christianity and world religions. The book covers the latest scholarly debates, yet it is written in comprehensible language. Rooted in his longtime Southeast Asian experience, the author succeeds in writing about polarities in thinking about interfaith dialogue in a holistic way."

    —Frans Wijsen
        Chair of Empirical & Practical Religious Studies
        Radboud University, The Netherlands

"Drawing on his broad scholarship and years of practical experience, Dr. Chia has indeed assembled a 'summa' of interfaith dialogue. He carefully and clearly introduces students/readers to the history, the methods, and the promise of religious traditions and peoples coming together to learn from each other and work together to fix the world. He both informs and inspires."

    —Paul Knitter
        Paul Tillich Professor Emeritus
        Union Theological Seminary, New York City

"*World Christianity Encounters World Religion* is a masterful summation of our multi-faceted religious reality that only the rare scholar and practitioner as experienced, insightful, and reflective as Edmund Kee-Fook Chia would dare to write. It is well-informed by the theology and lived experience of the church in Asia and attentive to the many ways in which Christians have encountered and do encounter people of other faith traditions in Asia's diverse contexts. A text for teaching, it will work well in an introductory course on world Christianity or in a course on interreligious dialogue—and yet it can also serve as a handy reference work for leaders and practitioners in the field."

—Francis X. Clooney, SJ
Parkman Professor of Divinity
Harvard University

"Dr. Chia discusses the changing shape of world Christianity and the history and theology of interfaith dialogue as an astute scholar and a leader of dialogue for decades. This book is a *summa* in the best sense: comprehensive, erudite, clearly organized, and yet accessible and not jargonish. It is a gift to students, teachers, and the church and deserves to be widely read."

—Kwok Pui-Lan
Visiting Professor at Candler School of Theology
Emory University

WORLD CHRISTIANITY
encounters
WORLD RELIGIONS

A Summa *of Interfaith Dialogue*

Edmund Kee-Fook Chia

Foreword by Archbishop Michael L. Fitzgerald

**LITURGICAL PRESS
ACADEMIC**

Collegeville, Minnesota
www.litpress.org

Library of Congress Cataloging-in-Publication Data

Names: Chia, Edmund, author. I Fitzgerald, Michael, 1937– writer of foreword.

Title: World Christianity encounters world religions : a summa of interfaith dialogue / Edmund Kee-Fook Chia ; foreword by Archbishop Michael Fitzgerald.

Description: Collegeville, Minnesota : Liturgical Press Academic, Liturgical Press, 2018. I Includes bibliographical references and index.

Identifiers: LCCN 2018016785 (print) I LCCN 2018020420 (ebook) I ISBN 9780814684474 (ebook) I ISBN 9780814684221

Subjects: LCSH: Christianity and other religions.

Classification: LCC BR127 (ebook) I LCC BR127 .C414 2018 (print) I DDC 261.2—dc23

LC record available at https://lccn.loc.gov/2018016785

To
Gemma

Contents

PART 3
THEOLOGIES AND PRAXES

Foreword

Religious pluralism is not a new phenomenon. If we look at the scriptures, we see that the Jewish people, chosen by God to bear witness to monotheism, had to accomplish their mission in a religiously pluralistic environment. Christianity also soon became aware of religious pluralism. Having developed as distinct from Judaism, it encountered polytheism and was confronted with emperor worship and Eastern cults such as Mithraism. As Christianity spread from the Mediterranean area to other parts of the world it met with other religious expressions. It found itself face-to-face with a new religion, Islam, but there were also Hinduism, Buddhism, and other religions that developed in Asia. On the Asian continent Christianity has always been, and, apart from in the Philippines, still is, a minority religion.

If even regarding the past it would be incorrect to see the world divided into religious "blocs"—Christianity, Islam, Buddhism, Hinduism, with only the Jews, because of their dispersal, scattered to various regions—this would reflect present reality even less. With the increased mobility of the modern world, the religions are brought into contact with each other more than ever. So there is a need for Christians to understand what the encounter with world religions means for them and for others. The purpose of the present book is to help them to fulfill this need.

Edmund Chia is well suited to this task. As a Christian of Asian origin himself, he has lived and practiced his Christian faith in a pluralistic environment. He has excellent academic qualifications, but moreover he has had professional experience in promoting interfaith relations. He certainly knows what he is talking about.

As Chia points out, interfaith dialogue can be learned only through actual practice. This *summa* can serve as a useful guide and a tool for verification. The suggestions for further reading at the end of each chapter provide indications for deeper understanding.

Archbishop Michael L. Fitzgerald
Past President of the Vatican's Pontifical Council
for Interreligious Dialogue
Former Apostolic Nuncio in Egypt and Delegate
to the League of Arab States

Preface

When we approach a person who professes his religion with conviction, his testimony and thoughts ask us and lead us to question our own spirituality. Dialogue, thus, begins with *encounter*. The first knowledge of the other is born from it. Indeed, if one begins from the premise of the common affiliation in *human nature*, one can go beyond prejudices and fallacies and begin to understand the other according to a new perspective.

—Pope Francis[1]

The notions of "world Christianity" and "world religions" are relatively new in the history of the study of religion. The former evolved in the academy when Western Christians became more conscious of non-Western Christianity, and the latter when Christian scholars became more conscious of religions other than Christianity. The encounter between them has become commonplace since the mid-twentieth century and is more widely known today as interfaith dialogue. The present book is about this encounter. It sums up practically everything that needs to be known about world Christianity's encounter with world religions; it is a *summa* on interfaith dialogue. It presents in a single volume a systematic and relatively comprehensive survey of all the dimensions related to or impinging on interfaith dialogue. The term "interfaith" is used here broadly to represent all forms of faith engagements: between different

---

1. Pope Francis, "To Participants in the Meeting Sponsored by the Pontifical Institute for Arabic and Islamic Studies on the Fiftieth Anniversary of Its Establishment in Rome" (January 24, 2015), https://w2.vatican.va/content/francesco/en/speeches/2015/january/documents/papa-francesco_20150124_pisai.html.

religious faith traditions, between different Christian faith denominations, and with peoples who do not identify with any religion.

This book's starting point is the importance of encounter between persons of different faith convictions. The encounters facilitate new knowledge, which can help us not only to correct prejudices and fallacies but also to appreciate the religious other from new perspectives. This is one of the principal aims of interfaith dialogue, a ministry that has become integral to the mission of the church in the religiously plural world of the twenty-first century. This is what the book highlights. It first explores, in part 1, the basics of Christianity, religion, and dialogue, moving on, in part 2, to discuss the bases for interfaith dialogue as found in Christian Scripture and tradition, and culminating, in part 3, with an exposition of the theologies and praxes of interfaith dialogue.

The three chapters of part 1 offer a quick glimpse of what is meant by world Christianity, world religions, and the encounter between them. Appreciating the history of Christianity, especially from its origins and looking at its heterogeneous tradition, helps in the appreciation of the advent of the notion of world Christianity. Likewise, appreciating the phenomenon of religion, by examining the history of its study and the related concepts of faith and spirituality, also helps in the appreciation of the nineteenth-century invention of the idea of world religions. As the encounter between Christianity and the world's religions is the concern of the book, the what, why, how, and when of interfaith dialogue are clarified from the outset. Specifically, it will be pointed out that there are different kinds or levels of dialogue, known in academic circles as the (1) dialogue of life, (2) dialogue of action, (3) dialogue of theology, and (4) dialogue of religious experience.

Part 2 consists of four chapters that survey the biblical and theological resources within the Christian tradition that can be garnered to attend to peoples outside of its fold. It begins by looking at the problem of biblical interpretation and especially how and where the Bible portrays themes of exclusiveness and also of inclusiveness. Likewise, how Christian theology over the centuries has been dealing with those who are not Christians or those who abandon their faith will be discussed, with special reference to the question of salvation. An integral part of the church's teaching tradition is the contributions of the Second Vatican Council. This will be assessed, especially what it teaches about other religions and how these teachings have been interpreted and implemented by the post–Vatican

II papacies. Also important to explore is the experience of the Asian Church, which has had a long and rich history relating with its religious neighbors. In particular, the thesis of the triple dialogue advanced by the Federation of Asian Bishops' Conferences will be spelled out.

The five chapters of part 3 offer an overview of the theologies and praxes that have developed in dealing with the reality of pluralism within as well as without the church. The actual praxis of dialogue between the different Christian denominations will be the first to be examined. The focus in this chapter is on the evolution of the modern ecumenical movement and the invitation to embrace the wider ecumenism. Next to be looked at are the numerous theologies of religious pluralism that have surfaced in recent decades, focusing on the contributions of eight pioneering figures and specific themes associated with each of them. The dialogue of theology and spirituality is then discussed by looking at the exercise of scriptural reasoning, the dynamics of cross-textual herme- neutics, the practice of comparative theology, and the cross-participation of believers in interfaith worship. An example of theological dialogue is then illustrated by examining the study of the Islamic critique of the Christian faith. This is no doubt the most urgent and sensitive dialogue for Christianity today since Islam is its most significant dialogue partner in the contemporary geopolitical world. Finally, the implications and challenges of religious pluralism will be deliberated by probing the phenomenon of religious syncretism and multiple religious belonging, as well as the response of theological education and Catholic educa- tional institutions. The book concludes by examining one of the most problematic challenges of religious pluralism to the church, that is, the mission-dialogue dialectics, but it will do so by engaging with a parable that, in turn, raises more questions for further discussion.

As is obvious from the chapter overview above, this book briefly addresses quite a number of topics related to interfaith dialogue and the encounter of world Christianity and world religions. Volumes have already been written on each of the topics, and so this book is intention- ally introductory in scope. It synthesizes the works of the most prominent scholars on each of the topics addressed. It can be used in undergraduate or graduate theology programs in seminaries or universities, especially where the curriculum has space for only one or two courses that address Christianity's relationship with other religions. Whether the course is titled "Comparative Theology," "Interreligious Dialogue," "Christianity and Other Faiths," "Theology of Religions," or "Religious Pluralism," the present book should be a valuable starting point. It is written for students and lecturers who come from Christian backgrounds—whether practicing or not—or who have greater familiarity with the Christian ethos as compared to their knowledge of other religions. It is also written for the intelligent and questioning layperson who may have little or no background in the study of theology but who wishes to explore the intricacies related to interfaith dialogue. The book is presented in as uncomplicated a fashion as possible, avoiding technical theological jargon, using minimal footnotes and references, and keeping to the textbook format so that it can be used in the course of a semester. The chapters can stand alone or be read sequentially. A list of suggested readings is provided at the end of each chapter and references are made in footnotes only to texts that are deemed important to the topic.

I have been teaching courses related to Christianity's encounter with other religions for more than two decades, both at a seminary in the United States and now at a university in Australia and also through formation programs run in various parts of Asia. But my interest in this field probably has its roots in my childhood, raised as I was in Malaysia as a Christian with grandparents and most other relatives who adhere to the Chinese religions of Confucianism, Taoism, and Buddhism. I was thus as used to participating in the rites and rituals of the Chinese religions as I was reciting the rosary or attending Sunday Mass. I also had more classmates who were Muslims, Hindus, Buddhists, and Sikhs than Christians, and the first school I taught at was in a predominantly Muslim village where only 1 percent of its student population was Christian. As a young De La Salle brother I was often invited to run faith formation youth camps for students of multireligious backgrounds. All of these experiences predisposed me to interfaith dialogue even as I had not really engaged in any formal studies on the subject. Moreover, I never took seriously the compulsory Islamic education courses that were offered when I went to college in Malaysia.

It was not until I went to Washington, DC, where I had the opportunity to study the world's religions with scholars such as William Cenkner, OP, and James Wiseman, OSB, at the Catholic University of America, as well as with Alf Hiltebeitel and Seyyed Hossein Nasr at George Washington University. My eight years as executive secretary for ecumenism and interreligious dialogue of the Federation of Asian Bishops' Conferences was yet another opportunity for further learning as I participated in numerous encounters with persons of other religions throughout the Asian continent. I was also mentored by my predecessor Thomas Michel, SJ, and greatly inspired by bishops I worked with, namely, Bishop Lawrence Thienchai, Cardinal Orlando Quevedo, Cardinal Chito Tagle, and Archbishop Ignatius Suharyo, as well as Archbishop Michael Fitzgerald and Archbishop Felix Machado who were at the Pontifical Council for Interreligious Dialogue at that time. Also inspirational were the Asian theologians I interacted with, especially Michael Amaladoss, SJ, Aloysius Pieris, SJ, Sebastian Painadath, SJ, Mary John Mananzan, OSB, Virginia Fabella, MM, Wesley Ariarajah, Felix Wilfred, and Wong Wai Ching. Working on my doctorate at the University of Nijmegen was of course a period of intense research and study, but it was my personal encounters with Edward Schillebeeckx, OP, and the support of Professors Wilhelm Dupre and Frans Wijsen, among others, that made it momentous. My seven years on the faculty of the Catholic Theological Union in Chicago were also occasions for more learning, particularly with colleagues Robert Schreiter, CPPS, Stephen Bevans, SVD, Diane Bergant, CSA, John Pawlikowski, OSA, and the other great scholars serving as role models. My involvement with the Catholic Theological Society of America was yet another blessing as I received a lot of support from Peter Phan, Francis Clooney, SJ, Ruben Habito, Paul Knitter, Jeff Gros, FSC, Gerard Mannion and many of the other Catholic theologians. In Australia, my dialogue partners include my colleagues of the Interreligious Dialogue Network of the Australian Catholic University, the Ecumenical and Interfaith Commission of the Melbourne Archdiocese, and the Living Faiths Commission and also the Faith and Order Commission of the Victoria Council of Churches. All of these encounters and moments of grace have prepared me well not only to engage in interfaith dialogue but to also write about it convincingly.

The publication of this book would not have been possible if not for the unyielding support of Hans Christoffersen and his staff at Liturgical Press. Hans told me to ensure that the book is not too intimidating and so I had a few of my best students read the drafts. I am grateful especially to Milani Arena and Victoria Caitlin Sophie-Louise Sharples, both of whom read through most of the chapters and provided me with valuable feedback. I began the research for this book when I had the good fortune of spending a few months in early 2017 as an international fellow at the

Jesuit School of Theology, Santa Clara University. I am grateful to the dean and the faculty for their warm welcome and support. My thanks also go to Archbishop Fitzgerald for writing the foreword to this book and to all those wonderful colleagues who endorsed it. But most of all, I am eternally thankful to my parents, Albert and Monica, and siblings, Gabriel, Magdalene, and Richard, all of whom are in Malaysia, who have been a true source of unconditional support for my career all these years, and I am especially indebted to my lovely and loving wife, Gemma Cruz, who is my everlasting support and daily theological dialogue partner.

PART 1

CHRISTIANITY,
RELIGION,
AND DIALOGUE

1

From Christianity to World Christianity

Introduction

Every now and then I notice stunned faces and sometimes even receive overt protests from students when I mention that Jesus was not a Christian and that he did not go to Sunday Masses or participate in Holy Communion. Of course, the more informed will immediately blurt out that he was a Jew and so a follower of Judaism, the Jewish religion. But those who know next to nothing about the Christian faith automatically presume that Jesus must have been the exemplary Christian whom Christians of all generations are called to follow in discipleship. Christians, after all, take their name from Jesus Christ and have been taught, as the lyrics of the hymn goes, "to follow Christ and love the world as he did." It is difficult to imagine a Christ who is not Christian or that he is not a member of our own Christian denomination.

This chapter begins with a discussion of the Jewish roots of Christianity, shedding light especially on the context and theology that gave rise to the Christian movement. It then examines Christianity's growth and development, mainly in its initial years, highlighting the challenges the emerging community had to confront from the external world. That the Christian tradition is by no means homogenous is then presented, particularly in the context of Christian divisions over the centuries. The origins and characteristics of the different Christian denominations are delineated, pointing to theological as well as socio-political causes for the splits. Finally, the advent of the notion of world Christianity will be interrogated in the light of the demographic shift of the Christian world from the global North to the global South.

Jewish Roots of Christianity

Christianity has its origins in Jesus of Nazareth who clearly inspired a following that, after his death, went on to establish themselves as a religious community independent of the Jewish religion that they all hailed from. To be sure, Jesus, like most Jewish people in Galilee and Judea of the first century, was a faithful Jew who adhered to the basic tenets of Judaism, including its laws and customs. They observed the teachings of the faith as revealed to them through the Hebrew Scriptures, which is also known as the Jewish Bible. The various books that make up the Bible (the Torah, Prophets, and Writings) developed over roughly a millennium, the oldest sections believed to have come from around the tenth century BCE. A lot of the most important texts were edited while the Israelites were in exile in Babylon, an ancient Mesopotamian city located in present-day Iraq.

The Bible begins with the two stories of creation in the book of Genesis that depict God as creator of heaven and earth and all that dwells therein. Unlike the Babylonian creation myth, *Enuma Elish* (with its depiction of earthly creation in the context of the battles and murders among deities), the first chapter of Genesis speaks of creation in the context of God's blessings and of human beings as the apex of creation, created in God's own image (Gen 1:26-27). Just before God rested at the end of creation, human beings were instructed to be "fruitful and multiply" and were bestowed with the responsibility of being co-creators with God on earth (Gen 1:28). While God saw that the whole of creation "was very good" (Gen 1:31), creation is by nature not perfect and, therefore, subject to making mistakes, being weak, and even committing sinful and evil acts. A condition of finitude is what it means to be created, and it is in this context that the second creation account relates the story of Adam and Eve, highlighting humanity's sin and the Fall (Gen 2–3). The theological anthropology presented by the Bible is that of a God who is omnipotent love and mercy amid the brokenness of the created world and despite human frailty. Such is the nature of God and, more important, such is the nature of creation and humankind. The biblical creation myths serve as the foundation for all of Israel's theology, shaping the history of the people, speaking to their faithfulness as well as sinfulness throughout the centuries.

The accounts of the first eleven chapters of Genesis are actually in the realm of prehistory. The history of the Jewish people generally begins in Genesis 12, with the call of Abram (whose name God changed to Abraham): "Now the LORD said to Abram, 'Go from your country and your kindred and your father's house to the land that I will show you. I will make of you a great nation, and I will bless you, and make your name great, so that you will be a blessing'" (Gen 12:1-2). Abraham and his family moved and eventually settled in the Promised Land of Canaan, which is variously referred to as Israel, Judea, or Palestine. God later enters into a covenant with Abraham: "I will establish my covenant between me and you, and your offspring after you throughout their generations, for an everlasting covenant, to be God to you and to your offspring after you" (Gen 17:7). This covenant becomes the basis for the later theology of the Jews as God's chosen people and Israel as the land promised them by God. Abraham and his descendants made Canaan their home until a famine struck when his grandson Jacob—whose name God changed to Israel (Gen 32:28)—brought the whole family down to live in Egypt (Gen 46).

While initially the people of Israel were living in Egypt as guests of Pharaoh, with time they served as slaves and suffered oppression for many generations. Hearing their cries (albeit only after four hundred years!), God calls on Moses to liberate them from the bondage in Egypt and lead them back to Canaan, "a land flowing with milk and honey" (Exod 3:17). The exodus from Egypt and the journey back to the Promised Land are constitutive components of the theological history of the people of Israel. Beginning with the ten plagues that befell Egypt and the Passover meal, the Israelites escaped the pursuing Egyptian army by crossing the Red Sea and then wandered around the desert of the Sinai Peninsula for forty years. It was from Mount Sinai that Moses brought down the Ten Commandments and renewed the people's covenant with God. The Mosaic covenant or Law of Moses is recorded in the first five books of the Bible, collectively called the Torah. The Israelites eventually made their way back to Canaan, where the land was carved out and given to the descendants of the twelve sons of Jacob. They were subsequently organized into a confederacy of the twelve tribes of Israel and ruled by a series of military rulers called judges.

After several hundred years in the Promised Land, the Israelite monarchy was established under Saul and continued under King David and his son Solomon. Jerusalem became the national and spiritual capital, and it was there that King Solomon built the First Temple. Upon his death, however, war erupted between the tribes, which led eventually to the united kingdom being split into the kingdom of Israel (consisting of ten tribes in the north) and the kingdom of Judah (consisting of two tribes in the south). The neighboring Assyrians conquered the northern kingdom in the eighth century, resulting in the dispersion of the ten tribes of Israel. The Babylonians conquered the southern kingdom in 587 BCE, destroyed the First Temple, and exiled many of the Israelites to Babylon. It was in Babylon where the Israelites engaged in much soul searching and interpretation about God's covenant with Israel: "By the rivers of Babylon—there we sat down and there we wept when we remembered Zion" (Ps 137:1).

It was therefore while they were in exile that the people of Israel reflected on and redefined their preexisting ideas about the theologies of monotheism, election, divine law, and covenant; these ideas eventually evolved into a strict monotheistic faith. When the Persians defeated the Babylonians the Israelites were allowed to return to their homeland in 537 BCE, and the Second Temple was built later. The Macedonian Greeks under Alexander the Great conquered Israel in the fourth century, and in 64 BCE the Promised Land came under Roman rule. It was in the context of being dispossessed from the Promised Land that the Jewish people developed the theology of the messiah. He was to be the anointed leader who would liberate them from foreign rule and oppression and reestablish the one united kingdom in fulfillment of God's covenant with the people of Israel.

Birth and Development of Christianity

Jesus of Nazareth was born in the messianic age when Judea was under Roman rule and the people of Israel were subjugated. His teaching ministry in Galilee attracted a small group of Jewish disciples, some of whom might have believed that he was the long-awaited messiah who would liberate them from foreign occupation. But the horrific torture and crucifixion of their leader and master forced the disciples to rethink and reflect on his life and message against Hebrew Scriptures. Prophetic texts such as Isaiah 53, which speaks of the Suffering Servant of Israel—who was "despised and rejected by others" (v. 3), "wounded for our transgressions" (v. 5), as it was "the will of the LORD to crush him with pain" (v. 10), and "yet he bore the sin of many" (v. 12)—helped in their appreciation of who Jesus really was. Collapsing Isaiah's theology of the Suffering Servant with that of the Jewish theology of the messiah, they saw Jesus as representing the "Suffering Messiah." This was a profoundly new doctrine the nascent community of Jesus' disciples developed that was not found within the Jewish tradition. The shameful suffering and death of Jesus then not only made sense but also empowered the disciples. The death on the cross was not the end as Peter, the head of the disciples, asserts: "God raised him up, having freed him from death" (Acts 2:24). This Jesus who was crucified and died is now experienced by his followers as the risen Christ. It was the experience of the resurrection that gave birth to the Christian movement.

The Christian disciples' new understanding of messiahship then transformed to seeing Jesus as the Messiah, the Christ, who had been resurrected by God and who would return to earth again at the end time to usher in the kingdom of God that was promised. All the other messianic prophecies would then be fulfilled. So, rather than being just the Jewish messiah, Jesus was now seen as the Messiah for the whole of humankind. He was also believed to be God's self-revelation here on earth: "And the Word became flesh and lived among us" (John 1:14). The early Christians believed that in the person and life of Jesus, God had revealed God's self in human form to humanity. That is the only way the finite human can ever know the infinite God: "No one has ever seen God. It is God the only Son, who is close to the Father's heart, who has made him known" (John 1:18). This new understanding of the identity of Jesus was liberating as well as empowering, leading the disciples not only to believe but also to take seriously the command that they should "Go therefore and make disciples of all nations, baptizing them in the name of the Father and of the Son and of the Holy Spirit, and teaching them to obey everything that I have commanded you" (Matt 28:19-20).

The early Christians' understanding of Jesus and their own role in history are reflected in how they then looked at Hebrew Scriptures. Being the only scriptures that they had ever known and believing that some of the prophecies within had been fulfilled by Jesus, they adopted the Jewish Bible as their own. They, however, renamed it "Old Testament" (old covenant), implying that a new covenant had already been inaugurated by Jesus, whom they believed is Son of God. They changed the order of the books in the Bible to reflect this. While the Jewish Bible concludes with the book of Chronicles, which carries the accounts of the Babylonian exile, the Christian "Old Testament" ends with the minor prophetic books (Malachi, Zechariah, Haggai, Zephaniah, etc.) that made reference to the coming of the messiah. The early Christians applied these references to Jesus. For example, the prophecy in Micah—"But you, O Bethlehem of Ephrathah, who are one of the little clans of Judah, from you shall come forth for me one who is to rule in Israel" (Mic 5:2)—was seen by the early Christians as referring to where Jesus was to be born. Haggai's "I am about to shake the heavens and the earth" (Hag 2:21) is interpreted as having been accomplished in Jesus as the book of Hebrews of the early Christians makes this reference to him: "At that time his voice shook the earth; but now he has promised, 'Yet once more I will shake not only the earth but also the heaven'" (Heb 12:26). Likewise, Malachi's "See, I am sending my messenger to prepare the way before me, and the Lord whom you seek will suddenly come to his temple" (Mal 3:1) is believed to refer to John the Baptist and Jesus of Nazareth, respectively. Many of these prophecies can be found lavishly integrated into the texts of the new scriptures that the early Christian community developed. They called this the New Testament, with the gospels focusing on the life, teachings, and ministry of Jesus, the book of Acts giving an account of the early church's expansion, the epistles revealing the developing theology, doctrine, and practice of the various Christian communities, and the book of Revelation depicting the teachings related to the apocalypse or end times. Like the Hebrew Scriptures, the Christian Scriptures or New Testament were meant to inspire the disciples of Christ to order their lives accordingly and to persevere in their faith despite the challenges incumbent on a new religious movement.

The challenges the early Christians encountered were many, especially from the external community. They began as a small sect of Judaism in a religiously plural, culturally diverse, and philosophically rich Mediterranean world. The Jews regarded the Judaic Christians as no more than apostates of the monotheistic faith, misled by a false messiah who blasphemously claimed identity with the absolute God. With time, the Judaic Christians became increasingly marginalized and unwelcome in the temple, and many were practically driven out of town on account of years of persecution. They in turn became more and more hostile toward the Jews and the practices of Judaism. When the Jews were revolting against the Romans beginning in the year 66 CE, culminating in the destruction of the temple in 70 CE, the Judaic Christians were nowhere to be seen and so were regarded as unpatriotic and traitors. Besides, the Good News or Gospel that Jesus taught encouraged them to make peace and not war. Christianity eventually developed an identity separate from Judaism, and the two traditions went their separate ways.

If the majority of the Jews rejected Christianity, the Gentiles were more receptive of the Gospel that was being preached. Paul, the apostle to the Gentiles, played a significant role in their conversion and also in explaining basic Christian beliefs in terms the Greco-Roman culture could appreciate. Christianity adapted to the Hellenistic and pagan world of philosophy and ideas by developing a more philosophically robust theology. Jesus' message of love and concern especially for the least and the lost appealed to the poor and those living at the margins. The impoverished and dispossessed found meaning and hope in the Gospel to the poor and the promise of an afterlife reward in heaven. With the inclusion of more Gentile Christians into the fold there was the question of whether they had to be circumcised and taught to keep the Mosaic Law. The decision taken at the Council of Jerusalem held around the year 50 CE instructed that the law was not necessary for salvation. It was predicated on the conviction, in the words of the Judaic Christian Peter, that "we believe that we will be saved through the grace of the Lord Jesus, just as they will" (Acts 15:11).

Another major challenge that confronted the early Christian community was the fact that they were emerging from within the Roman Empire. While its organized and sophisticated system of government helped with the expansion of Christianity, the early Christians had to deal with the reality of an emperor who claimed divine status and ruled by decree. In times of turbulence, Christians were easily made the scapegoats and persecuted as atheistic because they refused to worship the pantheon of Roman gods, including the emperor. The Romans charged that it was the Christians' refusal to offer sacrifices that caused the gods to be angry and not bestow blessings on the empire. Christians who refused to participate in what they regarded as the idolatry of emperor worship and who witnessed to the truth until death by torture are regarded as martyrs for the faith. Those who submitted and gave in to the authorities are known as *lapsi* or people who lapsed in their faith. Despite the persecutions, Christianity continued to attract new converts. By the beginning of the fourth century CE they constituted about 10 percent of the population of the Roman Empire. The persecutions ended when Emperor Constantine officially legalized the practice of the Christian faith with the Edict of Milan in 313 CE. Twelve years later, in 325 CE, amid the threat of doctrinal division, he convened the Council of Nicaea—the first of the ecumenical councils—to streamline Christian beliefs. It was Emperor Theodosius who, in 380 CE, established the Christian movement that adhered to the Nicene Creed as the official imperial religion, causing a surge in the conversion rates. By the end of the fourth century, Christians made up about half the population of the Roman Empire.

Christian Diversity and Denominations

Christianity, then and now, has never been a monolithic tradition. It was by no means a unified coherent religious movement, and this was evidenced even in the apostolic age. Christianity was and continues to be a pluralistic and diverse movement. This is in part because there was no real singular center or magisterium that controlled its development. Instead, there were many different centers established by small groups of the initial disciples of Christ and their followers. To be sure, there was diversity in how each group understood Jesus or practiced their new Christian faith. The four canonical gospels and the many more apocryphal gospels testify to this diversity. Mark's community probably had no idea what Luke or John's community believed about Jesus or how they were worshiping or what their concerns were in relation to Christian living. Pauline Christianity would have differed radically not only from Judaic Christianity but also within itself, in the different Pauline local churches spread throughout the Roman Empire. Many of Paul's epistles were written precisely to correct misleading doctrines or false practices. There was no set of agreed-on teachings, governance structures, or even sacred texts. The Bible was finally canonized only at the end of the fourth century, even if sets of established books had been gradually accepted by the many different Christian communities earlier. Despite the diversity between the communities of early Christianity, there was a general sense that they all belonged to the very same fellowship or *koinonia* (communion) of faith. It was a unity in diversity as there was a common acceptance of and expression of the apostolic faith. While each local church had its own particular identity, all the early Christians shared in the same faith of the one universal church.

Over the centuries, however, the ideal of unity in diversity was challenged, resulting in explicit breakaways of splinter groups from the mainstream on account of a variety of reasons. These differences included their views on doctrinal and ministerial issues such as the nature of authority, understandings of Jesus, the place of devotional practices, and the role of the papacy. Some breakaways resulted in an explicit break from the Christian tradition, such as Arianism (which denied the preexistence of Christ, thus subordinating the Son to the Father), which was condemned at the Council of Nicaea and regarded simply as a heresy. Others that were equally anathematized include Gnosticism (which emphasized the God-world or spirit-matter dualism) and the Ebionites (those who denied the divinity of Jesus). Most of these movements have all but disappeared and are generally not regarded as legitimate expressions of the Christian movement. The major divisions that are generally acknowledged within Christianity today are the Eastern and Oriental Orthodox, Roman Catholicism, and the various denominations formed during and after the Protestant Reformation.

Eastern Christianity

The first significant breakaway was more or less a follow-up on Arianism. Influenced by the teachings of Arius, Nestorius (patriarch of Constantinople) emphasized the distinction between the human and divine natures of the one person of Christ. His school of thought rejected the practice of bestowing the title of *Theotokos* (God-Bearer) on the Blessed Virgin Mary, arguing, rather, that she should only be known as the *Christotokos* (Mother of Christ). Nestorianism was denounced at the Council of Ephesus in 431 CE, as well as at the Council of Chalcedon in 451 CE, leading to a schism. The schismatic movement is more commonly known as the Nestorian Church, the Assyrian Church, or the Church of the East.

The next significant breakaway was a reaction in the opposite direction of Nestorianism. Pope Dioscorus (patriarch of Alexandria) felt that the Council of Chalcedon had caused ambiguity to arise when it advanced the christological dogma of Jesus possessing two natures, one divine and one human. The Alexandrian School of Theology advocated that any teaching should insist on the unity of the incarnation. It was emphatic that after the union of the divine and the human in the historical incarnation of Jesus Christ, there was only a single nature that was either divine or a synthesis of the divine and the human. The teaching became known as *monophysitism* (one nature), and the group that developed from it is better known as Oriental Orthodoxy. The Oriental Orthodox communion today consists of six groups: Coptic Orthodox, Syriac Orthodox, Ethiopian Orthodox, Eritrean Orthodox, Malankara Orthodox Syrian Church, and Armenian Apostolic Churches.

The third significant breakaway was a major one. This time it was a division between the entire Western and Eastern churches. These churches developed independently of one another and were largely shaped by the socio-cultural and ethno-linguistic developments within their own respective Western Roman and Byzantine empires. While the West used Latin as its lingua franca, the East used mainly Aramaic and Koine Greek. The transmission of theological thought and other ecclesial practices happened primarily within each tradition as there was little translation and sharing from one tradition to the other. The Westerners were more emphatic about legal ecclesial structures and approaches to the sacraments while the Easterners were more mystical in approach to their faith life and focused mainly on inner spirituality. Thus, the West's concern was more in the realm of people's sin and salvation while the East's concern was about becoming more God-like and the eventual deification of persons. These differences in perspectives shaped much of their Christian life and praxes.

While there were certainly political and cultural reasons for the schism between the Western and Eastern churches of the Roman Empire, the one theological controversy that served as the last straw was the inclusion and acceptance in the West of the *filioque* (and from the Son) clause into the Nicene Creed. The Eastern Church viewed this as erroneous. The other issue is with regard to the definition of papal primacy. While both the West and the East are in general agreement that the patriarch of Rome had "primacy of honor" among all the other patriarchs (those of Alexandria, Antioch, Constantinople, and Jerusalem), the West also expected that this primacy extended to jurisdiction. This was vehemently opposed by the Eastern patriarchs. Things came to a head and finally in 1054 the patriarchs from both traditions mutually excommunicated one another in an event that earned the label the "Great Schism." Since then "Greek Orthodox" or "Greek Catholic" have been used to identify churches that are in communion with Constantinople in the East and "Roman Catholic" used for churches in communion with Rome in the West.

Protestants and Reformed Churches

After 1054 the Western and Eastern churches went their separate ways. The next big fallout was within the Western Church when the Protestant Reformation took off. While the trigger was finally pulled in the sixteenth century, the reform spirit was already building in the fourteenth century. The issues this time were no longer just religious or theological but included political, intellectual, and cultural aspects as well. With the invention of the printing press and greater access to education, a new consciousness emerged among the people. This developed into the spirit of humanism of the Renaissance, leading to the establishment of a new questioning middle class. There was also the upwelling in nationalistic spirit and the rise of national rulers who were independent and strong. Society was more critical of institutions, especially the church, as new religious leaders, teachers, and preachers rose from the rank and file.

The religious leaders, mainly clergymen [sic], responsible for the Protestant Reformation had initially intended to only attempt reform within the Western Church, not cause a schism. They took issue with what they regarded as ecclesiastical malpractices, first, with issues such as the sale of indulgences and the selling and buying of clerical offices, and then later extended to concerns over false teachings about purgatory, papal authority, devotion to the Virgin Mary, devotion to the saints, the sacraments, mandatory clerical celibacy, monasticism, and so on. Essentially their problem was with the corrupt practices of the church's hierarchy, including the pope. Their demand was for a purification of the church and faith in the Bible (not in the church's teaching office) as the sole source of spiritual authority.

The trigger that set off the Protestant Reformation occurred when, in 1517, the Augustinian monk Martin Luther circulated his *Ninety-Five Theses on the Power and Efficacy of Indulgences*. His aim was to invite a debate on church teachings and practices for the purpose of freeing the Gospel exercised over it by the church's hierarchy. He wanted to enable individual believers to have control over their own destiny by faith in Christ or "by justification by faith alone," not through obedience to another human authority or the teachings of the church. The biblical text to support his position is from Romans: "For in it the righteousness of God is revealed through faith for faith; as it is written, 'The one who is righteous will live by faith' " (Rom 1:17). When the institutional church responded by excommunicating Luther in 1521, it served only to harden his position. The German princes backed Luther's reforms as they saw it also as an opportunity to be independent of the emperor and papal authority. The resultant breakaway group, known as Lutheranism, was established as the state religion in Germany, Scandinavia, and the Baltics.

The Reformation spread very quickly throughout many parts of Europe. The Swiss reformers were Ulrich Zwingli in Zurich and John Calvin in Geneva. Like Luther, their central claim was that it is *sola scriptura* (through scripture alone) or *sola fidei* (through faith alone) that we are saved. The church and its priests and their teachings, interpretations, and traditions are not necessary. Calvinist theology teaches that God's providence governs everything, and every person on earth is in God's hands. Since God is all knowing, the theories of divine election and predestination are advocated. The churches subscribing to these teachings are called the Reformed Tradition or Presbyterian Churches.

The next breakaway happened among some of the Protestant reformers who thought that the movement did not go far enough. They wanted a return to the root of the apostolic faith and pushed for a complete break from the Roman and papist traditions so as to live the way Jesus lived. This included distancing the Christian community from the world and its affairs. They also preached personal commitment, which meant infant baptism was invalid. A group who rebaptized those who had already been baptized as infants was called Anabaptists. Other smaller breakaways include the Hutterites, the Mennonites, the Religious Society of Friends (Quakers), the Seventh-Day Adventists, and the Disciples of Christ.

A fourth offshoot of the Reformation took place in England. While Lutheranism and Calvinism broke away for doctrinal, liturgical, or disciplinary reasons, the precipitating cause of the Tudor (Anglican) Reformation was personal. King Henry VIII wanted to be free from papal control in order to divorce his wife to marry another woman. Henry then declared that the king was head of the church, not the pope. Despite the royal primacy over papal primacy, Anglicans kept a lot of the teachings and practices of Catholicism. They embraced a sort of *via media* (middle road) between Catholicism and Protestantism, acknowledging the role of scripture, tradition, and reason and not so much the doctrine of by scripture alone.

The Catholic Church's response to the Protestant Reformation is sometimes called the Counter-Reformation. This took place during the Council of Trent (1545–1563). Instead of addressing the faults pointed out by the reformers, Trent reasserted church authority and insisted on its teaching that tradition was co-equal in authority with scripture. Two offices or structures within the church to ensure conformity were established: the *Inquisition* (to attend to charges of heresy) and the *Index* (to list forbidden books). But the Catholic Church did renew itself somehow and curbed corrupt practices related to the abuse of power denounced by the reformers, especially practices such as simony (buying/selling of ecclesiastical privileges), absenteeism (church leaders neglecting their duties), and nepotism (elevating relatives to positions in church). Moreover, it also initiated the foundations for seminary training of priests and reform of religious life by returning to the spiritual roots of their foundations.

Free Churches and New Christian Movements

The Protestant Reformation set off a spark that turned out to be a continuous movement. After the sixteenth century many more Christian denominations were founded all over Europe. This was multiplied greatly by the disintegration of medieval Christendom as well as the rise of the spirit of nationalism. Numerous Free Churches and new Christian movements grew out of the many Protestant movements that had already established themselves. Through missionary activity and also the movements of peoples across countries and continents, the new churches then spread to North America. Colonialism and the so-called discovery of the New World played an integral role in bringing not only Christianity to the Americas, Africa, and Asia but also the structures and enmity that had initially sparked off the Christian division in Europe.

The Puritans were a sixteenth- and seventeenth-century reform movement that sought to purify the Church of England. Two offshoots of the English Puritan movement were the Baptists and the Congregational Churches. When the Puritans were persecuted in England many sought refuge in Europe, especially in the Low Countries such as Holland. When it was safe enough to return to England, led by John Smith and Thomas Helwys, they made their way back and founded the Baptist Congregation. Like Anabaptists, they reject infant baptism. The Congregational Churches trace their roots to the English separatist and theologian Robert Browne. They advocate self-governing and independent, autonomous local churches that are free to choose their own ministers, administrative structures, liturgies, prayers, and so on. Some of their members who migrated to North America in the seventeenth century were the ones who founded Yale and Harvard Universities. The Unitarian Church later took control of Harvard in the early nineteenth century and advanced a more liberal, open, and ecumenical Christian faith. Today, the Congregational Churches have merged with the United Churches.

The Quakers or Religious Society of Friends also have their roots in England. Led by George Fox, they believed that a person's experience with Jesus Christ can happen directly, unmediated by the clergy. Convinced of the priesthood of all believers, they called themselves "seekers" and distanced themselves from creeds and ecclesiastical structures. Being Christian simply meant possessing the "inner light" and being "born again" in the Holy Spirit. Quakers are renowned for their antiwar and humanitarian campaigns. Likewise, the Methodists also emerged from the Church of England. Inspired by the life and teachings of John Wesley, who had led a very strict and methodical life, the movement began as a reform within the Anglican Church but later separated and became an independent denomination. Sanctity of the believers, a strict and rigorous life of prayer and holiness, and the impact of faith on one's character are the principal characteristics of Methodism.

The nineteenth and twentieth centuries saw even more breakaways from the mainline Protestant churches. In part as a response or reaction to the rise of scientific development, modernity, and liberalism, many of these breakaways are revivalist Evangelical or Restoration movements, aimed at reinforcing personal piety and faith or returning to the faith of the first Christians. The Brethren Church began as a reform movement of the Church of England and eventually broke away under the leadership of John Nelson Darby. They are apocalyptic in spirit and desire to unite Christians of all denominations in anticipation of the Second Coming of Christ. The Salvation Army is an offshoot of the Methodist Church in England and focuses on mission work to the poor in the slums of London. They later organized themselves along military lines and adopted uniforms, flags, titles and ranks, and a discipline system very much akin to those found in the army.

In North America, the Seventh-Day Adventists emerged in the nineteenth century as part of a universal apocalyptic revivalist movement. Founded by the Baptist preacher William Miller who was convinced that the Second Coming of Jesus Christ was happening soon, the followers eventually broke away or were expelled from their denominations and

established their own community. They are known for their strict observance of the Sabbath on Saturday, and they adhere to some of the puritanical practices of the Hebrew Scriptures, especially with regard to diet.

Two other movements that emerged from North America in the nineteenth century are the Mormons (or Church of Jesus Christ of Latter-Day
Saints) and the Jehovah's Witnesses. While self-identifying as Christian,
other Christians have questions as to whether they can indeed be called
Christian churches. The Mormons have as their founder Joseph Smith, who
believed that Jesus went to preach in America after his resurrection. Smith
claimed to have received visions revealing a new sacred text called the
Book of Mormon and, on the basis of its teaching, reestablished the original
church of Jesus Christ. The church's detractors charge that the community
cannot be Christian as they do not accept the creeds and confessions of the
post–New Testament church or believe that Christian Scriptures consist
of only the Holy Bible. The Jehovah's Witnesses are an offshoot of the
Adventist movement. Led by Charles Taze Russel, it spread its message
mainly through mass publications, especially with the foundation of The
Watch Tower Bible and Tract Society. Believing that the end of the world
is imminent, the movement espouses a theology that is basically otherworldly, pessimistic, and puritanical. Jehovah's Witnesses do not believe
in the Trinity but rather in the Jehovah of Hebrew Scriptures. They also
reject the divinity of Jesus and believe he is the Archangel Michael. It is
for these reasons that they are often not regarded as Christian.

The most significant movement to have emerged in the early part of
the twentieth century is Pentecostalism. Founded on the charismatic experiences of different groups of Christians, the movement does not really
acknowledge any particular founder. Two names, however, are often associated with its beginnings. The first is Charles Fox Parham, who started
a special Bible school in Topeka, Kansas, where he preached that a clear
sign of the baptism of the Holy Spirit is when Christians begin to speak
in tongues. The other is one of Parham's students, an African American
preacher named William J. Seymour who began preaching in Azusa Street
in Los Angeles. This set off the Azusa Street Revival in 1906, which has
since come to be regarded as the beginnings of Pentecostalism as a movement. The movement is made up mainly of independent churches that
are founded and led by a variety of Christian leaders and consider any
organization beyond the local as unbiblical. Pentecostals look on their
movement as a restoration of the apostolic age and the early Christian

community and believe that their practice of divine healing and speaking in tongues are manifest gifts of the Holy Spirit. They, therefore, often use terms such as "Apostolic" or "Full Gospel" to name their churches. In the twentieth century, Pentecostalism has been a major influence in the development of many churches around the world, especially in the global South, and is regarded as the fastest growing denomination of Christianity today. Its development has been crucial to the growing awareness of what has come to be called world Christianity.

The Advent of World Christianity

The phrase "world Christianity" was first used in academic circles in the earlier part of the twentieth century, particularly in reference to the study of the global missionary movement as well as the Christian ecumenical movement. The former explores the expansion of Christianity throughout the globe, while the latter refers to the efforts at forging unity between the numerous divisions of the Christian family. Together they were aimed at bringing about a more united Christian front for the purpose of proclaiming the Gospel and evangelizing all peoples living in the entire inhabited world. In more recent decades, however, world Christianity has come to mean something totally different. A look at how it is being used today will shed some light on what it means.

First, consider the advent of the *Journal of World Christianity* as well as the journal for the *Studies in World Christianity*. The former is published by Pennsylvania University Press and the latter by Edinburgh University Press. Second, note also the recent proliferation of academic centers dedicated specifically to the cause of world Christianity: the Nagel Institute for World Christianity of Calvin College in Michigan; the Centre for World Christianity and Interreligious Studies of Radboud University Nijmegen in the Netherlands; the Centre for the Study of World Christianity in Edinburgh; and the Centre for World Christianity of the University of London. An obvious point to note is that all of these journals and centers arose from or are located in the North Atlantic. They are also very new initiatives and were founded only in the last ten or twenty years. Thus, one can conclude that the phenomenon of world Christianity is something very new for Christian scholars, but only if Christianity is considered primarily from the Western perspective.

World Christianity's ascendancy may be attributed to two realizations. First was the realization that Euro-American Christianity is in decline, prompting scholars to posit the thesis of secularization as well as engage in conversations about the end of religion. But when viewed from a global perspective, the thesis is simply mistaken. To be sure, Christianity as a whole is not in decline, even if it may be so in the Western world. This led to the second realization, which is that Western Christianity is not the only one there is. Christianity exists in many forms. Its growth is happening in territories outside the West or the global North. Hence, a greater appreciation for the non-Western forms of Christianity, in particular that of the global South or Southern Christianity. Previously, even if Asian Christianity, African Christianity, and the other contextual forms of Christianity were in existence for centuries and millennia, Euro-American Christianity considered itself normative. It audaciously presented itself as "Christianity," devoid of any adjective or qualifier. But now that the focus has shifted from the West to the rest of the world, a distinction needs to be made of this "new" exploration of Christianity that is found outside the West and so the phrase "world Christianity" was coined. World Christianity, therefore, refers primarily to the global reality and awareness that the center of gravity of Christianity has shifted from the global North to the global South. Its interest is in how Christianity is expressed in the global South, usually in comparison with the West or global North.

This change in the global ecclesial landscape is well documented. Perhaps the most comprehensive empirical work on this is the one done by the Center for the Study of Global Christianity of Gordon-Conwell Theological Seminary in Boston.[1] According to its analysis, sometime between 1970 and 2010 the global South exceeded the global North in Christian population. While in 1900 more than 82 percent of the world's Christian population was found in the global North, by 2010 about 61 percent were already residing in the global South, and this is projected to increase to 72 percent by 2050. By then Africa will be the most populous Christian continent, followed by South America and then Asia. Europe, which had about 68 percent of the world's Christian population in 1900, reduced its share to 40 percent in 1970 and then to about 26 percent in 2010; this figure is expected to go down even further by 2050 to about

1. *World Christian Database*, Center for the Study of Global Christianity, Gordon-Conwell Theological Seminary, http://www.worldchristiandatabase.org/wcd/.

17 percent (refer to table below). By 2050, Brazil, Nigeria, the Philippines, D. R. Congo, Mexico, and Tanzania will have more Christians than any European country. Likewise, when referring to Christian cities one will more likely cite Manila, Dar Es Salaam, or Rio de Janeiro than Paris, New York, or Madrid. Thus, it would no longer be accurate to label Christianity as a European religion or the faith of the global North.

The changing distribution of Christian believers (across continents)

Year Region	1900	1970	2010	2050
Africa	10 million	143 million	493 million	1,031 million
Asia	22 million	96 million	352 million	601 million
North America	79 million	211 million	286 million	333 million
South America	62 million	270 million	544 million	655 million
Europe	381 million	492 million	588 million	530 million
Oceania	5 million	18 million	28 million	38 million
TOTAL	558 million	1,230 million	2,291 million	3,188 million

Source: World Christian Database: www.worldchristiandatabase.org/wcd/

Walbert Bühlmann's *The Coming of the Third Church* was among the first books to explicitly discuss the rise of the church of the global South.[2] He regards the church of the first millennium as being dominated by the concerns of Eastern Christianity and the second millennium by the hegemony of Western Christianity. He posits that the third millennium will see the rise of Christianity of the global South. He uses the term "Third Church" somewhat analogously to how the term "Third World" has been used to designate developing countries. It is thus a sociological term referring to what is also known missiologically as the "younger churches," the churches that were located in mission territories and that were on the receiving end of one-way missions. These churches have now come of age and are even blossoming, especially since the end of colonialism, which put a halt to the era of missionary activity from the West. Pope John XXIII made reference to this in an encyclical titled *Princeps Pastorum*, subtitled "On the Missions, Native Clergy, and Lay Participation," issued on November 28, 1959:

2. Walbert Bühlmann, *The Coming of the Third Church: An Analysis of the Present and Future of the Church* (Maryknoll, NY: Orbis Books, 1977).

It was, therefore, with good reason that Our predecessor Pius XII was able to affirm with satisfaction: "Once upon a time it seemed as though the life of the Church used to prosper and blossom chiefly in the regions of ancient Europe, whence it would flow, like a majestic river, through the remaining areas which, to use the Greek term, were considered almost the periphery of the world; today, however, the life of the Church is shared, as though by a mutual irradiation of energies, among all individual members of the Mystical Body of Christ. Not a few countries on other continents have long since outgrown the missionary stage, and are now governed by an ecclesiastical hierarchy of their own, have their own ecclesiastical organization, and are liberally offering to other Church communities those very gifts, spiritual and material, which they formerly used to receive."[3]

Bühlmann's use of the term "Third Church" is not confined to a geographical concept. It also refers to communities within the global North that have been marginalized by the dominant group. In North America the "Third Church" refers to the Hispanic Americans, African Americans, Asian Americans, and Native Americans, among others. But in terms of the demographic shift in Christian communities it is the Hispanics who have been on the increase and the Euro-Americans on the decrease. The findings of the Public Religion Research Institute's 2016 American Values Atlas, a survey of American religious and denominational identity, confirm this demographic shift. It states that in 1976 Americans who identified as white and Christian constituted 81 percent of the population. By 1996 it was down to 65 percent, and in 2016 its representation is only 43 percent, that is, less than half the total American population. Within the Catholic community, in 1991, about 87 percent of all US Catholics were white, non-Hispanic, but in 2016 Catholics who identify as white, non-Hispanic represented only 55 percent, while 36 percent of all Catholics identify as Hispanic.[4]

3. Pope John XXIII, *Princeps Pastorum: Encyclical of Pope John XXIII on the Missions, Native Clergy, and Lay Participation* (November 28, 1959), par. 10; http://w2.vatican.va/content/john-xxiii/en/encyclicals/documents/hf_j-xxiii_enc_28111959_princeps.html.
4. Daniel Cox and Robert P. Jones, "America's Changing Religious Identity," *Public Religion Research Institute* (September 6, 2017), https://www.prri.org/research/american-religious-landscape-christian-religiously-unaffiliated/.

Another dimension of the Southernization process, which is changing the face of Christianity in the West, is that many Western churches
are today recipients of missionaries from the global South. This is the
phenomenon of "reverse mission," where countries that were previously
mission territories are now sending missionaries to their mother churches
in the global North. Thus we see today Nigerian evangelists preaching
on street corners in London, Korean sisters working in nursing homes in
Baltimore, Mexican brothers teaching in Catholic schools in Dublin, and
Filipino priests celebrating the Eucharist in Sydney. Of course, the very
election of the Latin American Cardinal Jorge Mario Bergoglio to the
highest position of the Catholic Church as Bishop of Rome is very clear
evidence of this new face of world Christianity. To be sure, the universal
church is gradually embracing Southern features.

Christianity as World Religion

While the term "world Christianity" is sometimes used interchangeably with "global Christianity," a distinction needs to be made between
the two. Global Christianity was what we had for centuries before the
new awareness of world Christianity came about. It refers to how the
Christian faith of Europe had expanded throughout the globe, partly
through colonialism and missionary activity, with the faith of the mother
churches basically replicated in the mission territories. Thus we had
Spanish Christianity in the Philippines, French Christianity in Mada-
gascar, Portuguese Christianity in Brazil, and British Christianity in Sri
Lanka. World Christianity, on the other hand, is the appropriation of the
Christian faith, often through local agencies and expressed in cultural
forms and traditions more adapted to its local contexts. Church activities
and ministries in favor of enabling the contextualization and localization
of the church are given priority in view of transforming the imported
church into a local entity.

The interrogation of world Christianity, therefore, has primarily to
do with examining the different forms of Christianity around the world,
especially in the global South. Its concerns are with the pluralistic expressions of Christianity in its various dimensions: language, community,
structure, liturgy, theology, etc. This pluralism resonates well with the
postmodern ethos where diversity is not only a given but appreciated as

well. Hence, that Southern Christianity betrays all the hallmarks of pluralism is looked on with some degree of fascination and interest. Many of the churches in the South today are led by leaders inspired especially by Pentecostalism. Pentecostal churches are usually homegrown, locally born, led, financed, and propagated. The fact that it is primarily homegrown suggests that each "home" produces its own brand of Christianity. This is another characteristic of world Christianity; there is little uniformity across them. That is why it might be more accurate to speak of world Christianities in the plural. One is reminded here of the early church, especially during the New Testament era, where the Christian communities were characterized by their diversity and yet there was a certain unity between them. It looks like contemporary world Christianity is returning to the Christian origins of contextualized expressions of the faith.

Conclusion

World Christianity also means that Christianity can no longer be perceived through the lens of Christendom, with the power of the state and its concomitant bureaucratic tradition behind it. It ceases to have hegemonic advantage over others in society. Instead, it stands alongside the other religious and cultural traditions as a world religion among the many world religions, serving the local peoples in their quest for the fullness of life. Implied in this is the need and, indeed, obligation of Christianity to be in dialogue and engagement with the other religions of the world. This is not only to enable the various religions to work together for the common good and a better society but also to enable Christianity to discover its rightful place in the world of the many religions.

Suggestions for Further Reading

Jenkins, Philip. *The Next Christendom: The Coming of Global Christianity.* Oxford: Oxford University Press, 2002.
Johnson, Todd M., and Kenneth R. Ross. *Atlas of Global Christianity*. Edinburgh: Edinburgh University Press, 2009.

Kim, Sebastian, and Kirsteen Kim. *Christianity as a World Religion.* London: Bloomsbury, 2008.

Sanneh, Lamin. *Disciples of All Nations: Pillars of World Christianity.* Oxford: Oxford University Press, 2007.

Tan, Jonathan Y., and Anh Q. Tran, eds. *World Christianity: Perspectives and Insights.* Maryknoll, NY: Orbis Books, 2016.

2

From Religion to World Religions

Introduction

There are advantages and disadvantages to teaching religion at a Catholic university. I teach a regular introductory course that is mandatory for students majoring in education, especially those planning on teaching in Catholic schools. That is the advantage; there is no shortage of students enrolling in my courses. The disadvantage, however, is that a number of these students resent being there. I normally begin the semester asking them why they are taking the course. I once had a very mature first-year student politely say: "I've had twelve years of Catholic education. Religion was shoved down our throats on a daily basis. Frankly, I don't really know why I am here except that this course is needed for graduation. I think I've had enough religion to last me the rest of my life!" I quickly surmised that what he had was mainly catechesis or religious instruction, which differs significantly from theology or the study of religion. The student's point, however, is well taken and the best I could do was to appeal to him to "give religion a chance."

This chapter will not be presenting more of Christianity. Instead, it will explore the larger phenomenon of religion. While Christianity is a religion, religion is much more than Christianity. In fact, even if many younger people in the West are becoming disenfranchised from Christianity, the scenario in the rest of the world paints another picture. This will be looked at. Also to be looked at is the distinction between what is known as faith or spirituality and religion. With that as context, the chapter then explores more intricately the idea of religion and also the historical examination of the same, including the scientific study of it since the nineteenth century.

It culminates by interrogating the discourse on world religions and will briefly introduce some of the world's many religions.

A Case for Religion

Some people, in particular those living in the West, assume that religion has outlived its relevance in today's scientifically advanced and technologically sophisticated world. Religion, they argue, provided explanations to a lot of what were previously considered life's mysteries that today have already been answered by science. Only the uneducated and unenlightened will need to hang on to the superstitious beliefs that religion teaches. Besides, there is also the reality and danger of how the teachings and dictates of religion can be adhered to slavishly and without rational thought. This blind obedience is sometimes at the root of the evil and violence of our times, as evidenced by some religious adherents who are willing not only to die for their religion but also to kill for it. Religion, therefore, it is argued, should be done away with by thinking and thoughtful people; it has no place in today's world, especially among the educated masses.

Despite what we make of the assertions above, the data still shows that the vast majority of people around the world continue to subscribe to one form of religion or another. The findings of the 2015 Pew Research Center's Forum on Religion and Public Life survey reveal that 84 percent of the global population identify themselves as affiliated to a particular religion. Its more detailed report reads: "Christians were the largest religious group in the world in 2015, making up nearly a third (31%) of Earth's 7.3 billion people. Muslims were second, with 1.8 billion people, or 24% of the global population, followed by religious 'nones' (16%), Hindus (15%) and Buddhists (7%). Adherents of folk religions, Jews and members of other religions make up smaller shares of the world's people."[1]

So, there you have it. If religion has indeed been superseded, if it is really irrelevant and has outlived its usefulness, how do we explain the

1. "The Changing Global Religious Landscape," *Pew Research Center: Religion & Public Life* (April 5, 2017), http://www.pewforum.org/2017/04/05/the-changing -global-religious-landscape/.

fact that such a high percentage of the world's population (84 percent) still pledge allegiance to it? It cannot be that they are all unthinking and wrong and that the only ones who got it right are the 16 percent who claim they are religious "nones," that is, those who do not affiliate with any religion. While numerical majority is by no means a measure of truth or authenticity, it is important to note that there are many very thoughtful people and critical scholars who are religious believers as well. Of course, there are also as many thoughtful people and critical scholars who are not religiously affiliated. So, religious affiliation is certainly not a function of rationality. People choose to be religious for a variety of reasons or in a variety of circumstances. Likewise, people choose to be unaffiliated to religions also for a variety of reasons. The 16 percent or 1.2 billion religious nones in the world include atheists, agnostics, secularists, and people who simply prefer not to identify with any particular religion. Representing the third-largest category, behind only Christianity and Islam, they are a significant group to contend with. Moreover, the data also indicates that they are growing in numbers by the year and making their presence felt, especially in public discourse. It might come as a surprise, however, to learn that the vast majority of the religiously unaffiliated in the world are actually from East Asia. In fact, East Asians represent 76 percent in this category, or 888 million people, and they come mainly from China, Japan, Vietnam, and Korea.

The data about East Asia having such a huge percentage of the religiously unaffiliated is surprising because East Asians are generally known for their religiosity. Unlike the religious nones of the West, East Asians who identify with the "no religion" category do so sometimes for political reasons. Those living under atheistic communist regimes such as in China and Vietnam, for example, do not acknowledge that they belong to any religion basically to avoid scrutiny from government agencies. Others claim they are unaffiliated with religion because they see religion—a term that does not feature in their local vocabulary—very differently. What the West calls religion is something East Asians see as integral to life, as there is no separation between the sacred and the secular. Religion is not something a person joins or decides to believe in or to reject. It is something that one simply accepts as part of existence. Moreover, even if they do select the religious "none" box in surveys, many of these peoples from East Asia continue to participate in ancestor veneration or prayers to the dead, as well as the many other rites and rituals of life often associated with Confucianism, Taoism, Buddhism, and Shintoism. They do so, however, without necessarily identifying the practices with religion as such. Another reason for selecting the religious "none" category is because people from the East Asia region are generally not used to identifying with only one particular religion. In fact, many might engage in the practices of several religions at the same time without necessarily "belonging" to any of them. To be sure, they are religious practitioners even if they do not claim any religious adherence.

Spiritual but Not Religious

Religion is often confused with but is actually not the same as faith or spirituality, two terms that are often used interchangeably. Most people consider religion as distinct from faith or spirituality, where the latter are seen as much more encompassing realities than the former. While religion is associated with an organized and institutional entity, faith is a universal experience intrinsic to all persons. Faith arises in human beings on account of the basic constitution of the human person and especially the fact that humans are finite creatures. The vulnerable and dependent nature of the human person facilitates the realization that they are never completely in control of everything that goes on around them. Faith is that innate principle or energy or life force that enables people to trust in themselves, in others, and in whatever is regarded as higher than or beyond the finite world. It also drives them to engage the depth of their human experience in search for meaning, purpose, and significance in life. The search is premised on the sense that there is something more than just our personal and egoic self, prompting us to search inward, outward, and upward. A person is said to have lost faith when this trust or search is severely distorted or abandoned. Spirituality, in turn, refers to the way or path a person takes to cultivate this trust or to engage in the search. It is the efforts exerted for the purpose of discovering meaning, purpose, and significance within oneself (inward search), in relation to others (outward search), and in relation to that which transcends humankind (upward search). Hence, unlike the institution of organized religion, faith and spirituality are universal realities that are found in all persons and are integral aspects of being human. They transcend religion but could also be expressed through the many and varied religions of the world.

Many atheists and agnostics declare themselves to be religiously unaffiliated because they do not believe or believe it is not possible to verify
the existence of God or the gods. Not all atheists and agnostics are
religiously unaffiliated though, as the original forms of Buddhism and
Jainism, as well as strands within some other religious traditions, are
also atheistic by nature. So, by definition, Buddhists and Jains are atheists or agnostics even as they are religiously affiliated. But, in general,
for the religious nones of the West, unbelief—or the cognitive rejection
of the theistic understandings of the divine—can result in the rejection
of some or all of the other dimensions of religion, such as its scriptures,
ritual practices, and moral codes. Together with the secularists, atheists
and agnostics are generally those who have been disaffected by organized religion and are often vehemently opposed to the more legalistic
and dogmatic aspects of them. This is a phenomenon that has become
increasingly pronounced in many countries in the West in recent decades,
as the results of national surveys clearly indicate.

A nationwide survey in Britain reveals that 53 percent of the British
public professes "no religion" in 2016, a figure that has significantly increased since the survey began in 1983 when the proportion who marked
the "no religion" category was only 31 percent. Among the younger Brits
the figure is even more drastic as 71 percent of those below the age of
twenty-four today claim they have no religion.[2] The trend is not much
different in Australia. While in 1966 those who identified with the "no
religion" category constituted a mere 0.8 percent, the figure in 2016 has
shot up to 29.6 percent, nearly double the 16 percent recorded in 2001.[3]
Likewise, about 24 percent of the population in the United States claim
they are religiously unaffiliated, a figure that has roughly tripled in size
since the early 1990s. The proportion is slightly higher among those who
are under the age of thirty (34 percent) as well as those above fifty years

2. "BSA 34: Record Number of Brits with No Religion," *British Social Attitudes*,
http://www.bsa.natcen.ac.uk/media-centre/latest-press-releases/bsa-34-record
-number-of-brits-with-no-religion.aspx.

3. "2016 Census Data Reveals 'No Religion' Is Rising Fast," *Australian Bureau of
Statistics, 2016 Census: Religion*, http://www.abs.gov.au/AUSSTATS/abs@.nsf/media
releasesbyReleaseDate/7E65A144540551D7CA258148000E2B85?OpenDocument.

of age (29 percent).[4] These survey data enable us to safely conclude that the number of people who claim they are religiously unaffiliated is definitely on the rise in the West as more and more of its citizens become increasingly secularized or, at least, disengaged from religious institutions.

This does not suggest, however, that the religious nones are without faith or are unspiritual. In fact, a number of those who identify themselves as religiously unaffiliated also insist that they are spiritual persons. They can be called those who "believe but don't belong" but are more commonly known as the "spiritual but not religious" (SBNR). The rise of the SBNR has been well researched and documented since its ascendancy in the postmodern era. The common complaint of the SBNRs, most of whom are former Christians, is that religion (read: Christianity) is far too prescriptive about what one is to believe, how one is to worship, and what one is to regard as right or wrong. Christianity's exclusivist theologies of God and of salvation leave little room for the SBNRs to appreciate the beliefs and practices of their religious neighbors or friends who do not identify with Christianity. Its central belief in a theistic God who is depicted as a supernatural entity "out there" or "up there" is often taken to mean that the locus of authority for believers resides outside of the individual. Being religious seems to entail submission in loyal obedience to the dictates of this higher power as taught by its priestly representatives and as discerned by interpreting its scriptures. These dictates are usually seen as excessively rigid and dogmatic, expressed in religious doctrines and practices that serve the interests of the religious institution more than the needs of the individual believer. Their concern seems to be more about history and tradition than about the present and contemporary realities.

Those who call themselves SBNR claim that such doctrines and practices are not only irrelevant to people's growth and well-being but potentially harmful and detrimental to their personal development as well. Or, at the very least, they could be a hindrance to the advancement of authentic spirituality. In contrast to religion, which is seen as focusing primarily on a person's external life, spirituality is more often associated with the interior life. It is often regarded as the experience of the heart rather than that of the head. Its emphasis is on the integration of mind-body-spirit, and its focus is on the individual's personal religious experi-

4. Daniel Cox and Robert P. Jones, "America's Changing Religious Identity," *Public Religion Research Institute* (September 6, 2017), https://www.prri.org /research/american-religious-landscape-christian-religiously-unaffiliated/.

ence. William James's standard definition of religious experience as the "feelings, acts and experiences of individual men in their solitude, so far as they apprehend themselves to stand in relation to whatever they may consider the divine" informs this quest for the spiritual.[5] The personal religious experience of the individual is integral to their spiritual search for truth. The search for truth is a neverending quest of various dimensions, where the inward quest attempts to answer the "who am I?" question, the outward quest aims to discern one's place in community, and the upward quest is driven by the "is there something more?" question.

Thus, while the SBNRs may have rejected organized religion, they have also developed new forms and systems that are employed in the cultivation of their faith. A byproduct of the postmodern culture, they place a premium on individuality, authenticity, freedom, empowerment, and personal choice and are open to approaches that are nonconventional, eclectic, and heterogeneous. Some of the spiritual practices that have developed from these experimentations adopt elements from the Eastern traditions such as Vedanta and Zen and holistic practices such as yoga, reiki, tai chi, and transcendental meditation. Their aim is to embrace the best of the developmental psychology tradition of the West, blending them with the best of the transcendental consciousness tradition of the East in an attempt to postulate what is seen as an integral spirituality. There is, of course, no shortage of criticism of the SBNRs. They are accused of submitting to the consumeristic and narcissistic culture of self-centeredness and shallowness and of stealing from the great religious traditions without necessarily committing themselves to them. Their act of adopting the practices of a variety of systems divorced from their contexts and histories is alleged to be an act of religious and theological vandalism. Whatever it is, the SBNRs are here to stay and will probably create even newer ways for apprehending their faith and spirituality, much of it in reaction to the ways of mainstream religions.

The Idea of Religion

There is no certainty as to where the word "religion" comes from, but the various possible etymologies can shed some light. Some believe it

---

5. William James, *The Varieties of Religious Experience: A Study in Human Nature* (New York: Longmans, Green, and Company, 1902), 30.

is connected to the Latin *religio*, which roughly translates as respect or obligations to the gods. The Romans of antiquity, where the word comes from, probably took it to mean being pious or what we today refer to as being religious. This refers to the attitude of reverence or respect or even awe that one has for the forces of nature and life, especially those that are beyond rational understanding. Thus, the ancients believed that the roar of thunder signaled that the gods are angry, or that when an animal is killed for food one asks forgiveness from its spirit, or that an unexplainable illness may signal possession by the evil one. These are natural and instinctive responses that fall under the ambit of respecting the gods or the forces of life. They are different manifestations of religious experiences. Rudolf Otto describes religious experiences, especially those of God or the divine, as "numinous" and elaborates through the use of the Latin phrase *mysterium tremendum et fascinans*. As unknown and unknowable mystery, the numinous is an "otherworldly" and "wholly other" experience, qualitatively different from that of an ordinary sensory or rational experience. It evokes feelings of terror or fear and trembling, on the one hand, but also feelings of fascination, attraction, and awe, on the other, all of which cannot be intellectually or easily explained.

Another possibility is that the word "religion" comes from the Latin word *ligare*, which means the act of being bound, joined, linked, or connected. With the prefix "re-" added to *ligare*, religion refers to individuals being bound again, rejoined, relinked, or reconnected with others as well as with the divine. Émile Durkheim's definition of religion as "a unified system of beliefs and practices relative to sacred things, that is to say, things set apart and forbidden—beliefs and practices which unite in one simple moral community called church, all those who adhere to it" accentuates the role of religion in the reconnection of people with others in the community in relation to the sacred.[6] Religion serves a social function by bringing people together into a community with common bonds and interests. This social emphasis does not stand alone but must always be understood as complementing the reconnection of the individual with the sacred or whatever is regarded as divine or a higher power. The horizontal connection is therefore always in relation to the vertical, as people are as much in need of reuniting with one another as

6. Émile Durkheim, *The Elementary Forms of the Religious Life*, trans. Joseph Swain (London: George Allen & Unwin Ltd., 1915), 47.

with divinity or the source of one's being. Many religions teach that the present state of humankind is one where there is a disconnection with divinity—because of original sin, arrogance, forgetfulness, etc.—and that religious living aims to rediscover one's original condition or to return to one's primordial status or to realize one's true and authentic self. Thus, remembering (reestablishing membership), or reminding ourselves of our original pristine nature, features prominently in many religions.

It is important to point out that the word "religion" as we understand it today was not how it was understood in the ancient or medieval worlds. It was only in the sixteenth and seventeenth centuries that developments within European history, especially in the context of the European Enlightenment, saw it to mean a sphere of life distinct from the more ordinary and so-called secular spheres of life. Religion is, according to Durkheim, that "unified system of beliefs and practices relative to sacred things," which are by nature "things set apart and forbidden" and so are to be differentiated from the routine or mundane experiences of one's social existence. This is also referred to as the separation of the realm of the sacred from the realm of the profane. In the Western world today these two qualitatively different realms are not only clearly distinguished but also distanced from one another. This is the basis for the Western democratic nations emphasizing, in the terminology used by Thomas Jefferson, the separation between church and state. What belongs to religion should be confined within the walls of the church or temple and not allowed to mix with the everyday nonreligious or secular aspects of lives, which is the responsibility and purview of the state. This is how religion has come to be understood today in the West and accounts for some of the antipathy experienced in Western cultures toward anything associated with it.

For many other peoples around the world, however, what is referred to in the West as religion is really a "way of life" and not just a "view of life." Religion is certainly much more than a set of beliefs that distinguishes the sacred from the profane. It is also much more than the corpus of texts that one is supposed to believe in or submit to. Religion engages most aspects of one's life and has an impact and influence on most people, whether consciously or unconsciously. Religion is found not only within the church, synagogue, or temple but also in society at large. There is no separation between the holy and that which is deemed unholy. Issues and values of religious import permeate and guide many aspects of one's personal and social life. Many cultures around the world, including those of the indigenous communities in North America and Europe, do not have a specific word that translates meaningfully into what the West terms as religion. Religion is often roughly translated as *din* when referring to Islam, but the word actually means the way of life that every righteous Muslim ought to adhere to in compliance with the *Shari'a* or divine law. When referring to the religion of Hinduism the Sanskrit word *dharma* is often used in its translation. *Dharma*, however, is also used when discussing one's duty or virtue in relation to the divine power that upholds the universe and society. Thus, what the West refers to as religion is appreciated elsewhere as integrated and nondistinct from the other spheres of everyday life. Religion is an encompassing reality, as there is no binary distinction between what is regarded as sacred and profane or what is deemed supernatural and natural. Indeed, what is often thought of as supernatural or in the realm of spirit is also considered immanent to life and not transcendent. This is characteristic of the nondual approach to life that does not distinguish between our experience of the natural world and our experience of the spiritual world. The whole of life is sacred, as our being is but a manifestation of the Divine Being. Every person and, indeed, all beings are by nature sacred. Enlightened souls realize this while the unenlightened ones don't. The task of life is to shed one's ignorance in favor of knowing fully well the true nature of all beings in the ordinariness of daily existence. Some African cultures capture these sentiments with the assertion that "religion is life and life is religion."

Even if the West relegates it as distinct from the ordinary realms of social existence, it still speaks of religion as encompassing and engaging many aspects of the individual's existence. Religion is usually discussed in terms of the following four interrelated dimensions: (1) creed, the set of teachings and doctrines that are to be believed and adhered to; (2) code, the legal rules and principles that constitute the prescribed moral and ethical codes for the adherents; (3) cult, the ritual activities of prayers and sacrificial offerings that adherents participate in; and (4) community, the membership group of the followers with the appropriate leadership structures. Furthermore, religion generally entails the following three aspects: (1) sacred time, prescribed time for worship in a day or week or year; (2) sacred spaces, specially consecrated places for prayer or devotional purposes; and (3) sacred persons, recognized individuals who are the leaders and custodians of the tradition.

The Study of Religion

Religion has been the subject of intellectual inquiry throughout most of history. The more prominent examples are the inquiries of the great philosophers of the Greco-Roman period in the centuries leading up to the Common Era. The subject matter that these Greek philosophers investigated includes appreciating the myriad cultic practices as well as the variety of gods found in the many different Greek mythologies; these philosophers also posited a unitary entity that transcends these gods and serves as an overarching controlling principle, such as *logos* or reason. Another example of the study of religion is the scholarship among the Muslim philosophers of the Middle Ages. Worthy of mention are the works of the influential Persian scholar Muhammad al-Shahrastani, who pioneered the development of what was then regarded as an objective and philosophical approach to appreciating religion. His most celebrated work, *Treatise on the Religious and Philosophical Sects*, is considered to be among the first projects advancing the history of religion from an Islamic perspective. With the European colonial powers venturing out in voyages to the Americas, Africa, Asia, and beyond, the discovery of cultures and religions hitherto unknown to Europe not only fascinated the academic community but also opened their eyes and minds to beliefs and forms of worship that differed significantly from those of the Abrahamic faiths. The sixteenth-century contributions of the two Italian Jesuits, Matteo Ricci and Roberto De Nobili, to the study of religion were unparalleled until the modern era. The former's engagement with the Chinese religions shaped, to a great extent, how Catholicism was received by the peoples of China as he was able to explain the Catholic faith in Confucian terminology. De Nobili did the same by explaining Christianity and its teachings to the peoples of India and used terms coined in the local Tamil language to draw parallels between the faith of his Christian ancestors and the religious practices of his newly adopted home country, India, especially those associated with Hinduism.

The more formal study of religion, however, emerged only in the modern period, with its formative stages beginning in the nineteenth century. This was an era in which there was immense work being done to advance the application of scientific methods in literary studies, history, and philology, including on the scholarship of the historical and critical analysis of the Bible. The era also saw the discovery on a mass scale of the sacred texts of the Eastern cultures, which were then thoroughly edited and made accessible through translations into European languages. Max Mueller's edition of *Sacred Books of the East* was published by Oxford University Press between 1879 and 1910. It is a fifty-volume compilation of English translations of Asian religious writings of Hinduism, Buddhism, Taoism, Confucianism, Zoroastrianism, Jainism, and Islam. Archeological findings of prehistoric artifacts and cave paintings also provided new data and evidence to scientists and scholars about the religious beliefs and practices of preliterate societies, including those from pre-Christian Europe. They also shed light on the course of religious evolution from as far back as the ancestors of the first humans. Stories and news reports from merchants and explorers and those who had traveled to the East about the exotic cultures and religions they had witnessed also became more available throughout Europe and had a special influence on the members of the religion academy.

This same period also saw the beginnings of the advancement of the different intellectual disciplines in the social and human sciences such as anthropology, psychology, and sociology. Together with the arts and humanities, such as history and economics, they were all brought to bear on the study of religion. The aim was to establish a science to investigate religion through the use of methodologies that were more consistent with the scientific approaches that were gaining currency among scholars at that time. Max Mueller, in view of his 1873 book *Introduction to the Science of Religion*, is often associated with the beginnings of the scientific study of religion. While previously religion was studied on the basis of theological presuppositions and categories peculiar to the Christian religion (such as the primacy of the Bible or an analogous sacred text, the idea of God or of a divine entity, the linear conception of time, and the doctrines of salvation or Christian uniqueness), the new science of religion placed an emphasis on what were considered more objective and nonjudgmental criteria. The traditional dogmatic starting point (such as God's revelation in Christ) that revealed religions (read: Christianity) are *a priori* guarantee of truth and authenticity was no longer relied on. This obviously challenged the presumption of the supremacy of the Gospel or the Christian faith over the other religions.

This new science of religion is known variously as the history of religions, comparative religions, and also religious studies and is emphatic that it differs radically from the discipline of theology. While theology begins on the premise of faith, the study of religion strives to be adamantly neutral and objective. Set against the backdrop of European wider consciousness of religions other than the Abrahamic faiths, emphasis was placed on how the particular beliefs and practices of the individual religions can be studied, appreciated, and evaluated in their own right. Thus, there developed a method known as *epochē*, or bracketing off or setting aside one's own beliefs, fears, and biases in favor of a more detached and descriptive attitude toward what is observed in the religions. The idea of *epochē* was first used as a method in the phenomenology of religion as advocated by its proponent Edmund Husserl.

The Science of Religion

With the heightened awareness of the fact of religious pluralism, Western scholars of religion developed a preoccupation with identifying and theorizing, from a comparative perspective, the definitions of religion, its origins, and also its characteristics. Defining religion is, however, no mean task. There is practically no definition that can be applied to all the religions or that cannot be challenged. Some definitions are simply too narrow to be of any use, while others may be so broad that they include entities that have almost nothing to do with religion. But in general, the definitions fall under several categories. There are the monothetic definitions, which are based on a single idea or principle, and there are the polythetic definitions, where the many characteristics of religion are identified. There are two main types of monothetic definitions: (1) the substantive or essentialist theories that focus on the content of religions, identifying an element that is central to it (such as belief in a higher power or the ritual of worship); (2) the functional or utilitarian theories that focus on the social and psychological functions of religion, identifying what it does for people or society (such as allaying people's fears or bringing people together). Oftentimes, the search for the definition of religion overlaps with the quest for its origins and attempts at postulating its characteristics.

With the rise of the Darwinian theory of evolution in the field of biology in the late nineteenth century, social theorists began to postulate an evolutionary approach to understanding the origins of religion. John Lubbock's 1870 book, *The Origin of Civilization and the Primitive*

Condition of Man: Mental and Social Conditions of Savages, advanced the idea that in the beginning the *Homo sapiens* was without religion (atheism). This then switched to ascribing supernatural powers to objects (fetishism) and engagement with nature worship. The later progression was toward a mystical relationship with spirit-beings such as an animal or plant (totemism). The next stage was when worship involved a special person who has psychic and curative powers (shamanism). This slowly led to the practice where human characteristics were attributed to god (anthropomorphism), gradually giving way to the belief in one god (monotheism) and eventually culminating in the belief that god is the source and guide for all moral activities (ethical monotheism). Edward Burnett Tylor also developed an evolutionary theory of religion along the same lines. Considered the father of modern anthropology, he suggests, in his 1871 book *Primitive Culture*, that animism is the earliest and most basic form of the religious instinct. This evolved into fetishism, the belief in demons, then belief in many gods (polytheism), and finally monotheism. Tylor theorized that animism includes the belief that the human soul lives on after bodily death, as well as the belief in other non-human spirits and deities. He thus defined religion as "belief in spiritual beings" as it answers questions about natural life events that are in the main incomprehensible to the rational mind. As is clearly obvious, both Lubbock and Tylor were shaped by the Christian bias that considered Christian monotheism to be the most evolved—and, by extension, the most complex and superior—form of religious beliefs.

The philosopher and anthropologist whose thesis provided a paradigm for some of the functionalists' ideas about religion is Ludwig Feuerbach. In his most celebrated book, *The Essence of Christianity* (1841), he engaged in a serious critique of religion in general and Christianity in particular. Feuerbach's starting point is that it is in human consciousness and contemplation that people find out who they are and discover their true selves. So, when they contemplate God they are in fact learning more about themselves, their own needs, and individual nature. God is, therefore, somewhat of an outward projection of what the human person experiences of the inner self. The social philosopher Karl Marx extrapolated this idea of projection by analyzing religion from a strictly materialist and economic perspective. Reflecting on the suffering of the popular masses, especially the proletariat and subjugated peoples, and the comfort offered by religion, he defined religion as "the sigh of the oppressed creature, the heart of a heartless world, and the soul of soulless conditions. It is the opium of the people."[7] Marx considered religion to be the antidote to an otherwise painful situation that serves as the opium that numbs the people's senses to reality. This enables them to live in a wishful world of bliss and happiness, much like the metaphorical pie in the sky. Religion, therefore, is a symptom that the conditions of the people, particularly the working class, are pathetic and in need of being challenged. While religion provides an interpretation of the world that makes it temporarily bearable, Marx believed that the point is to change the living conditions that have led to the need for religion. He thus advocated a revolution to overthrow the status quo and fight against the oppression of the ruling and bourgeois class.

From the psychological perspective, Sigmund Freud employed Feuerbach's theory of projection to advance the thesis that religion is no more than an illusion based on the inadequate infantile feelings of helplessness of individuals longing for protection from a father or powerful figure. In his 1927 book, *The Future of an Illusion*, Freud asserted that religion is necessary in early human development because it offers a defense against the challenging forces that the environment presents while the child is maneuvering through the difficult task of growing up. Through its simplistic but effective teachings, religion also serves the role of spelling out the dos and don'ts of human behavior and so helps control the violent and destructive instincts of younger children in favor of more productive behaviors that strengthen the ego. Freud drew a parallel between religion and neurosis, emphasizing that they are both conjured up by the mind and that they are both made manifest through compulsive and repetitive behaviors. Religious rituals, for him, are no more than an obsessive neurosis, but displayed on a universal scale involving mass numbers of believers. Freud's thesis is that those who have grown up and become more informed ought to know that religion can be done away with instead of holding on to it as a psychological crutch and thus risk distorting their own growth. With reason and science, Freud insists, people should regain their independence by walking on their own without the crutch

7. Karl Marx, *A Contribution to the Critique of Hegel's Philosophy of Right*, trans. Annette Jolin and Joseph O'Malley (Cambridge: Cambridge University Press, 1970), https://www.marxists.org/archive/marx/works/1843/critique-hpr/index.htm.

of religion and take responsibility for their own lives without the need for the illusory reassurance provided by religion.

The Invention of World Religions

Like the idea of religion, the idea of "world religions" also came into dominant discourse only in the nineteenth century, especially toward its end. It shaped and is very much shaped by the study of religion, particularly since, previous to that, it had been customary for Western scholars to use the term "religion" when referring primarily and almost exclusively to the Christian tradition. Discussions or books on the topic of religion were usually about only the Christian religion, but their assertions and conclusions were generalized as if applicable to all the other religions. On the contrary, their findings sometimes do not make sense to some of the other religions of the world. This was but a reflection of the Christian bias that had been augmented by the European hegemony of the world. The advent of the term "world religions," therefore, was momentous as it signified that religions other than Christianity would be appreciated in their own right. It appeared, according to Tomoko Masuzawa, to be "a turn away from the Eurocentric and Eurohegemonic conception of the world, toward a more egalitarian and lateral delineation."[8] The use of the term "world religions" was indeed a major shift in attitude and worldview in favor of a more respectful and pluralist approach to apprehending the phenomenon of religion. Or, so it seems!

On closer scrutiny, however, the use of the term "world religions" was actually a continuation of the European academy's attempt at maintaining control and asserting its superiority. It served as a conceptual framework for othering and classifying "the rest" in contradistinction with what "the West" had hitherto considered religion to be. It provided a seemingly objective structure for identifying and differentiating a variety of social, cultural, and political practices of peoples in the rest of the world, subsuming them all under the rubric of religion and distinguishing them under the genus as world religions. It sacralized and spiritualized

8. Tomoko Masuzawa, *The Invention of World Religions: Or, How European Universalism Was Preserved in the Language of Pluralism* (Chicago: University of Chicago Press, 2005), 13.

a host of otherwise ordinary and mundane practices and enshrined them as suprahistorical supernatural religious observances. The more exotic the beliefs and practices, the more legitimate they become, as they then served the academic classification of Christianity's other.

This magnanimous openness to the diversity of religious expressions served also as a front for the underlying subtle but universalist Western agenda and tendencies. The interest in the other religions of the world served as a cover for asserting Christianity's uniqueness and superiority. Stephen Bevans offers an incisive description of this with reference to the first ever interreligious gathering in 1893, as well as the World Christian Missionary Conference at Edinburgh of 1910: "A century ago there was no doubt of the superiority of Christianity over the other world religions: the modern 'master narrative' was in full force. This was evidenced at Chicago's 1893 World Parliament of Religions and at Edinburgh itself, where the demise of the other world religions was confidently predicted if Christians would take the initiative boldly and quickly."[9] This is by no means an exaggerated claim as the Christian organizers of the World Parliament of Religions event did harbor some of these colonizing desires. For instance, in welcoming the plans for the parliament, President W. F. Warren of Boston University reflected on how he had once preached that by assembling the leaders of the great religions together to discuss the problem of faith, they would all reach "the conclusion that there could only be one perfect Religion, that the perfect Religion must reveal a perfect God, that it must assure man the greatest ultimate good, that it must bring God into the most loving and lovable relations with humanity, and that this could be achieved only by his taking upon a human form, and suffering for man."[10] There is no dispute that he was referring to Christianity in this proclamation.

---

9. Stephen Bevans, "From Edinburgh to Edinburgh: Toward a Missiology for a World Church," in *Mission after Christendom: Emergent Themes in Contemporary Mission*, ed. Ogbu U. Kalu, Peter Vethanayagamony, and Edmund Kee-Fook Chia (Louisville: Westminster John Knox, 2010), 6.

10. Rev. John Henry Barrows, ed., *The World's Parliament of Religions: An Illustrated and Popular Story of the World's First Parliament of Religions, Held in Chicago in Connection with the Columbian Exposition of 1893*, vol. 1 (Chicago: Parliament Publishing Company, 1893), 9.

In hindsight we can see that the parliament eventually accomplished the opposite result. This is because, according to John Henry Barrows, the chair of the Parliament General Committee, "the Asians at the Parliament set out to accomplish a number of things—to check Christian missionaries, counter western aggression, assert the integrity of their own religious traditions, and gain public support for their objectives."[11] Not only was the organizers' agenda for universalizing Christianity dashed, the other religions actually received a boost from the parliament and set out on a path of renaissance. Thus, instead of Christianity advancing to the East, the Ramakrishna mission, Zen Buddhism, and some other Eastern religious movements made significant inroads in the West and its mission to the West continued into the twentieth century.

The World's Religions

There are various ways in which the religions of the world are termed and classified. The term "world religions" is often used when discussing the many religions of the world, though what makes it "world" is often in dispute. Is it in reference to religions that are transcultural and international, religions that have proselytizing motives, religions that make claims to possessing universal truth, or religions that have a worldwide population? Likewise, there are a variety of ways the many religions are categorized. A common paradigm is to classify the main religions according to the three distinct regions in Asia where many of them have grown out of:

(1) Middle East or West Asia—Judaism, Christianity, Islam
(2) Indian subcontinent or South Asia—Hinduism, Buddhism, Jainism, Sikhism
(3) Oriental or East Asia—Confucianism, Taoism

This does not take into account a number of other religions, some with fewer adherents, less widespread, or lesser known and so not counted among the world religions. Many of these are religions that are more localized, culture specific, and found only within a particular nation or

11. Richard Hughes Seager, *The World's Parliament of Religions: The East/West Encounter, Chicago, 1893* (Bloomington: Indiana University Press, 1995), 97.

context, such as the variety of indigenous religions (previously referred to as primitive, primal, or tribal religions) and the new religious movements, including the New Age religions.

Below is a very quick introduction to the world religions above, excluding Christianity (since it was already introduced in the preceding chapter), but looking at only their origins and where they feature in the world stage today.

Judaism

Judaism is the religion of the Jewish people, whose name comes from one of Jacob's sons called Judah. It is also known as the religion of the people of Israel, the first of the three Abrahamic faiths that evolved through history. The foundations of the Israelite religion begin with Moses and the exodus, the reception of the covenant at Mount Sinai, leading up to the conquest and settlement of the Israelites in Canaan, the Promised Land. With the destruction of the temple of Jerusalem by the Romans in 70 CE, Rabbinic Judaism came into ascendancy. The codification of the Talmud complemented and interpreted the Torah to encourage religious practice in the absence of temple sacrifices with rabbis to serve as teachers and leaders of the Jewish communities. Today there are about fourteen million Jews in the world, most of whom live in Israel and the United States.

Islam

Islam is the third of the Abrahamic faiths—after Christianity—and arose in the seventh century on the Arab peninsula. The Arabs are believed to be descendants of Ishmael, the son of Abraham and Hagar (the Egyptian maid of Abraham's wife, Sarah). One of the descendants, Muhammad, received divine revelations of the practice of the true faith in the one God, *Allah*. This is the same primordial faith that had already been revealed through the prophets of old, including to Adam, Abraham, Moses, and Jesus, all of whom are considered prophets of Islam. The revelation to Prophet Muhammad, the Seal of the Prophets, was codified into the Qur'an and regarded as the Word of God. Together with the *Sunnah* and *Hadith*, its teachings provide the norm for Muslim living. Today, Islam is the second largest religion in the world, with a population in excess of 1.6 billion and growing. The majority of Muslims live in Asia, with Indonesia, Pakistan, Bangladesh, and India housing nearly half its global population.

Hinduism

Hinduism is a religion that is usually not associated with a particular founder, body of scriptures, or set of philosophies or beliefs. It is more a synthesis of many different Indian cultures and traditions. Its name comes from the Indus River called *Sindhu,* used in the fifteenth or sixteenth century to distinguish the local people from the Muslim foreigners. It is sometimes called the *Sanatana Dharma* or "eternal tradition," and the Vedic scriptures are also regarded as eternal truths revealed to the ancient sages. Together with other sacred texts, such as the *Upanishads, Bhaga-vad Gita,* and the *Ramayana,* the *Vedas* are revered and studied and are the basis for Hindu beliefs. One prominent belief is that the pantheon of deities and divine beings that Hindus accept are manifestations of a single impersonal absolute known as Brahman. Hinduism is the third largest religion in the world today, with more than 1.1 billion followers, the majority living in India and Nepal.

Buddhism

Buddhism is sometimes regarded as a reform movement against the Brahmanic philosophy that gave rise to Hinduism. It has its origins with Prince Siddhartha Gautama, who left his ostentatious lifestyle in a quest for the truth that will end the cycle of birth and rebirth and suffering in humankind. He began his search by studying under Vedic teachers, switched to asceticism, and finally turned to the practice of intense meditation. He discovered the truth about *karma* (spiritual principle of cause and effect) and taught the Middle Way of the Noble Eightfold Path between the extremes of sensual indulgence and self-mortification. As an enlightened being or awakened one, he was then called the Buddha. Buddhist practices include taking refuge in the Buddha, the *Dharma* (teachings), and the *Sangha* (monastic community). Even as its origins is in India, Buddhism spread rapidly to East Asia and adapted itself efficiently so that today it is recognized more as a Chinese religion. There are about 500 million Buddhists in the world, the majority living in China and East Asian countries such as Japan, Korea, Thailand, and Myanmar.

Jainism

Like Buddhism, Jainism is also a reform movement against Brahmanism and was born at around the same time in the sixth or fifth century BCE.

Like Hinduism, Jainism also regards itself as an eternal religion. It was established by Mahavira, who was born into a royal family. Jainism is emphatic about the practice of asceticism and has *ahimsa* (nonviolence), including not killing any living being, as a core principle of the religion. The other two core principles include nonabsolutism and nonattachment. These principles have shaped the way Jains live their lives, including adopting a predominantly vegetarian lifestyle and avoiding occupations that are connected with harm to any beings, including animals. Thus, one finds them mainly in the trade and financial sectors. There are about seven million Jains in the world and the majority live in India.

Sikhism

Sikhism is one of the younger religions of the world, originating in the Punjab region of northern India only in the fifteenth century. It is sometimes looked on as having incorporated the ideals of Hinduism and Islam as its teachings embrace both the radical monotheism of Islam and rejection of idolatry, as well as the Hindu concepts of *karma*, *dharma*, and *samsara*. Sikhism owes its origins to Guru Nanak, who, after a mystical experience, preached that "there is no Hindu, there is no Muslim." Its religious teachings place less emphasis on ritual activities in favor of encouraging individuals to cultivate their internal state through contemplation especially of the divine name. Succeeding Guru Nanak were nine Sikh *gurus* (teachers), after which the Sikh scripture, the *Guru Granth Sahib*, was named as successor, bringing an end to the line of human gurus and conferring eternal status to the community's sacred text. There are about twenty-seven million Sikhs today, most of whom continue to reside in the northern Indian state of Punjab.

Confucianism

Confucianism is often regarded not as a religion but more as a system of social and ethical philosophy or merely a way of life or governance of the peoples. In the sixth century BCE, in an era of the warring Chinese states, Kung Fu Tzu (Confucius) taught the societal values of compassion and tradition. These teachings were later encoded in the *Analects*, which is the key text for appreciating Confucian philosophy of ethics, public life, and education. Depending on the ruler of the time, Confucianism was at times conferred the status of imperial philosophy of China but at other times repressed by the state. Most people of Chinese descent embrace Confucianism, in particular values such as *xiao* (filial piety), *ren* (humanness or benevolence), and *yi* (justice or righteousness). While there are more than 1.5 billion Chinese around the world, demographics usually indicate that there are about six million Confucians, most of whom live in China.

Taoism

Taoism is the complementary system to Confucianism in a *yin-yang* Chinese cosmology that sees seemingly opposite forces as interdependent. While Confucianism emphasizes rigid rituals and social order, Taoism encourages spontaneity and the natural flow in view of facilitating harmony, as expressed in the principle of *wu wei* (effortless action). The concept of *Tao*, which informs most Chinese schools of philosophy, literally means "the way" but is used to denote the creative principle of the universe or the source and pattern of all existence. Taoism is associated with Lao Tzu (old master), a contemporary of Confucius believed to be the author of the *Tao Te Ching*, which has become the foundational text for its philosophical system. This system forms the bases for the Chinese practices of astrology, martial arts, traditional medicine, and *feng shui* (the Chinese metaphysical and quasi-philosophical system). Like Confucianism, it is difficult to determine the number of Taoists since most people of Chinese descent embrace the religious practices of Taoism, Confucianism, and Buddhism all at once. Like Confucians, the majority of Taoists live in China.

Conclusion

The study of religion has seen many interesting investigations over the course of the past centuries and millennia. To be sure, these investigations will continue to multiply as more data and knowledge about the varieties of religious beliefs and practices become available in the contemporary information age. Even if it may appear that religion is in its death throes in the global North, it continues to serve as a dynamic, ongoing force in the lives of most people in the rest of the world. One of the key themes that dominates research today is the phenomenon of religious pluralism. The postmodern adventure occurs when we are able to pass over to another religious tradition and then return to our own enriched with new insights not only into the world of the other but also into our own religious tradition as well. This is where interfaith dialogue will have a significant role to play, with its thrust toward facilitating relationship across the traditions in view of building bridges of understanding and cooperation.

Suggestions for Further Reading

Eck, Diana L. *A New Religious America: How a "Christian Country" Has Now Become the World's Most Religiously Diverse Nation.* New York: HarperSanFranciso, 2001.

Esposito, John L., Darrell J. Fasching, and Todd Lewis. *World Religions Today.* 3rd ed. Oxford: Oxford University Press, 2009.

Nongbri, Brent. *Before Religion: A History of a Modern Concept.* New Haven, CT: Yale University Press, 2015.

Sharpe, Eric J. *Comparative Religion: A History.* 2nd ed. London: Duckworth, 1986.

Smith, Huston. *The World's Religions.* New York: HarperSanFranciso, 1991.

3

Principles and Methodology for Dialogue

Introduction

The parish priest had invited me to give a talk on interfaith dialogue. It was a small group of about twenty parishioners, and I thought it would be a good idea to begin by asking them to share their experience and/or attitude toward interfaith dialogue. This was a parish in a cosmopolitan city, and so I expected most of the parishioners to have friends or colleagues or even relatives who adhere to other faith traditions. The first person to speak nearly derailed my plan to use an interactive method to conduct the session. She introduced herself as a high school teacher and then said, "I'm not a priest, I'm not a theologian. I barely know much about my own Christian faith, much less about other religions. How can you expect me to have any experience in interfaith dialogue?"

This is what the present chapter will discuss. Its starting point is that interfaith dialogue is for everyone, not just for the trained theologian. It looks at the what, why, when, and how of the dialogical experience and the basic principles recommended for those engaged in this ministry. Specifically, interfaith dialogue will first be defined so as to clarify what it is and to emphasize the crucial role of witnessing and learning. Then, the reasons why it is important will be discussed, focusing on the real differences that exist between the religious traditions. That interfaith dialogue is not just an intellectual and academic exercise will be examined as we delineate its various forms and how they are engaged under different circumstances. Finally, for interfaith dialogue to be effective it would be necessary that the interlocutors possess certain dispositions and attitudes and that certain methods and precautions are adhered to during the dialogical encounter itself. All of these will be examined in view of building a case for considering interfaith dialogue an essential activity for all persons of goodwill.

Definition of Interfaith Dialogue

Because interfaith dialogue is a relatively new activity and remains very much in its infancy stages, many people have misconceptions about what it really stands for. Some misconstrue it for a debate where adherents of different faiths come together to face off against each other on fundamental issues of religion, such as God or salvation or truth. Such exercises, they believe, are meant to ascertain the truth or falsity of how each religion appreciates the issues and end when one party's views emerge as more convincing and the other party's views are discredited, if not altogether disparaged. That is not what interfaith dialogue is about. It is certainly not an argumentative event where there is a winner and a loser. In interfaith dialogue, all the parties involved emerge victorious.

Besides, interfaith dialogue is more than just a verbal exercise or intellectual exchange. It is an encompassing term used to include all forms of positive encounters and relationships between persons of different faith experiences or who hold different worldviews, especially those that are explicitly religious. Some of these encounters are formal while others may be informal and unorganized, taking place on the streets or in the marketplace in the form of spontaneous interactions between persons of different religions. The level or extent of each person's participation really depends on their situation in life and the opportunities they are presented with. Some are more active in it while others are less so. But, ideally, all of us should be engaged in interfaith dialogue in some form or another. This is, in fact, the contemporary teaching and mandate of many churches and especially the Roman Catholic Church.

We participate in interfaith dialogue as individuals, even as we adhere to and represent a particular religious or faith tradition. As individuals, we come to the dialogue with our whole beings, bringing with us our wisdom, thoughts, feelings, insecurities, fears, preconceptions, education, and everything that make us who we are. In interfaith dialogue we realize that we are encountering not only the other person's mind but their body, heart, will, and history as well. It is essential that all parties are totally respectful of and sensitive to the totality of being of their dialogue partners. Interfaith dialogue is an encounter not between the religions or religious institutions but between their adherents. It is the religious persons who are engaged in the encounters. But the religious persons participate in the dialogue as members of their own religion, without having to give up their religious identity. No one should think that interfaith dialogue means having to set aside or bracket off our religious viewpoints so that we do not have to deal with the difficult and sometimes conflicting beliefs or practices between the religions. On the contrary, it is precisely because of the differences that those engaged in interfaith dialogue should be consciously willing and able to identify with their faith traditions. In other words, the dialogue partners should not be ashamed of their religious identity or apologize for it; they are an essential component of the dialogical encounters. Otherwise, the encounters would be no more than two human beings in dialogue with one another on specific issues, including those of religion, but attending to them from perspectives that have nothing to do with their own faith or religion. That has a place in the academy and in life but is not usually regarded as interfaith dialogue.

The reason why the faith dimension is essential is because each person in the dialogical encounter is expected to share what they believe and to witness to their own faith. Interfaith dialogue is a two-way, interactive process where there is teaching and learning, giving and receiving, and sharing and listening. In order for us to witness to our faith or share our beliefs, it is necessary for us to be committed to it in the first place. We also need to have adequate knowledge of what our faith teaches and to courageously and sincerely represent it as authentically as possible. That is why the activity of interfaith dialogue can sometimes be an impetus for the participants to revisit and renew the knowledge of their own faith. The idiom "teachers make the best students" is most apt here, as those who are expected to teach will force themselves to learn so that they have a reasonably good grasp of their own faith. While it would be expected that we share our faith convincingly in view of enabling the other to understand and appreciate it, we do so fully aware that our sharing is but a gift to the dialogue. There is no expectation that the other will necessarily agree or accept it. What we could hope for is that our sharing will enable the other to view our religion from a more informed and holistic perspective and, in the process, dispel any distortion or falsehood that the other may have previously acquired about our religion.

If sharing and witnessing to our faith is important in interfaith dialogue, so is receiving and learning. Both parties in the dialogue will have to be open to not only hearing what the other has to say but also to listening sincerely and attentively. Interfaith dialogue is premised on the hope that people are willing to open their eyes and minds as well as their hearts and souls to receive what the other has to offer. The process of listening requires that we suspend and bracket our previous understandings of what we think we know of the other's religion and also that we not make judgments about what the other is sharing with us. Such courtesy facilitates authentic and respectful listening. Dialogue is aimed at enabling us to better appreciate what the other is sharing and not about whether what they are saying is right or wrong, good or bad. Of course, where we do not fully understand what the other is saying it is perfectly appropriate to seek clarification. Reiterating an earlier statement, it is never expected that we agree or accept what the other is sharing, but it is certainly hoped that we can come to a better understanding of their faith and religious beliefs.

What can also be hoped for in interfaith dialogue is that the encounters result in the "conversion" of the parties involved. This does not refer to institutional conversion, where one person switches over to another religion, but to intellectual, moral, and spiritual conversion. Obviously, it will take many years of dialogical experiences for such conversions to happen. But when they do, they enable us to apprehend reality in new ways, have widened horizons for understanding life and faith issues, and develop an expanded consciousness to govern our thinking and acting. One could also call this *metanoia* or personal transformation where there is a total change in one's attitude and way of life. We would then develop empathy for what our dialogue partner shares with us, a more encompassing moral and social awareness, as well as an inclusive and dialogical worldview.

Reasons for Interfaith Dialogue

Having discussed the "what" of interfaith dialogue, it would be reasonable to ask why interfaith dialogue is necessary. The most obvious reason motivating interfaith dialogue, as alluded to above, is that there are indeed differences across the religious and faith traditions. Those who subscribe to the "all religions are the same" or the "they all say the same thing" theories are oversimplifying the phenomenon at best. While it is true that there are similarities between the many different religions, it is also true that they are inherently different, not only in their histories and organizational structures but also in what they teach and the practices they prescribe. For example, not only is the Ultimate Reality called by different names in the different religions, there are also significant differences between what is understood by Brahman or Allah or God or the Tao or Nirvana or the Great Spirit. Besides, there is certainly no consensus as to whether this Ultimate Reality whom Christians call God is a personal being or nonpersonal and nonbeing or whether it is singular, plural, or nonexistent. To be sure, there are many other teachings and doctrines as well as moral codes and cultic practices that vary from one religious tradition to another.

In light of these real differences, a sincere search for truth ought to include what we can learn from the other religions. If, as Christians, we have a fair idea of what God has done according to the teachings of our own tradition, would we not want to find out what the other religions teach about God and God's activity in the world? The earnest seeker would surely be open to new and additional knowledge about God, and this can be acquired if we are in dialogue with our religious neighbors. Moreover, as we learn more about what the other religions teach about particular truths, we will need to revisit our understandings of what our own religion teaches about those same truths. Interfaith dialogue brings us back to our own faith so that we can look at it again, but with new eyes, that is, eyes that have been transformed on the basis of the fresh knowledge we attained from outside of our faith tradition. This is why it can be asserted that interfaith dialogue serves to enhance the knowledge of our own faith. Aside from relearning our own faith, interfaith dialogue enables us to discover common features shared by the different religions. This could lead us to having a greater appreciation for other religions as we can identify with those beliefs that resemble ours. The gap that divides the different religious traditions can then be gradually bridged, thanks to the dynamics of interfaith dialogue. Thus, interfaith dialogue will definitely enhance our understandings of reality and the pursuit of truth about religion and life in general.

While differences across the religions have to be acknowledged, the practical consequence of this reality has to be dealt with. But, first, it would be useful to take note of how the various religions negotiate the fact of religious pluralism. Historically, most religions developed independently of one another and sometimes even consciously in isolation from other religions. Their sacred texts and traditions indicate that they are not interested in or have no need for another religion. The attitude of a religion's adherents toward other religions is often characterized more by feelings of superiority and condescension than of mutual respect or interdependency. There is a tendency within particular religions to view religious diversity negatively, as an undesirable situation that has to be tolerated if doing away with it altogether is not a viable option. But in our increasingly globalized world where we are almost forced to come face-to-face with others who adhere to different religions, either in our own backyards or in our living rooms or on our iPhones, denying the need to engage with the religious other is probably no longer an option. Transnational migration, tourism, mass and social media, and a host of other avenues are thrusting religious diversity on to us, forcing us to attend to the fact that the strangers we encounter come with their strange beliefs and alien practices as well. While all these social changes are happening at exponential rates, religious people are generally not too well equipped with the necessary attitudes, concepts, visions, and skills to assist in apprehending them. Many continue to operate out of their ignorance about the religious other and are easily susceptible to negative feelings such as fear, threat, and insecurity. Those who wield social and political power may allow these feelings to manifest in behaviors such as discrimination, marginalization, persecution, and other forms of violence, including rioting against and even killing off the religious other. To be sure, numerous incidences of extremism and violence have been committed against groups of people primarily because of their religious difference. This is why interfaith dialogue is urgently needed. It offers an alternative response in the face of the innumerable negative reactions to religious diversity. It sees diversity as not a necessary evil but a potential for good. It witnesses to the fact that developing positive and harmonious relations with those who are religiously other than us is not only possible but enriching as well. It sends another message to society and proclaims another narrative in the media: that religious pluralism is a blessing that has to be relished and that we can and should strive toward developing wholesome and holy relationships with our religious neighbors.

Forms of Interfaith Dialogue

As mentioned earlier, interfaith dialogue is an activity that all persons can engage in and is not only for scholars or trained theologians. Christians, whether ordained or lay, are certainly called to it as part of their Christian duty, especially if they live in multireligious contexts. But not everyone is expected to participate in interfaith dialogue the same way or to the same extent. There are various forms of interfaith dialogue, and each person's participation depends very much on their situation in life and/or position in the social-cultural sphere.

The most basic form of interfaith dialogue is what is called the *dialogue of life*. This is the day-to-day dialogue that people engage in and is obviously nonformal, unstructured, and unplanned. It is a dialogue that everyone can and should participate in. It is a dialogue that involves our whole selves as individuals and persons. It happens when we consciously relate with our neighbors of other faiths in the lecture hall or dining room or sports complex instead of avoiding them because of their religious difference. There is no need for any discussion on religion; the simple act of interacting positively with someone who is of another religion is already the dialogue of life. It happens when we are nice to people of other faiths and extend our hand of friendship and hospitality to them for no reason other than because it is the appropriate thing to do. Of course, it is also the Christian thing to do, especially when authentic values and convictions are brought to the fore. In other words, the dialogue of life is "purposeless" and manifests itself when peoples of different religions welcome one another wholeheartedly while respecting the religious difference between them. It may sound easy and effortless, but it is a much-needed alternative to the demeaning and disparaging ways some people treat those who are of another religion. Social media is replete with stories of people being hostile and violent toward those of other faiths or who speak or think evil of their intentions or who are simply not prepared to be pleasant to them. The sad reality is that many of them display these behaviors even if they have never talked to any person of a different religion. Obviously, stereotypes and misinformation are depended on to trigger these knee-jerk defensive and offensive behaviors. Those engaged in the dialogue of life are presenting an alternative narrative to such inauspicious conduct and malicious attitudes. It is for this reason that the dialogue of life is the most important of all the different forms of dialogue and should ideally become a way of life for as many people as possible.

A second form of dialogue is called the *dialogue of action*. When people of different religions come together to address an issue or problem of common concern, they are engaged in the dialogue of action. It is also sometimes known as the dialogue of the hands, as people join hands and lock arms as they go about confronting together the challenges posed to their communities. The dialogue of action has, as its principal aim, the alleviation of the pain and suffering of humanity and also that of the earth. It can take the form of cooperative ventures across religions in attending to problems such as homelessness, drug addiction, or poverty. It could also take the form of advocating for the environment, for an oppressed group of workers, or for victims of domestic abuse or human trafficking. What makes it an interfaith dialogue of action is when religious people consciously reach across to their partners of other religions to work collaboratively on behalf of society in general and in the service of life. A church group, for example, intending to start a soup kitchen goes out of its way to seek help from the adherents of the neighborhood mosque. Or a Catholic school sending their students to tutor children in an asylum-seeker camp does so in partnership with students from the city's Buddhist school. That way, these activities are not merely social and humanitarian in nature but become interfaith bridge-building opportunities as well. Christians are exhorted to participate in the dialogue of action because it serves also to reinforce the fact that people of other religions are to be regarded not as competitors but as allies and partners of Christian mission. The liberation of the people and the environment is a mission common to all religions; all their adherents can and should play a central role in it, and, more important, they must do it together.

A third form of dialogue is known as the *dialogue of discourse*. It is also sometimes called theological dialogue or the dialogue of the head. As the name suggests, this dialogue is intellectual in nature and the task of those who have specific knowledge of theology, especially comparative theology. It is a dialogue particular to trained scholars and happens most often in academic settings. It is the most published form of dialogue and for that reason is often mistakenly thought to be the only type of interfaith dialogue possible. That accounts for why those who perceive themselves as theologically incompetent feel they should not be involved in the dialogue ministry. The dialogue of discourse addresses all areas of religion, from comparing scripture to clarifying cultic practices to discussing doctrines and beliefs to analyzing the myths and stories of each other's religious tradition. It presumes that we engage in interfaith dialogue not only because people of different faiths have different perspectives but because there are real and significant differences across the various religious beliefs and practices. In acknowledging this, the dialogue of discourse sometimes aims at discerning and understanding which elements of religion are more likely to find convergence and which are more likely to end up in divergence. Engaging in the dialogue of discourse effectively means doing theology together with persons of other religions. The concrete presence of the religious other makes it unlikely that the theological reflection ends up being negatively biased against the other's religion. Moreover, understanding the other's religion through an actual process of dialogue differs from the understanding one acquires from a process of book research. In the dialogue of discourse we engage not only the beliefs or doctrines but the whole being of the dialogue partner as well. Such dialogues are not only academic but become religious or sacred encounters. This is why the dialogue of discourse is critical to all the religions, even as it usually involves only the more educated and elite sectors of the religious communities.

A fourth form of dialogue is the *dialogue of religious experience*. Also called the dialogue of spirituality or the dialogue of the heart, this is the spiritual dimension of dialogue where an openness of heart is essential. How do we pray? Why do we pray? Who is God for us? What motivates us to live virtuously? These are some of the questions addressed in this form of dialogue. Our experiences in pilgrimages, a spiritual insight, a religious vision, or a prayer image are some of the contents of this dialogue. As dialogues of religious experience entail the sharing of personal experiences that can at times be intimate, it is generally understood that there will be no arguments or even discussions on what is shared. Instead, it is made clear that each dialogue partner is encouraged to share about the depths of their own religious experience with no direct preoccupational concern for its rightness or wrongness. As sharing of religious experience, they remain personal and subjective and can only add to the treasury of how people experience their God and live their faith. The dialogue of religious experience could also include opportunities where the dialogue partners come together to accompany the other in a religious practice such as fasting during the month of Ramadhan or participation in prayer in the other's place of worship. This form of dialogue is most exemplified in the church through the Christian spiritual or ashram movements, which are centers of the monastic tradition established for the purpose of contemplative and ascetic prayer. These centers are privileged places for interfaith dialogue in view of the ambience they provide, which is generally welcoming of all persons regardless of religious affiliation. The contemplative nature of their prayers makes for universal acceptability and facilitates spiritual bonds between persons even if they may each subscribe to a different institutional religion.

While the above are the four forms of dialogue that people generally engage in, it does not suggest that they are rigid descriptions to be adhered to with no overlaps. At times the different forms of dialogue flow into one another and then back-and-forth. For example, a Christian who has befriended a newly arrived Muslim migrant from Iraq in college (dialogue of life) invites her new friend to join her in a rally organized by the #BlackLivesMatter movement (dialogue of action). While protesting under the scorching sun, she asks her Muslim friend what it is like to be wearing the *hijab* (head covering) and this leads to an enriching conversation on the theological significance of putting on the veil and the practice of modesty according to both their religious traditions (dialogue of discourse). As evening draws near, the Muslim invites her new Christian friend to join her as she performs the sunset or *Maghrib* prayers. Reciprocating, the Christian invites her Muslim friend to accompany her to the church's Sunday worship (dialogue of religious experience). This is but an example of Christian-Muslim dialogue at all the levels and forms of interfaith dialogue. These multiple forms of dialogues are happening all the time without people even thinking that they are involved in what is now labelled as interfaith dialogue.

Attitudes for Enhancing Interfaith Dialogue

While everyone, especially Christians, is called to the ministry of interfaith dialogue, not everyone has the necessary attitudes and disposition to ensure a successful outcome. Those who bring to the dialogue table certain negativity guarantee that their experience will be similarly negative. On the other hand, those who are generally positive and optimistic about the dialogical encounter usually end up with outcomes that are not only positive but life-giving and life-changing as well. What is essential is that the interlocutors are serious about the dialogical encounter and bring with them the two basic attitudes of rootedness to their own tradition and relatedness with others.

As mentioned earlier, we engage in interfaith dialogue as members, if not representatives, of our own religious community. We do not surrender or diminish this aspect of our identity. It is in fact a requirement that we come to the encounter fully rooted in our religion and familiar with its convictions. Only then is interfaith dialogue meaningful, both for the dialogue partners and for their respective traditions. This is what it means by rootedness in one's tradition. There are two integral components to this. First, we speak not only for ourselves but also on behalf of an entire religious tradition. As such, it is crucial that we have a certain degree of commitment to our religion, are conversant with what it teaches, and are able to represent it reasonably well. Our dialogue partner must be able to learn something about the most authentic aspects of our religious tradition through their encounter with us. Second, rootedness also means that we are committed to returning to our community to share with its members the fruits of our dialogical encounters. In other words, it is necessary that the insights and experiences gained from interfaith dialogue be beneficial to our own co-religionists and that the community learns and grows from it as well. Hence, the attitude of rootedness entails a commitment to engaging with our religious neighbors to help them understand our tradition and also to returning to our community to share with its members elements that can enrich our own tradition.

This takes us to the second basic attitude needed for successful interfaith dialogue, that is, relatedness. One of the principal aims of interfaith dialogue is that both parties learn and grow through the encounter in a mutually enriching and reciprocal relationship. This happens only if the interlocutors are open to learning from their partners in dialogue. While committed to the teachings of our own religion, we should also be generally open to learning what the other religions teach. The commitment that we have to our own faith must therefore be a gentle and respectful commitment. It is not arrogant in thinking that we have nothing more to learn from the religious other and therefore will not even bother to listen to what they have to say. Instead, it is a commitment that humbly recognizes the limitation and especially the finiteness of our own religion or our understanding of what it teaches. This epistemic humility means that we believe that there are areas for growth in our understandings of truth and that this can be enriched by learning from our dialogue partners. It also means that we are hospitable and generous in acknowledging that the other religions do contain elements of truth that we can learn from. These attitudes are premised on the conviction that there is a relatedness and interconnection between the different religious traditions and that they are all attempting to wrestle with the same existential questions of life, God, spirituality, and the universe.

It is therefore with receptive minds that we approach the convictions and values of the religious other, since, even if we believe in the fullness of truth in our own religion, there is no guarantee that we have grasped this truth appropriately and fully. It is imperative that we cultivate an attitude of empathy in interfaith dialogue so that we can truly stretch our imagination and appreciate what our dialogue partner is sharing with us, stepping into their shoes if possible. This passing-over to the world of the religious other would enable us to gain an empathic understanding of their faith, beliefs, and practices. Of course, if we are able to participate in their rituals and spiritual exercises, that would be a further help in our appreciation of their faith tradition. These are all fruits of the dialogical encounter. Far from weakening our own faith, authentic interfaith dialogue should enhance and deepen it as new dimensions of the faith are discovered. A balanced attitude is crucial, one that is open and receptive but not ingenuous or overly critical. Dialogue also requires a spirit of generosity and impartiality, acceptance of differences and of possible contradictions. Above all, it is the will to engage together in commitment to the truth and the readiness to allow ourselves to be transformed by the encounter that makes interfaith dialogue a life-changing and life-giving ministry.

Strategies for Enhancing Interfaith Dialogue

Interfaith dialogue is about developing positive relationships between persons of different religious and faith traditions. Like all relationships, it is not an easy endeavor. Positive relationships are not cultivated overnight. A lot of investment needs to be made to ensure the viability of the dialogue ministry and to minimize distractions and possible pitfalls. Challenges from both within and without the relationship can make it sometimes seem insurmountable. Even with the best of intentions we can sometimes fail miserably if we are not careful about the approach we take in developing interfaith relations. Socio-psychological knowledge can be employed in foregrounding appropriate strategies to ensure that our efforts are enhancing and not obstructing interfaith dialogue.

A first strategy is to employ the socio-psychological factor of similarity. As the old adage "birds of a feather flock together" predicts, we generally get along better with people who display characteristics, attitudes, or interests that are similar to ours. This is because they not only resonate closely with us but also confirm our very own convictions. As such, interfaith dialogue needs to begin with discussing or engaging issues of similarities between the religions. It is undoubtedly more beneficial for us to be highlighting shared principles, beliefs, stories, or values than those that are markedly different. In other words, more efforts should be made in drawing parallels between the traditions or in identifying areas of convergences so that the dialogue partners are aware of the common ground they share. When this happens, the religious other is no longer an alien with strange beliefs but one who understands the realities of life and of the universe in some of the same ways we do. Because dismissing or disparaging another religion that is quite similar to ours creates cognitive dissonance, this strategy has greater promise for enhancing interfaith dialogue and promoting positive relationships between the followers of the different religions.

A second strategy is to invoke the familiarity effect. The more familiar we are with something or someone, the more likely we are to like it. Scholars call this the "familiarity breeds liking" effect. People prefer the familiar to the unfamiliar simply because they have more experience with the former. Not only is it more comforting, we are also better able to predict the person's or thing's behavior. An object we are familiar with is more reassuring to us and less likely to hurt us or, at least, less likely to hurt us in unexpected ways. Thus, we usually tend not to risk the familiar for the unfamiliar. Familiarity can be increased by repeated exposures as processing the object becomes easier each time since we have more information about its characteristics. When the processing is made easier and less complicated for our lazy brain, it facilitates our liking of the object. Advertisers capitalize on this mere exposure effect and so repeatedly expose us to a product in view of making it more familiar and conditioning us to desire it. This is also what needs to be done in interfaith dialogue. We can be exposed more regularly to the teachings, values, stories, practices, and also the institutions of other faiths. This is what exposure programs are aimed at achieving. Churches can organize excursions or visits to mosques and gurdwaras to enable Christians to simply be exposed to the Islamic or Sikh cultures and religions. Or churches can have exhibitions or conduct classes where the principles and practices of other religions are disseminated widely. These events provide Christians the opportunity to become more familiar with the other religions and hence develop a greater openness toward their adherents. Direct exposure to the adherents of these other religions would be even better. This can be facilitated by joint social programs involving other religious communities. They are invaluable occasions where believers of different religions not only mix with one another but also begin cultivating long-lasting friendships.

Closely related to the principle of familiarity is the principle of proximity. We generally relate more with people who are physically closer to us for no other reason than that they are accessible and striking up a relationship is more convenient. When we get to see or hear or speak to someone more frequently, chances are that we are more prepared to foster a positive relationship with that person. This is because the exposures and contacts provide opportunities for us to better understand the person's character, attitudes, and values, thus enabling us to become more familiar with them. Moreover, as it is psychologically distressing to frequently meet or be alongside someone we hate, proximity encourages us to strive for a positive relationship. Thus, one effective way to enhance interfaith relations is to reduce the physical distance between the religious communities. Where possible, persons of different religions should be encouraged to mix with one another rather than be segregated. Schools or residential communities that remain segregated by religion have more challenges to confront in the task of promoting positive encounters across the religions. Conversely, those who grow up in desegregated pluralistic communities or who attend multireligious schools are generally more open to people of different religions. Where churches are built alongside the houses of worship of other religions they have a greater chance for enhancing interfaith relations. On the flip side, where they are situated far away from other religions there is the risk that they become exclusivist in their worldview and think nothing of interfaith dialogue.

All three factors mentioned above—similarity, familiarity, proximity—are true only to the extent that the increased encounters do not turn out to be negative occasions or experiences where the more detestable traits of the religious other are showcased. If this happens, then the "familiarity breeds contempt" rule will override all the positive possibilities discussed above. In other words, the religious other must be presented in as attractive a way as possible. The attractive principle is crucial for the promotion of any relationship, not only interfaith relationships. Unless something or someone appears attractive or at least not unattractive, positive relationships may be hard to come by. Friendships that begin with discussion about each other's bad breadth are doomed to fail. Likewise, it would be disastrous if a Christian-Muslim encounter begins with the Christian raising the issue of Islam and terrorism and the Muslim the issue of Catholic priests and pedophilia. While both the issues of terrorism and pedophilia are not Islamic or Catholic issues, what is more important is that they are nasty issues to deal with and will almost certainly sour the relationship. Bad-breadth issues are best left to the doctor or specialist and come more under the purview of medical treatment rather than relationship building. They may have a place elsewhere but not within interfaith dialogue where facilitating goodwill between the religions is the primary goal. Aside from more attractive content, interfaith dialogue should also always begin with more "attractive" persons or models. Having bigoted and narrow-minded persons represent our faith tradition in dialogue will do a disservice to the entire project. But when those most open to the religious other take the initiative in this ministry, chances are they will be successful and leave a positive impression on the interfaith encounter. With every successful interfaith encounter, the project can be widened to include more people and slowly become a ministry everyone can be involved in.

Conclusion

Interfaith dialogue is a relatively new ministry with few roadmaps or models to guide it. What we know is that it has to progress slowly, gradually, and patiently. The interlocutors need to be prepared for the dialogue, possess the requisite attitudes, and adhere to some basic principles. There are no shortcuts to this; dialogue is a tedious and enduring affair. As dialogue is an active verb, it cannot be done any other way except through the actual praxis of dialogue. We have to attend to it steadfastly if we hope for the desired, valuable, and positive results. Otherwise, we risk turning it into a negative experience and cause more harm to the already vulnerable relationships across the religions that we find in many societies today.

Suggestions for Further Reading

Amaladoss, Michael. *Interreligious Encounters: Opportunities and Challenges.* Edited by Jonathan Y. Tan. Maryknoll, NY: Orbis Books, 2017.

Chia, Edmund, ed. *Dialogue? Resource Manual for Catholics in Asia.* New Delhi, India: ISPCK, 2002.

Cornille, Catherine. *The Im-Possibility of Interreligious Dialogue.* New York: Crossroad, 2008.

Swidler, Leonard. *After the Absolute: The Dialogical Future of Religious Reflection.* Minneapolis: Fortress Press, 1990.

Yong, Amos. *Hospitality and the Other: Pentecost, Christian Practices, and the Neighbor.* Maryknoll, NY: Orbis Books, 2008.

PART 2

SCRIPTURE
AND
TRADITION

4

The Bible and Other Religions

Introduction

I was once at a seminar where questions of what the Bible teaches about interfaith dialogue and other religions came up. One of the speakers was very blunt, beginning his response by reference to 1 Timothy 4:1, which states that "in later times some will renounce the faith by paying attention to deceitful spirits and teachings of demons." He cautioned against falling into the trap and deception of the interfaith movement and then asserted that all the other religions are human attempts at reaching God while Christianity is about the one true God reaching out to humans. The various religions, he continued, are preoccupied with rituals and religious practices while Christianity's focus is on developing a relationship with God. His conclusion was simple: the truth of biblical Christianity means that true Christians have to proclaim the falsity of all other religions and at the same time have the duty of announcing the Good News of Jesus Christ to those trapped by them!

This chapter explores the attitude of the Bible toward the other religions of the world. It begins by reflecting on what it means when Christians claim that the Bible is the "Word of God" and then goes on to examine some of the complexities involved in discerning God's Word, especially in the contemporary context of multireligious societies. It then offers an overview of the Bible by looking first at key themes in what Christians call the "Old Testament," which is really the Jewish Hebrew Bible, and then examining some major themes found in Christian Scriptures, more commonly known as the "New Testament." Focus will be on showing that the themes of both exclusiveness or particularity and also inclusiveness or universality are clearly found throughout the Bible.

How to appreciate exclusive verses that proclaim Jesus as the one and only Savior will also be discussed from the perspective of a contextual reading of the biblical texts.

The Bible as Word of God

Christianity is a biblical faith. Christians regard the Bible as the "Word of God." Some read the Bible regularly and devotionally while others turn to it when looking for answers to life's questions and challenges. Christians believe that the Bible is an important source of knowledge and information about life. Its teachings and truth carry a lot of weight. Its authority is premised on the belief that it is a record of God's revelation to humanity. Some Christians take this to mean that the actual and literal words of God were dictated to and recorded by the biblical authors and evangelists. They cite as proof that, though the Bible is a collection of many books written by many authors in different languages and styles and spanning many centuries, its message is consistent. It is oriented toward the proclamation of Jesus Christ as Lord and Savior of the world. Prophecies from the Hebrew Scriptures are cited as being confirmed in the New Testament, especially in the person of Jesus Christ, who is "the Word became flesh and lived among us" (John 1:14). And since God is the source of all truth, which Jesus claims when he says, "I am the way, and the truth, and the life" (John 14:6) and, "your [God's] word is truth" (John 17:17), it is beyond doubt that the Bible is from God and that it is true in all its senses. So, when asked what the Bible has to say about other religions Christians who read the Bible literally usually refer to it for guidance. Verses such as Deuteronomy 4:35 ("To you it was shown so that you would acknowledge that the LORD is God; there is no other besides him") and Mark 13:22 ("False messiahs and false prophets will appear and produce signs and omens, to lead astray, if possible, the elect") are sufficient proof for them that there is no place for other religions and interfaith dialogue in Christian living.

There are major problems with the above lines of thought. While we might get some insights on the leanings of the Bible with regard to how Christians ought to think about other religions, what it has to say is actually very little. This is because the Bible contains elements that were first addressed to the Judaic faith and later additions that tell the story of Jesus Christ and his followers. Its compilation addresses the Christian faith. One can then expect mainly to find issues pertaining to Christianity's development and its interaction with the Jewish religion to be contained within. But since the first part of the Christian Bible is the Jewish Bible or Hebrew Scriptures, the people of Israel's theology shapes to a great extent Christianity's attitude toward people of other religions. For example, in view of Israel's profound consciousness of its own religious identity as God's chosen people, its negative judgments on other religious systems was taken over in the New Testament by the early Christians in their evaluation of the other religions as idolatrous. This does not, however, suggest that the entire Bible teaches negatively about other religions, as there are indeed biblical stories and teachings advocating positively for out-group members. But, on the whole, discussions about other religions are at best ancillary to the primary concern of the Bible, which is to witness to the Christian faith. There is certainly no theology of other religions explicitly articulated in the Bible. It is an in-house document with lots to say about and to those within the group but almost nothing substantive about or to those without. At best we can only discern some basic principles that can then be applied to today's reality of religious pluralism.

The Problem of Biblical Interpretation

Another reason why it is disingenuous to assert that the Bible preaches against other religions is because there are many ways in which the Bible is being interpreted today. Biblical hermeneutics or interpretation is a science unto itself, positing a variety of tools and methods, such as the allegorical, moral, and anagogical approaches, some of which yield radically different interpretations from one another. The literalist approach, which considers the Bible to be inerrant and infallible, for example, differs significantly from the contextualist approach, where texts are interpreted in the light of the context of the author as well as that of the reader. It is important to note that interpretations are also a function of the interpreter's education, theological orientation, social location, existential concerns, and a variety of other nontheological factors. Contemporary biblical studies also insist that it is necessary to take into account the "world behind the text," "the world of the text," and "the world in front of the text." All three worlds are significant because they influence how scriptural texts are read and interpreted. There is also the problem of exegesis as opposed to eisegesis. While the former listens carefully to what the text is saying, the latter brings into the text one's own agenda and viewpoints and reads meaning into it. The diversity of these methods and their differing conclusions highlight the difficulties involved in the unquestioning acceptance of some of the basic assumptions of biblical teachings that have been historically passed down from generation to generation.

Moreover, there is also the problem of the text itself. It is somewhat inaccurate to suggest that there is absolute consistency in the Bible. Biblical scholars have unraveled lots of errors in the copying and translation of key texts from their original languages of Hebrew, Aramaic, and Greek. Some of these errors are really mistakes but some may have been intentional as the "wrong" translation fits more squarely with the scribe's or translator's worldview or theology or beliefs. Internal inconsistencies are also found in the Bible. The apostle Paul, for example, teaches that "For by grace you have been saved through faith, and this is not your own doing; it is the gift of God—not the result of works" (Eph 2:8-9) while the Letter of James, on the other hand, is explicit that "a person is justified by works and not by faith alone" (Jas 2:24). An even more obvious example is the Ten Commandments, which teaches "You shall not murder" (Exod 20:13) while just a few chapters down we have the story of the Golden Calf, where Moses was so furious that he ordered, "Thus says the LORD, the God of Israel, 'Put your sword on your side, each of you! Go back and forth from gate to gate throughout the camp, and each of you kill your brother, your friend, and your neighbor' " (Exod 32:27).

There are even incorrect citations of texts from the Old Testament in the New Testament. One small example suffices. The Gospel of Luke states in Luke 4:18-19 that it was quoting a text from the book of Isaiah. But when we compare the quoted text with where it was quoting from, namely, Isaiah 61:1-2, it is clear that "and recovery of sight to the blind" in Luke was an addition and that "to bind up the brokenhearted" in Isaiah is missing from Luke. With regard to prophecies from Hebrew Scriptures being fulfilled in Jesus, scholars have hypothesized that the reverse could also have been the case. The gospel authors, they argue, could have consciously framed the life of Jesus based on these prophecies that they were all too familiar with so that Micah 5:2— "But you, O Bethlehem of Ephrathah, who are one of the little clans of Judah, from you shall come forth for me one who is to rule in Israel, whose origin is from of old, from ancient days"—shaped Matthew's and Luke's decisions to locate Jesus as being born in Bethlehem when composing the infancy narratives. These concerns, along with numerous other opinions and theories about the Bible, enable one to conclude that there are many complexities associated with biblical interpretation. Merely insisting that the Bible is the literal words of God and that it has to be taken at face value is problematic, to say the least. To be sure, there is no one way of biblical interpretation that is perfectly accurate or acceptable to all. Just as those who argue negatively about other religions quote scriptural texts selectively, it is also possible for those who have a more positive attitude about other religions to do the same. Proof-texting, or the misuse of isolated verses from scriptures, is not a convincing method or argument to use.

The Bible has to be read holistically, taking the entirety of its message, discerning what it says about other religions through specific texts, and intelligently looking for clues between the lines. Because its primary purpose is to proclaim the Christian faith, we would expect to read texts in the Bible that endorse that proclamation. But where we come across biblical texts that speak positively about the religious outsider, we ought to pay special attention to them. These are texts that could be regarded as groundbreaking. An illustration might help: If I were writing a book to glorify my red football team it would be surprising if in the book I say something nice about the competing blue team. But if you do find me complimenting the blue team in the book, it is probably because the comments are true, what I said actually did happen, and not writing about it would simply make the book less credible. Meantime, it would also be safe to say that many of the nice things I say about my own red team—for example, that it includes all the best footballers on the face of the earth—can be taken with a grain of salt since my professed aim is to excite my supporters, in which case exaggeration helps. In biblical scholarship this is known as the "criterion of embarrassment," as the nice things I say about my competitor is embarrassing and serves only to weaken the overall thesis of my book. But I had no choice but to mention them because it is truthful information that cannot be hidden.

So, if the Bible—which is a Christian document written to nurture the Christian's faith—has something positive to say about other religions, one must regard those views as not only insightful and authentic but also truly revolutionary. These revolutionary insights and teachings cannot be dismissed as aberration. They are God's teachings for us and have special relevance in today's increasingly pluralistic world. So, given the nature of the biblical texts and the problems inherent in interpretation, it is important that we are more conscious when referring to the Bible in our assessment of other religions. A sincere reading of scriptures ought to open minds, soften hearts, and encourage Christians to look to the Bible as God's Word inspiring everyone to build bridges rather than walls across the different religious traditions. We can begin the cultivation of more positive attitudes by offering alternative ways of looking at biblical texts, as well as by pointing out that some traditionally held views, such as the Bible opposing interfaith dialogue, need not always be accurate, much less absolute. The Bible is the Word of God and has thus to be treated as a dynamic and not static text. It has much to say to every culture and in every era and about practically everything that matters in life, including the contemporary phenomenon of religious pluralism in society.

Universality in Hebrew Scriptures

The Bible begins with the story of creation. Creation therefore serves as the starting point and foundation for how all the other biblical texts are interpreted. The biblical story of creation differs from the other ancient Near Eastern thinking on how the earth came into being. It speaks of God as creator of everything on earth and everyone who has ever lived. Creation comes out of nothing, with God simply uttering the "Let there be . . ." command in words and the light, dome, sky, land, etc. comes to be. The first chapter of Genesis offers a theology to the "How did it all begin?" and "What is the human's place in relation to the world?" questions. Nothing or no one on earth or in the heavens is outside of God. Thus, all peoples, not only Jews and Christians, are God's people. This cosmic perspective on creation is the basis for the doctrine of the universal lordship of God.

The Bible is also emphatic that there is only one creator and that there is no other. All human beings are children of this one and only God. This is the strict monotheism of biblical theology. Those who claim that the Israelite God is different from the Babylonian God or that the Christian God is not the same as the Muslim or Hindu Gods are not monotheists. That is not what the Bible teaches. There is no such thing as a Christian

God or a Muslim God, since there is but only one God. This monotheistic insight evolved sometime during or shortly after the Babylonian exile when the Israelites realized their folly of having conceived of God in tribal terms. The exile taught them that God was even able to use their Babylonian enemies to subjugate them in order to bring them back to the right path of faithfulness to the one and only God. This means that the God whom they called by the name Yahweh was the same God of the Babylonians. The first chapter of Genesis is the fruit of this reflection. It depicts the myth of creation culminating in the creation of the first human beings, as representing the one human family: "So God created humankind in his image, in the image of God he created them; male and female he created them" (Gen 1:27). The biblical text also records that they participate in the life and image of God. This was how humanity was designed to be, and God saw that it was good. The Bible clearly emphasizes that as, at the end of creation, "God saw everything that he had made, and indeed, it was very good" (Gen 1:31).

But the biblical authors then had to account for the existential reality of brokenness and sin in the world. Thus, the next two chapters of the Bible depict the accounts leading to humanity's alienation from God, beginning with the Fall (Gen 3). Ironically, it was the sin of Adam and Eve that facilitated their growth and development as human beings with the appropriate conscience, including "knowing good and evil" (Gen 3:22). In other words, growing up means being endowed with the freedom and responsibility of choice, which in turn means being susceptible to sinfulness. The Bible's narrative is that God then sends the humans off from the Garden of Eden so that they are able to lead their lives on their own and be responsible for the earth's affairs (Gen 3:23). The finite realities of the world, with all its depravity, are then amplified in the subsequent chapters of the Bible. Genesis 4 speaks about the effects of the Fall, including its giving rise to the sins of jealousy, anger, and murder. Ironically, again, these acts of violence take place in the context of worship of God and sacrificial offering. Worship of God does not necessarily guarantee a blissful life. Humans have to take charge of their lives even if in the presence of God. This is the Bible's way of portraying God as unconditional love and acceptance, on the one hand, and human beings as truly free individuals but having responsibilities, on the other. This theme of God's saving activity is interspersed with the theme of the sinfulness of the human condition throughout the rest of the Bible.

The reality of human irresponsibility becomes so bad at one stage that God contemplates wiping it all away: "I will blot out from the earth the human beings I have created—people together with animals and creeping things and birds of the air, for I am sorry that I have made them" (Gen 6:7). With Noah and the Flood, however, humanity is allowed to begin anew as God establishes a universal covenant with the whole of creation: "As for me, I am establishing my covenant with you and your descendants after you. . . . I establish my covenant with you, that never again shall all flesh be cut off by the waters of a flood, and never again shall there be a flood to destroy the earth" (Gen 9:9-11). The rainbow is the sign of that covenant. Noah, like Adam before him, is seen as humanity's representative in that this was God's covenant with the entire human race. The rainbow is seen even until today; the covenant remains valid. God's love for the human race continues to be available to everyone, Jews or Christians, Muslims or Buddhists, secularists or atheists. The Bible teaches that every person on earth has the potential of being reconciled and brought into the heavenly embrace of the kingdom of God that is made possible through the universal love and salvation for all.

The Tower of Babel and Diversity

The first nine verses of Genesis 11 narrate the story of the Tower of Babel. It is often used etiologically to explain the origins and causes of linguistic diversity in the human family. The story begins by stating that "the whole earth had one language and the same words" (Gen 11:1). It then describes how the people came together in a plot to build a tower to reach the heavens, saying, "let us make a name for ourselves; otherwise we shall be scattered abroad upon the face of the whole earth" (Gen 11:4). But God was not pleased, saying, "Look, they are one people, and they have all one language; and this is only the beginning of what they will do; nothing that they propose to do will now be impossible for them" (Gen 11:6). Thinking that their plans could be stopped if they do not understand one another, God decides to confuse their language and then "scattered them abroad over the face of all the earth" (Gen 11:9).

This text risks being interpreted as suggesting linguistic homogeneity was the original divine intent and that linguistic heterogeneity is a result of God's punishment. This literalist reading of the myth can be countered by another that reads Genesis 11:1-9 in the context of the wider Genesis story. A close reading of the text would point out that the primary motivation for building the tower is the fear of being "scattered abroad upon the face of the whole earth" (Gen 11:5). Ironically, at the end of the day, it is because of their attempt at building the tower that caused them to scatter all over. Anyway, acting on the fear of being scattered, the people in Babel thought that if they were to build an edifice high enough to storm the heavens they would not be subjected to God's dictates anymore. They would then be masters of their own lives and destinies, a desire evidenced by their saying, "let us make a name for ourselves" (Gen 11:4). So, the biblical author's intent is to point out that the ultimate sin in this story is really the people's desire to do away with God so that they can then take charge of their own lives, without any recourse to God. This is comparable to Adam and Eve's sin of wanting to eat of the tree of the knowledge of good and evil (Gen 3:5) so that they can become all-knowing, like God. Thus, sinfulness in the Bible is usually in reference to the human being's rejection of the finite conditions of worldly and human existence and wishing that they can be like the infinite God. But just as Adam and Eve were banished from the Garden of Eden for yielding to their sinful desires, the people at Babel were also scattered "abroad over the face of all the earth" (Gen 11:9) for wanting to defy their true human nature.

The Bible's thesis seems to be that the people at Babel would have liked to remain where they were and not move away. In that sense they would view being banished and being scattered as punishment from God. The fact of life, however, is that change and being scattered around the earth is simply a reality of the human condition according to God's divine plan for the world. If we revisit the story of creation, we will be reminded that humanity was commanded to "be fruitful and multiply, and fill the earth" (Gen 1:28), a command repeated after the flood when "God blessed Noah and his sons, and said to them, 'Be fruitful and multiply, and fill the earth'" (Gen 9:1). Filling the earth means human beings have to spread out far and wide. That is just what life is all about and the way the world was created. Human desires, however, are not always in consonance with the divine blueprint. The fear of the unknown and the comfort of the status quo can lead one to prefer stagnation and be afraid of living out the mandate of the creator God. Moreover, being scattered can be challenging even as it is the process by which new thinking, beliefs, and languages evolve. These were the very realities that the biblical authors had been experiencing in their lives in the millennium before the Common Era when the texts of Genesis were being composed. They were merely reflecting on these challenges and projecting it onto the Bible in their description of the beginning of time. Heterogeneity, rather than homogeneity, therefore, is the state of the world and of created reality. It is how the world was created, and God saw that it was very good.

So, far from advocating that a single language or culture or religion was the original will of God, the Babel story is asserting, instead, that human reality entails dealing with diversity. There is no running away from it and no human tower can change the course of nature. This is in fact verified in the opening chapters of the Acts of the Apostles where the Pentecost event is seen as a recapitulation of Babel, except that the story is reversed. Filled with the Holy Spirit, the disciples, all of whom were Galileans, spoke in tongues so that the crowd, who had come from all over the face of the earth, could say "in our own languages we hear them speaking about God's deeds of power" (Acts 2:11). There was no indication that the crowd had learned the language of the Galileans, and there was no indication that the disciples had learned the many different languages of the crowd. Yet they all heard the message of God in their own native languages. The Word of God cannot be localized to any specific people or nation. It is meant for all peoples and all nations, and they will hear it in the diversity of their language, culture, race, and nation. This is the message of universality that the Bible relates over and over again. Its universality is not so much in its uniformity but precisely in its pluriformity or diversity.

Particularity in Hebrew Scriptures

Beginning with the call of Abraham as recorded in chapter 12 of Genesis, the Bible shifts its focus from a story about the wider universal human community to the story of a specific people, namely, the people of Israel. The rest of the Hebrew Scriptures have to be appreciated in light of this; its concerns are with Israel as people and nation. The stories of other nations are mentioned from the perspective of Israel, especially in the context of its special relationship with God. The accounts of Abraham, such as his calling, his faithfulness, and his descendants, are best read with the covenant that God establishes with him in mind (Gen 15:18). The Abrahamic covenant, in turn, has to be read in concert with the Mosaic covenant (Exod 24:7-8) that establishes Israel as God's chosen people. This covenant reminds the people that there is but one true God and that they are to be faithful and obedient to God's commandments and the divine will for human living: "Hear, O Israel: The LORD is our God, the LORD alone. You shall love the LORD your God with all your heart, and with all your soul, and with all your might" (Deut 6:4-5). But, over time, the people of Israel swayed in their faith and began to lapse, at times not fulfilling their part of the covenant. They rebelled and sinned and even adopted as their own what were called "pagan" gods that the surrounding nations were worshiping. This was a major transgression against the commandment: "You shall not bow down to them or worship them; for I the LORD your God am a jealous God" (Exod 20:5). Israel's forgetfulness and tendency toward sin, especially after possession of the Promised Land, is met with rebuke by the prophets, and these are at times accompanied by divine rebuke as well. The prophetic message is consistent: "Obey my voice, and I will be your God, and you shall be my people; and walk only in the way that I command you, so that it may be well with you" (Jer 7:23). Thus, if the foundation of Hebrew Scriptures is the universality of God's revelation and salvation as depicted in the doctrine of creation, the theme of Israel's election and uniqueness is most dominant throughout the rest of the scriptures.

Given this very particular concern for Israel's faithfulness to God, oftentimes at the expense of its relationship with those outside its fold, accounts in the Bible that speak positively about people of other nations ought to be highlighted. That these stories, which have the potential for being an embarrassment to the doctrine of election of the people of Israel, were included in the Bible signals that they are important. The anointing of the pagan Cyrus the Great of Persia by God as the king who would liberate the Israelites from the Babylonian Captivity is an example of how the Hebrew Scriptures seem to go out of their way to portray the religious outsider positively in the history of the people of Israel (Isa 45). Another example is the famous story of the Israelite prophet Jonah, not so much with the whale, but with the city of Nineveh, the capital of the Assyrian Empire, Israel's dreaded and sworn enemy. The Bible records the conversion of what was initially a pagan and wicked city after which God decided to spare it from destruction, much to the protest of Jonah

(Jonah 3–4). These texts confirm the thesis of the universality of God's love, that Yahweh is the God of all and not only of the people of Israel.

God cares for all, including Israel's enemies. While Israel is the favored child, the Bible insists that its election is not for its own sake but to serve as "a light to the nations" so that God's "salvation may reach to the end of the earth" (Isa 49:6). The people of Israel, therefore, become humanity's representative of God's love and providence. God's blessing on the nations is through the nation of Israel. Israel announces God's salvation to all peoples, including the Assyrians, the Babylonians, the Hittites, and so on. The God of creation who wills the redemption of all is the only God and will care for all of God's people. This theme of the universal God is interspersed with the theme of Israel as God's chosen people throughout the Bible. The dialectic of universality and particularity continues even through to the New Testament.

The New Testament as New Covenant

The New Testament begins with accounts of the life and ministry of Jesus of Nazareth. Jesus and his disciples, all of whom were Jews, were naturally steeped in their understanding of the people and nation of Israel as God's chosen people. In fact, even after the early Christian community's separation and expulsion from the mainstream Jewish community, they continued to embrace the theology of election and eventually made it central to their own self-understanding of what it means to be church. They not only considered themselves to be God's special and elect community but even insisted that the church had displaced Israel and that the Christian community was now the "new" and "true" Israel. They believed that they had entered into a new covenant with God. The church's new status and role are clearly articulated in Peter's epistle: "But you are a chosen race, a royal priesthood, a holy nation, God's own people" (1 Pet 2:9).

Where did this idea of the new covenant come from? Familiar with the teachings of Hebrew Scriptures, the early Christians took as their basis a text from the prophet Jeremiah: "The days are surely coming, says the LORD, when I will make a new covenant with the house of Israel and the house of Judah" (Jer 31:31). This new covenant, they assumed, was initiated and fulfilled by the coming of God's Son Jesus Christ, the promised Messiah, who by his death on the cross and subsequent resurrection redeemed all of humanity. Paul's Letter to the Galatians spells this out: "Christ redeemed us from the curse of the law by becoming a curse for us—for it is written, 'Cursed is everyone who hangs on a tree'—in order that in Christ Jesus the blessing of Abraham might come to the Gentiles, so that we might receive the promise of the Spirit through faith" (Gal 3:13-14). The evangelist John distinguishes between the old and the new covenants: "The law indeed was given through Moses; grace and truth came through Jesus Christ" (John 1:17). Matthew adds that Jesus had, in fact, fulfilled the law but gave humanity much more on top of that (Matt 5:17). The Letter to the Hebrews testifies to Jesus' role in establishing a new covenant with God: "But Jesus has now obtained a more excellent ministry, and to that degree he is the mediator of a better covenant, which has been enacted through better promises" (Heb 8:6). God's church was now known as the "spiritual" or "heavenly" Israel.

Jesus' role as the promised Messiah and God's revelation is most adequately depicted in the four canonical gospels found in the New Testament. Taken together they tell the story of God as revealed in the human person of Jesus of Nazareth. There is no singular account of the story of Jesus; there are multiple. The gospels offer different perspectives of who Jesus is and are by nature meant to be not historical or biographical but theological. Each gospel is written in a different context, by different authors, and for different audiences. No single gospel can capture the complete picture of the life, ministry, death, and resurrection of Jesus. They have to be read in concert with one another to obtain a more holistic picture of who Jesus is and what he means for the world. The themes of particularity and universality are again evident in the gospels. This is most clearly seen through a comparison between Matthew's and Luke's gospels.

Particularity in the Gospel of Matthew

Matthew's gospel was written for Jewish Christians. It portrays Jesus as the new Moses and the newly proclaimed kingdom of heaven as a reality for the Jews. It emphasizes the continuity between the Hebrew Scriptures and the life of Jesus the Messiah. Jesus fulfills many of the biblical prophecies the Jewish Christians were familiar with. His genealogy is traced back to David and Abraham (Matt 1:1), and many of the expectations about the Messiah's birth are recounted in Matthew's gospel. Like the Israelites who sought refuge in Egypt during the time of the famine (Gen 46), Jesus too was forced to seek refuge in Egypt shortly after his birth (Matt 2:13-14). Like Moses who brought the law to the people of Israel from Mount Sinai (Exod 20), Jesus too delivers the new law, the Beatitudes, as a sermon from the mount (Matt 5). Jesus' choosing of the twelve disciples (Matt 10:1-4) recapitulates the twelve tribes of Israel (Deut 33:6-25), and his betrayal by Judas (Matt 26:14-16) seems to have been foretold in Zechariah 11:12: "So they weighed out as my wages thirty shekels of silver." Throughout Matthew's gospel, Jesus' message is that he has come not to abolish the law or the prophets but to fulfill them (Matt 5:17). Focused on the Jewishness of Jesus' message, Matthew even has Jesus instruct his disciples to "Go nowhere among the Gentiles, and enter no town of the Samaritans, but go rather to the lost sheep of the house of Israel" (Matt 10:5-6). Matthew's gospel, as we can see above, portrays the more exclusivist and particularistic dimensions of Jesus' mission.

That notwithstanding, there are still accounts in Matthew's gospel where the message is otherwise. One account is most revealing as it shows him using a religious outsider to convince Jesus that he should open up his heart to include even those outside the house of Israel. Matthew 15:10-20 narrates the Canaanite woman's faith. By labelling her Canaanite, the evangelist was intentional in making known that she was an outgroup member. The text is, from the outset, highlighting issues of identity, boundaries, and cultic purity. For sure, it presumes, good Jews should have nothing to do with Canaanites. True to form, Jesus and his entourage give her the silent treatment and his disciples have this to say: "Send her away, for she keeps shouting after us" (Matt 15:23). Following the script, Jesus responds: "I was sent only to the lost sheep of the house of Israel" (Matt 15:24). The exclusiveness of his mission in Matthew's gospel is beyond doubt. Rather than going away, the unnamed woman persists and even "came and knelt before him, saying, 'Lord, help me' " (Matt 15:25). As if pushed to the wall, Jesus responds harshly: "It is not fair to take the children's food and throw it to the dogs" (Matt 15:26). This is a stinging rebuke, unkind, insensitive, offensive, and racially and religiously inappropriate. Some interpreters suggest that it is merely a test that Jesus is putting the woman through to ascertain her faith. They cite how the episode concludes with Jesus proclaiming, "Woman, great is your faith! Let it be done for you as you wish" (Matt 15:28). The Gospel of Mark, however, where the same story is told, has the additional clause, "Let the children be fed first" (Mark 7:27), suggesting that the real reason for Jesus' cold treatment is, according to the divinely appointed order, that the gospel is meant, first, for the house of Israel. Reaching out to the non-Jews or the Gentiles can wait. The slandered woman's response sets the stage for further theologizing. Her riposte, "Yes, Lord, yet even the dogs eat the crumbs that fall from their masters' table" (Matt 15:27), was clearly a challenge to Jesus' exclusivist attitude. She was not asking to be treated like the master's children. She was looking for leftovers, crumbs. Both the master's household and the dogs eat simultaneously; there is no need to wait until the former has finished. Moreover, bread is plentiful, as illustrated by the feeding of the five thousand (Matt 14:13-21) and four thousand (Matt 15:32-39), two stories the evangelist strategically inserted just prior to and after the story of the Canaanite woman in the same gospel. Another important point to note is that the woman was asking not for bread but for healing. The former is an economic entity, which is limited. The latter, however, is a transcendental entity, which is unlimited. Healing, like salvation, compassion, or love, does not run the risk of running out. This was the genius of the Canaanite woman who, in her dogged persistence, was converting Jesus to God's mission, moving him out of his exclusive and particularistic mode to one of inclusiveness and universality.

Universality in the Gospel of Luke

Luke's gospel, in contrast to Matthew's, is written specifically for the non-Jews, the Gentiles. He is believed to be a companion of Paul, who is known as the Apostle to the Gentiles. The gospel's aim, therefore, is to portray Jesus as Savior for all of humanity, not only for the Jews. Like Matthew, Luke also begins by delineating Jesus' lineage but traces it back all the way to Adam, the progenitor of the human race. He is writing to an audience that was asking the question of how the Gospel can be relevant to those who are not Jewish despite it being rooted in Hebrew Scriptures. Luke portrays Jesus as delivering the new law, not so much from the mount, but from the plains or "a level place" (Luke 6:17) since the Gentiles have no allegiance to Mount Sinai. His focus is on Jesus, the universal savior for all of humankind, and Christianity, the universal religion for all. Luke's universal emphasis is evidenced in his concern for the outsiders such as the Samaritans, Gentiles, sinners, poor, outcasts, and women. It is only in the Gospel of Luke that one finds the parables of the Lost Sheep, Lost Coin, and Lost Son (Luke 15). It is Luke's gospel that commends the tax collector instead of the Pharisee (Luke 18:9-14). It is also in Luke's gospel that we read of the ten lepers who were cleansed, only one of whom, a Samaritan, returned to thank Jesus (17:11-19). Luke's theology follows Paul's, which presupposes that all peoples are in need of the salvation that Jesus alone can offer.

An example of Luke prioritizing the outsider over the Jews can be found in the all-too-familiar parable of the Good Samaritan (Luke 10:25-37). Here, it is Jesus' teachings that are explored, not so much his own witness or demeanor. As is true of all parables, there are multiple interpretative paradigms for understanding the teaching intended in this Lukan parable. St. Augustine's allegorical interpretation is probably the most common. The man going down from Jerusalem to Jericho represents every person. The robbers are the satanic forces. Over the centuries Christians reading the text from an anti-Semitic or anti-Jewish perspective have come to regard the priest and the Levite mentioned in this parable as representing the Prophets and the Law of Hebrew Scriptures. They are too concerned with issues of purity and so touching a wounded person would render them unclean. In other words, according to Christian theology, the religion of the Old Israel will not bring the ordinary person to salvation. The next person to come by is the Samaritan, who "was moved with pity" (Luke 10:33). This, according to the Christian interpretation, is the Lord Jesus who, "having poured oil and wine" (sacramental symbols) on the wounds (sin), "put him on his own animal" (the Lord's body, which bears our sins) and "brought him to an inn" (the church) (Luke 10:34). "The next day he took out two denarii" (baptism and Eucharist or knowledge of Father and Son?), asked "the innkeeper" (church leader) to "take care of him; and when I come back [second coming], I will repay you whatever more you spend" (Luke 10:35). This is the traditional interpretation that has often been taught to our children over the years and decades.

A closer look at this interpretation, however, reveals that there is nothing really unique in the teaching. Helping those in need is a given. Numerous biblical passages teach that. Another is not necessary. Moreover, the lawyer already mentioned that one must love your neighbor as yourself, and Jesus told him to "do this, and you will live" (Luke 10:28). But his question was "what must I do to inherit eternal life?" (Luke 10:25). His concern was about life after death and not simply about living. He wanted to know what one must do besides fulfilling the Law. More thought needs to be given in our reflections, and our starting point makes all the difference. The Augustinian interpretation discussed above takes as starting point that Jesus is the Good Samaritan. He is the one who comes to the battered man's aid. Within the theology of Jesus as Savior, that seems most fitting. But what if our starting point is that the battered man is the one who represents Jesus in the parable? After all, did not Jesus identify himself with the stranger, prisoner, sick, hungry, and wounded? With this alternative starting point, the question becomes "who does Jesus see as neighbor to him?" This is a much more intriguing question, and Jesus' response is even more intriguing. It takes us into new territory in the theological reflection process. The Jewish New Testament scholar Amy-Jill Levine suggests that, in the Jewish context of the first century, we can begin by thinking of the Samaritan "more as the enemy, as those who do the oppressing. From the perspective of the man in the ditch, Jewish listeners might balk at the idea of receiving Samaritan aid. They might have thought, 'I'd rather die than acknowledge that one from that group saved me.'"[1] If we look at Samaritans that way then perspectives change. This is because it means that the teaching of the parable is that the one who comes to the aid of Jesus, the helpless one, is someone who is hated and feared by the community at large. Discipleship, according to Luke's gospel, challenges the Christian to open their minds and hearts to those whom society perceives as outsiders or enemies. According to the teachings of the parable of the Good Samaritan, they are the true neighbors. They could even be instruments of salvation for Christians, saving them from the ditch and caring for them until full recovery. The lawyer was unable to acknowledge that it was the Samaritan who was neighbor to the wounded man. To Jesus' question, he responded with "The one who showed mercy on him" (Luke 10:37), while avoiding the mention of what to him might be a dirty word, "Samaritan." But this was the thrust of Jesus' teaching; God's salvation comes to us from all quarters, including through the kind works of the religious outsider. Again, the

---

1. Amy-Jill Levine, *Short Stories by Jesus: The Enigmatic Parables of a Controversial Rabbi* (New York: HarperOne, 2014), 96.

theme of the universality of God's love and salvation that the Gospel of Luke emphasizes is reiterated.

Jesus as the One and Only Savior

A final issue that needs to be addressed is the particularity and exclusivity of biblical verses about Jesus or those attributed to him. How do we deal with statements, especially in John's gospel, the Acts of the Apostles, and the Pauline Epistles that insist on the necessity of Jesus for salvation? This is a contentious issue, as our religious neighbors have experienced evangelically minded Christians telling them to their faces that unless they believe in Jesus they will burn in eternal hellfire. The scripture verse normally cited in support of this is the proclamation of Peter who was arrested and brought in front of the high priest and the Sadducees. In defending himself, he witnessed to Jesus Christ theologically: "There is salvation in no one else, for there is no other name under heaven given among mortals by which we must be saved" (Acts 4:12). This is a clear statement that Jesus is the only name in the entire world by which all peoples can be saved. The apostle Paul confirms this in his instruction on prayer to Timothy when he says, "For there is one God; there is also one mediator between God and humankind, Christ Jesus, himself human, who gave himself a ransom for all" (1 Tim 2:5-6). Again, this is another unambiguous claim about Christ as the only mediator of every person to the one and only God. In another epistle, this time to the Romans, Paul spells out what needs to be done: "if you confess with your lips that Jesus is Lord and believe in your heart that God raised him from the dead, you will be saved" (Rom 10:9). So, if we take these biblical texts literally, it is necessary not only to believe but to also explicitly profess one's faith in Jesus as Lord if one wishes to attain salvation.

Perhaps the most cited passage by Christians in asserting the necessity of Christ for salvation is the claim attributed to Jesus himself in John's gospel: "I am the way, and the truth, and the life. No one comes to the Father except through me" (John 14:6). The use of the definite article "the" makes it clear that there is no other or that Jesus' way, truth, and life are the most profound. But, like all the other biblical verses about or by Jesus mentioned above, it is important to interrogate the specific context within which John's statement was made. As mentioned earlier in this chapter, a literal reading of it is insufficient; one needs to take into account the "worlds" surrounding the text. First, exploring the "world of the text" leads one to appreciate that the context was Jesus and his closest disciples preparing for the Passover. One can imagine the twelve in a room listening to their Master, much like little children huddled together in front of the fireplace with their father who is about to leave them. The questions posed by Thomas ("Lord, we do not know where you are going. How can we know the way?" [John 14:5]) or by another disciple, Philip ("Lord, show us the Father, and we will be satisfied" [John 14:8]), hint at the disposition of the disciples. Anxious, nervous, confused, and tense could be words used to describe their feelings. Appreciating the "I am the way, and the truth, and the life" statement in this context, it is possible that they were Jesus' way to comfort and reassure his disciples. This is substantiated by the "I will not leave you orphaned" (John 14:18) statement about the Holy Spirit that Jesus promises them.

It would not be difficult to draw a parallel between the response of Jesus and the response of the father bidding farewell to his children. The father might use superlatives such as "I will be thinking of you every single minute when I am away" or "You are the loveliest kids in the whole world" to console his children and to lift their spirits. Reciprocating, the children may tell the father that he is the best daddy in the whole world. Based on the father's words, it would be disingenuous for the kids to go out to proclaim that they are lovelier than all their friends and every other child on earth. Likewise, it would be equally disingenuous for the father to go around telling his friends that he is a better dad than everyone else. Both the father's and the kids' heartening words can be appreciated only within the context of the relationship of love in the family. They are love proclamations, not meant to be empirically factual or scientifically valid, and make no sense outside of the relationship. Likewise, Jesus' words or any claims made about Jesus in the Bible can be appreciated only within the context of Christian discipleship and faith in Christ. They are faith claims and, like love claims, are made in a language that makes no sense outside of the special relationship from which they evolved. The statements of John 14:6; Acts 4:12; and all other scriptural verses about Jesus are meaningful only within the Christian community. They serve to nurture faith and encourage love of and devotion to Christ the Savior. Used outside of Christian circles, however, they are not only meaningless but also dangerous, especially if used to pass judgments on those who are not Christians.

Second, interrogating the "world behind the text" would reveal to us that John's gospel was composed toward the end of the first century, more than sixty years after the crucifixion of Jesus, and one or two decades after the appearance of the other three canonical gospels. Scholars believe that it is the product of a school of followers of the Beloved Disciple, named John. Among their sources for the gospel are the numerous poems, hymns, and homilies that had been circulating among the Johannine church for several decades. John's gospel focuses on the presentation of the mystery of Jesus and his identity as Son of God. John employs a lot of symbolic discourse in the gospel, especially in stressing Jesus' unique relationship with God the Father. These discourses need to be understood in the context of the Johannine community being expelled from the synagogues by the Jews and the continued persecution they were experiencing, eventually forcing them to flee Palestine for the diaspora. Jesus' claims to being the way, the truth, and the life, therefore, provide meaningful sources of hope and relief for the community that was in crisis and transition.

Third, exploring the "world in front of the text" focuses on how the text resonates with the twenty-first-century reader living in a world that is religiously pluralistic. One could point out that because the text mentions Jesus as the "way" first, the gospel is prioritizing the praxis or action dimension of the Christian faith. Considering that Jesus had washed the feet of his disciples (John 13:1-11) just before the utterance of the "I am the way, and the truth, and the life" statement, one can understand the gospel as emphasizing humble service and loving actions for the truth and life of Jesus to be revealed. In other words, truth is not a cognitive notion that is to be intellectually understood or believed, it is something that has to be actualized and "done" by those who claim to be Christian. Likewise, life is not a wishful notion that is prayed and hoped for; it has to be acted upon and "lived" by those who identify as followers of Christ. Jesus taught as much when, after washing his disciples' feet, he told them: "If you know these things, you are blessed if you *do* them" (John 13:17; emphasis added). This is also reflected in the famous teaching of St. Francis of Assisi: "Preach the Gospel at all times. When necessary, use words." In other words, our preaching ought to be through our life and actions rather than our words.

Conclusion

We began this chapter by reflecting on the Bible as "Word of God" and discussed how problematic it can be for a literal approach to the appreciation of its teachings. Discerning what the Bible has to say about religions other than Christianity has to take into account that the Bible is more or less an in-house document written for Christians for the purpose of nurturing their faith. In this context, the other religions are viewed as competitors and so one cannot expect too much from the biblical testimony about them. Having said that, a close reading of the Bible, especially if done contextually, will reveal that it treats the religious outsider very generously and hospitably. There are texts within that can even be classified as life-giving and revolutionary. They reveal not only a God whose universal love for all of humankind exceeds all expectations but also a God who calls on the Christian community to be more radically inclusive in their dealings with those who are not Christians. Its central message is that we accept every human person as brother or sister, as God's people, and abide by one of Jesus' last words to his disciples: "I give you a new commandment, that you love one another. Just as I have loved you, you also should love one another. By this everyone will know that you are my disciples, if you have love for one another" (John 13:34-35).

Suggestions for Further Reading

Ariarajah, Wesley. *The Bible and People of Other Faiths.* Geneva: World Council of Churches, 1985.
Knitter, Paul. *Jesus and the Other Names: Christian Mission and Global Responsibility.* Maryknoll, NY: Orbis Books, 1996.
Maccammon, Linda M. *Liberating the Bible: A Guide for the Curious and Perplexed.* Maryknoll, NY: Orbis Books, 2008.
Newbigin, Leslie. *The Gospel in a Pluralist Society.* Grand Rapids, MI: Eerdmans, 1989.
Rogerson, J. W. *An Introduction to the Bible.* Rev. ed. London: Equinox, 2005.

5

Christian History and Other Religions

Introduction

I once attended a Christian evangelical rally and happened to be seated beside someone I recognized as a Buddhist monk, dressed as he was in saffron robes. Midway through the rally, the preacher proclaimed something to the effect that God has taught us that there is absolutely no salvation outside the church. He went on to assert that this means that those who have not accepted Jesus Christ as Savior and been baptized into the church will not have a place in heaven and so are destined to suffer the torments of hell. I squirmed in my seat while noticing that my new Buddhist friend sat there rather detached and acted as if he were not paying attention to the preacher. It was only years later, when I first took up theological studies, that I realized that there was no truth to what the preacher had proclaimed. First, the teaching is not from God. Second, the teaching was initially formulated not so much for those who had not accepted Christ but for those who were considering leaving the church.

This chapter discusses the history of Christian attitudes and what the church has been teaching about religions other than Christianity over the centuries. It will engage in a cursory study of some of the main doctrines and approaches Christian leaders have taken in attending to the fact of other religions, beginning with the post-resurrection period up until the earlier part of the twentieth century. Locating these church teachings within the socio-political and ecclesial contexts of the times, each age of church history examined will include a brief reference to issues of the contemporary situation and cultural milieu. Focus will be on how Christian attitudes about other religions developed as a response to the contextual circumstances and challenges, both internal and external, to church life. The chapter will address these in five historical or kairological ages of Christian history, where each is pivoted by a specific and critical focus, with chronological overlaps between them.

The Age of the Apostles

The first period is known as the age of the apostles as it refers to the beginnings of Christianity with the twelve apostles, ending with the death of the last toward the end of the first century. This was the period when most of the New Testament books were being composed and, in fact, only those books associated with the apostles were eventually canonized as Christian Scriptures. The scriptures provided the necessary guidance to what the Christian communities were to believe in and how they should practice their faith. It is also within these New Testament books, specifically in the Acts of the Apostles and the Pauline Epistles, that we find accounts on the attitudes of the first Christians toward those outside the faith.

All the apostles and the other first Christians were primarily Jews, either by birth or by conversion. They continued to adhere to Jewish customs such as temple worship and Jewish home prayers, the practice of fasting and the observance of Jewish holy days, and also the reverence for the Torah. They saw themselves as a Jewish sect distinguished by their belief in Jesus as the Messiah. That the Holy Spirit descended upon them on the Jewish Feast of Weeks, *Shavuot* (Pentecost), which commemorates the deliverance of the Torah to Moses at Mount Sinai, is confirmation that they were still thoroughly Jewish by identity but also signals that a new age was dawning on them (Acts 2). The early Christian community saw themselves as representing the new covenant and the New Israel, having replaced the old covenant of God with the Jewish people and the Old Israel. Inheriting the Jewish theology of election, they believed that it was they who were now to be regarded as God's chosen people. This exclusivist stance informed their attitudes toward those who were outside the faith. As theirs was also an apocalyptic and eschatological faith, awaiting the final coming of the kingdom of God, the early Christians proclaimed rather impatiently and aggressively that Jesus was "the one ordained by God as judge of the living and the dead" (Acts 10:42). In so doing, they were indirectly passing a negative judgment on the Jewish people and all others who had not accepted the messiahship of Jesus. The anti-Semitic texts in the New Testament—for example, "You snakes, you brood of vipers!" (Matt 23:33); "You are from your father the devil" (John 8:44)—have to be appreciated in this context of competition and rivalry. By the end of the first century, the Christian movement had grown into a totally separate religion from the Jewish religion.

Early Christianity developed within the Greek Hellenistic context and the Gentile world. Like Jesus, the first Christians also initially saw their movement as confined to the people of Israel but eventually opened their doors to the Gentiles as well. The story of Peter and Cornelius illustrates the Christian community's gradual acceptance of the Gentiles. After a vision of how God has made every animal clean, Peter's speech to the household of the Gentile Cornelius begins with "I truly understand that God shows no partiality, but in every nation anyone who fears him and does what is right is acceptable to him" (Acts 10:34-35). The text then goes on to say at the end of his speech, "The circumcised believers who had come with Peter were astounded that the gift of the Holy Spirit had been poured out even on the Gentiles" (Acts 10:45). A few chapters later the Acts of the Apostles has Paul make two speeches. The first is in Lystra, where, after healing a paralyzed man, he proclaims: "In past generations he [God] allowed all the nations to follow their own ways; yet he has not left himself without a witness in doing good—giving you rains from heaven and fruitful seasons, and filling you with food and your hearts with joy" (Acts 14:16-17). Paul was recognizing that in the religion of the Greeks God's providence was already present, as evidenced by the faith of the man he had just healed. Then, in another speech, this time in front of the Areopagus, Paul confirms that the Gentiles were equally religious people: "Athenians, I see how extremely religious you are in every way. For as I went through the city and looked carefully at the objects of your worship, I found among them an altar with the inscription, 'To an unknown god.' What therefore you worship as unknown, this I proclaim to you" (Acts 17:22-23). Here, Paul is first acknowledging that the religions of the Greeks are not without value and that, second, he has come to shine light on this "unknown god" whom they had been worshiping all along. Of course, Paul's thesis is that faith in Jesus Christ surpasses all the other religious beliefs of the Greeks. So, while the early Christians see the religions of the nations as finding their eventual fulfillment in Jesus Christ, they also acknowledge that these religions are by no means worthless.

The early Christian movement also had to discover its political identity within the Roman Empire from which it was emerging. Confident that the entire world was under their rule, the Romans promoted an imperial cult to sustain the empire as well as to support its expansionist programs. The nascent Christian community was seen as problematic when its members refused to obey the Roman religious practices, especially those that were considered sacrilegious or idolatrous from the Christian perspective. In the light of persistent persecution, the Christians had to have a reinforced faith, which meant being doubly zealous about their identity with the crucified messiah. Assertive language about their faith developed as a defense against the onslaught of the imperial assault. Absolute claims about the lordship of Jesus Christ and triumph of Christian salvation served as survival mechanisms and helped in the nurturance and protection of the vulnerable faith of those who would otherwise cave to Roman pressures.

The Age of the Church Fathers

The second age is that of the ancient and influential bishops, church leaders, thinkers, and theologians, all called by the generic label "church fathers." This age is also sometimes known as the patristics and generally refers to the period between the end of the apostolic age and sometime in the fourth century. This was the time when, for the Christians, witnessing to their faith in Jesus was most important. Fidelity to the teachings of the apostles and the church fathers was paramount, steadfastly held on to, even unto fearless death by martyrdom. In the context of the surrounding Hellenistic culture rife with polytheistic beliefs, pagan mythologies, and mystery religious practices, the church fathers vehemently defended the "you shall have no other gods before me" (Deut 5:7) dictate of the Decalogue.

Concurrent with this opposition to some of the Greco-Roman religious practices, the church fathers did display some sense of openness toward other aspects of the peoples' culture. Evidence of this can be seen in the number of interpretations that arose with regard to the salvific ministry of Christ vis-à-vis the place of those outside the Christian dispensation. Two questions dominated much of their reflections. The first is what happens to the many people who lived before the incarnation, which is but a recent event given the long history of the world. If Christ is indeed the salvation of all, why did he come so late? The second question is what happens to those Christians who consciously break away from the church. Do former Christians enjoy the salvation that Christ died for?

Salvation of Those in the Pre-Christian Era

With regard to the first question about the possibility of salvation for the pagans and Jews who lived and died before the coming of Christ, the Johannine gospel's identification of Jesus Christ as the incarnate Logos became the starting point for reflections. As the Greek Stoic philosophers had referred to the Logos as the divine principle ordering the cosmos, Christ was presented by the church fathers—many of whom were steeped in Greek philosophy and converts to Christianity from the pagan religions—as the source and summit of all salvation history. That the Logos existed from the beginning of time (John 1:1) and was incarnated in the human person of Jesus (John 1:14) means that the same God who reveals and saves in Jesus was also revealing and saving all peoples and cultures before the incarnation. Logos theology became one of the most significant investigations during the patristic era.

The second-century Justin Martyr posits that the universal and active presence of God predated the incarnation of Christ and appeared in the form of the seminal logos or *logos spermatikos* (seeds of the word). His thesis was that while the Logos extends to everyone from every culture and to all of creation, it was revealed more decisively to Israel and most completely in the coming of Christ in the flesh. So if Christians have access to the fullness of Truth in the Logos, all other persons who have known the Truth and live righteously also participate and live according to the Logos of God. In fact, Justin asserts that those who "lived according to reason [*logos*] were really Christians, even though they were thought to be atheists, such as, among the Greeks, Socrates, Heraclitus and others like them."[1] Revelation and salvation, therefore, can be found outside the boundaries of the church, even if anonymously or partially and not as fully as that available within.

Another second-century church father, St. Irenaeus of Lyons, through his most well-known book, *Against Heresies*, put forth a theology of

---

1. *First Apology* 46 in Falls, trans., *The Fathers of the Church*, 6:83–84, as cited in Francis A. Sullivan, *Salvation outside the Church? Tracing the History of the Catholic Response* (Mahwah, NJ: Paulist Press, 1992), 15.

history. This is the theology of how God acts in the natural and human affairs in the history of the world, which begins with the beginnings of time, as laid out in the Hebrew Scriptures, and continues through to the New Testament until the end of time. Locating Christ at the center of this history, Irenaeus believes that it is through the Logos or Christ that God is revealed to everyone from the very beginnings of creation, including to the adherents of prebiblical religions. It is therefore in and through creation that God reveals to all of humankind, and it is through the Logos that all divine manifestations take place. So, for Irenaeus, where the human person knows God through the natural events in history, that person is already responding to a personal divine initiative. In other words, God's self-revelation and divine manifestation are discerned by human beings through the ordinary occurrences of their life in the world. This is the initial phase of God's manifestation through the Logos. The belief, of course, is that this is to be followed by the Jewish and Christian dispensations, the phase of revealed religion. A famous quote attributed to St. Irenaeus is *Gloria Dei est vivens homo* (The glory of God is the human being fully alive), suggesting that where the human being is at its best, we can be sure that God is manifestly present and glorified.

Clement and his disciple Origen, of the School of Alexandria in Egypt, were the Greek thinkers of the late second and early third centuries who brought Logos Christology to its fullest development. A great center of Hellenistic wisdom, Alexandria was a city not only where the dialogue between the Jewish and Greek heritage took place but also where many other cultures intersected. Buddhist monks had come to Alexandria from India as a result of Ashoka's missionary endeavors, while Indian sages were also there with their Upanishadic wisdom. Clement refers to them as *sarmanae* (ascetics), *brahmins* (priestly elites), and *gymnosophists* (practitioners of yogic bodily disciplines). Alexandria, therefore, represented a cross-cultural center where many different religious people were in a passionate search for the truth that cuts across the traditions. In keeping with Upanishadic philosophy, Clement asserted that truth is one and that the different streams of thought and philosophies are but fragments of this one truth. He believed that the Greeks were given philosophy to open their minds to the truth of God, just as the Jewish people were given the law. Understandably, he concludes that the fullness of this truth is contained in Christ, the Logos of God. Philosophy, like the Mosaic Law, serves as a preparation for the perfection by faith in Christ.

In the early fourth century, church historian Eusebius of Caesarea wrote a volume consisting of fifteen books, titled *Praeparatio evangelica* (Preparation for the Gospel), where he postulates that all the Jewish and pagan religions and philosophies are means by which the cultures were prepared for the reception of the Gospel of Christ. The book was actually written to introduce pagans to the Christian religion and also used as a doctrine for explaining God's presence in cultures that had not yet been evangelized. Likewise, Gregory of Nyssa, of the later part of the fourth century, also considered the pagan religions as partners in the search for God's truth. In sum, most of the church fathers taught that while Christ is the fulfillment of the other philosophies and religions, the universal and active presence of God was nevertheless very much present in each of them.

No Salvation outside the Church

For a response to the second question, on the place of former Christians in the economy of God's gift of salvation, the first church father to turn to is St. Ignatius, the bishop of Antioch in Syria in the first century. A lot of his teachings come from letters he wrote while on his way to Rome where he was martyred. One of his main concerns was the increasing disunity among the members of the early churches, with some breaking off from their bishops to follow illegitimate leaders. Ignatius warns that those who do so deviate from the church and so will not inherit the kingdom of God. Like St. Ignatius, St. Irenaeus of Lyons was equally concerned about those on the verge of separating from the church. But the group St. Irenaeus had in mind was the Gnostics, those who claim to have higher knowledge of the Christian mysteries. To them, he also warns that anyone who breaks away from the church, becoming heretics and schismatics, will be excluded from God's divine economy of salvation.

Origen expounded on this same teaching in a homily on the second chapter of Joshua of Hebrew Scriptures. A pioneer in Christian allegorical exegesis of scriptures, Origen offers an interpretation of the actions of the two Hebrew spies sent by Joshua who took refuge in the house of the prostitute Rahab (Josh 2:1). Origen sees the woman as representing a sinner (one rejected by society), who has now been converted to Christianity (and so is welcomed by Jesus) and whose house refers to the church. The bright red scarlet cord that the woman was to tie in the window (Josh 2:18)—which serves as a sign to the Hebrews that the house is to be spared from destruction when the Hebrews invade the city—represents the blood of Christ, which has redeemed the church. The two men instructed her to gather all her family members into the house and warned that "If any of you go out of the doors of your house into the street, they shall be responsible for their own death" (Josh 2:19). This is Origen's way of warning Christians contemplating leaving the church that they will not be saved by the blood of Christ as long as they were outside of its doors.

The church father most associated with the teaching of *extra ecclesiam nulla salus* (outside the church, no salvation) is St. Cyprian, the bishop of Carthage in North Africa, who served in the early third century. His concern was whether Christians who had been previously baptized by those whom the church considers as heretics need to be rebaptized. His position was that those who had separated from the official church do not have the guidance of the Holy Spirit and cannot admit others into the church validly. In short, his interest was with preserving the purity and unity of the church, and so he insists that, since there is only one house of God, anyone admitted by those outside of it will not be saved. St. Cyprian was in no way directing his warning to the Jewish peoples or the pagans or those of other faiths. He was merely warning against heresy and schism within the one true church of Christ.

The Age of Christendom

Christianity underwent a 180-degree turn in the fourth century with Emperor Constantine's Edict of Milan of 313 decriminalizing Christianity and ending centuries of Christian persecution. Christianity not only became legal but also gradually became the favored religion of the empire. By 380 the Edict of Thessalonica declared Christianity the official religion of the state, and all the citizens of the Roman Empire were expected to profess the faith of the bishops of Rome and Alexandria and pledge adherence to the Nicene Creed. We could call this the beginnings of Christendom, where Christianity had become not only the dominant religion but also a geopolitical force that was to last until well into the twentieth century. In the interest of uniting the Roman Empire, pagan religious practices and celebrations were gradually outlawed. The rituals, customs, and worship places of the pagan religions were also gradually but mercilessly destroyed. Theologically, everything that did not augment the practice of the Christian faith was deemed to be demonic.

With this newfound status, Christians had now moved from the cata-combs to the throne. The persecuted religion had now become the official religion. The dictum *cuius regio, eius religio* (whose realm, his religion) meant that the people were expected to follow the religion of the region's ruler. Unsurprisingly, mass conversions took place throughout Europe. Becoming Christian came with perks and privileges, including social, political, and economic advantages. Church officials were empowered to serve as city and state administrators as well. Christianity advanced significantly and also rather arrogantly and aggressively. Christians no longer regarded the Jewish people, and later the Muslims, as belonging to the one people of God. This gave rise to sentiments of anti-Semitism and the rhetoric that Jews were Christ-killers or God-killers (deicide) became more pronounced and used—especially when Christians and Jews were competing economically—to incite violence against the Jews.

In this new context, the judgment of no salvation outside the church becomes lethal. It is now no longer applied only to those who lived in the pre-Christian era or to Christians who were abandoning their faith but also to Jews and pagans and those who did not become Christian under the new Roman imperial government. Theologians of the late fourth century such as St. Ambrose, the bishop of Milan, St. Gregory of Nyssa, and St. John Chrysostom were unequivocal that those who had not embraced the Christian faith were doomed to eternal hell. Part of their reasoning was that the Gospel had by now been preached to the ends of the earth (at least as they knew the earth at that time). This is what Chrysostom wrote:

> Do not say: "How is it that God has neglected that sincere and honest pagan?" You will find that such a one has not really been diligent in seeking the truth, since what concerns the truth is now clearer than the sun. How shall they obtain pardon who, when they see the doctrine of truth spread before them, make no effort to come to know it? For now the name of God is proclaimed to all, what the prophets predicted has come true, and the religion of the pagans has been proved false. . . . It is impossible that anyone who is vigilant in seeking the truth should be condemned by God.[2]

---

2. *In Epist. Ad Rom. Hom.* 26:3–4; *Patrologia Graeca* 60:641–642, as cited in Jacques Dupuis, *Toward a Christian Theology of Religious Pluralism* (Maryknoll, NY: Orbis Books, 1997), 89.

In the late fourth and early fifth centuries, the North African theologian and bishop of Hippo, St. Augustine, reiterated a lot of the teachings of the earlier church fathers. He too asserted that salvation is possible for Jews and pagans who lived before the coming of Christ if they lived a good and devout life. This is premised on his conviction that God had provided sufficient revelation to everyone, albeit at times obscurely. Their salvation, however, still comes through Christ. But Augustine added that where salvation was not afforded it is because God already foreknew that the people would not be receptive to it. This doctrine of predestination concludes that because God knew beforehand that they would have refused divine grace and salvation on account of their ignorance, they were the ones to be held responsible for their own damnation. God acts justly. Likewise, Augustine also asserts that there is no salvation for the heretics and schismatics if they stood outside the church. He believed that they could have everything else, including a valid baptism and the other sacraments, the Gospel, or even martyrdom, but they would be deprived of salvation if they choose to remain separated from the church. This damnation applies even to those who were unknowingly baptized into a schismatic group, although they would be less guilty compared to those who consciously break away from the true church of Christ.

As expected, Augustine was equally harsh in his condemnation of those who had not accepted the Christian faith and baptism. Taking Mark 16:16 ("The one who believes and is baptized will be saved; but the one who does not believe will be condemned") literally and rigorously, he was insistent that those who had heard the Gospel but had not embraced Christianity were guilty of sinful rejection of God's mercy and gifts and so were rightfully damned. While in his earlier career he believed that no one should be excused from this damnation, as the Gospel had already been preached worldwide, he realized later that there were still tribal peoples—whom he called barbarians—in his African home continent who remained unreached and so had no opportunity of becoming Christian. In keeping with his predestination argument, he believed that if they were worthy of salvation God would have afforded them the revelation and proclamation of the Gospel. So, they have themselves to blame for not being given the opportunity to come to the Christian faith. In his later career he used another argument to condemn the unbaptized while responding to the threat of Pelagianism (which advocates that human beings are inherently good and have the capacity for choosing good or evil without divine assistance). As to why masses of people who had not heard the Word of God—including unbaptized infants—would be justifiably condemned, Augustine proposed that it was because they were stained by the guilt of original sin. So, because every person is tainted by original sin and deserves to be condemned, those who attain salvation are saved solely by the sheer mercy of God. In short, salvation is a free gift and grace from God; some are fortunate to receive it while others are not. This is how Augustine explains it:

> Now this grace of Christ, without which neither infants nor adults can be saved, is not given in return for merits, but is a free gift; for this reason it is called "grace." Wherefore, all those who are not set free by that grace, whether because they could not hear [the message of the Gospel], or because they refused to obey it, or, being unable to hear it because of their infancy, they did not receive the baptismal bath by which they could have been saved—all these, I say, are justly damned, because they are not without sin—either the original sin that they contracted, or the sins that they added by their own wicked deeds. . . . The entire mass, therefore, incurs the penalty, and if the deserved punishment of condemnation were meted out to all, it would without doubt be justly meted out. . . . Anyone who judged rightly could not possibly blame the justice of God in wholly condemning all mankind.[3]

While Augustine's theology had been influential throughout most of Christian history, some of his theories did not really prevail. In particular, his condemnation of unbaptized infants for the inherited guilt of original sin was reworked when the medieval theologians came up with the speculative idea of *limbus infantium* (limbo of infants), which allows for an intermediary space between heaven and hell for these infants. Likewise, his teachings on God holding back salvation from some adults on account of their guilt of original sin or simply because they were predestined to damnation also met with ambivalent reception by later church leaders and theologians.

---

3. *De natura et gracia* 4–5; *Patrologiae cursus completes, series graeca* 44:249–50, as cited in Sullivan, *Salvation outside the Church?*, 38.

The Age of the Crusades

The 1054 split between the Eastern Byzantium Church (Greek-Constantinople) and the Western Church (Latin-Rome) represents a major blow not only to Christian unity but to the imperial powers of the church as well. These powers had already been severely affected by the rise of Islam in the seventh century and its spread to various parts of the Mediterranean and into the Iberian Peninsula and Europe. The response of the church took the form of the Crusades, a generic term used here to stand for a series of religious wars and church-sanctioned campaigns fought for a variety of reasons, including the suppression of paganism and heresy, the resolution of conflict among rival Christian factions, or simply to gain more power and expand the empire. The age of the Crusades, then, represents the period of Christian self-understanding characterized by religiously inspired aggressions extending from the eighth century to the capture of Constantinople (the capital city of the Byzantine Empire) by the Ottoman Empire in 1453.

In the eleventh century when the Seljuk Turks advanced into Asia Minor (modern-day Turkey), a Christian-dominated region since the time of St. Paul, the emperor of Constantinople appealed to the pope (mind you, not to the emperor!) of Western Europe to send reinforcement to defend the territory. In 1095, at the Council of Clermont, Pope Urban II launched the first of the nine Crusades that were to take place in the next two hundred years. The pontiff's aims included freeing Jerusalem and the Church of the Holy Sepulcher, aiding the Eastern Christians in the hopes of healing the division between the Roman Catholic Church and the Orthodox Church, and channeling the forces of the constantly warring feudal lords and knights into a singular common religious cause. The Crusades were pitched as pilgrimages but were actually more like religious wars to retaliate against Muslim aggression in defense of Christian territories and to reclaim the Holy Land. The crusaders took the vow of the cross and put the sign of the cross on their foreheads and breastplates. They saw their acts as religious devotions of Christian piety and self-sacrifice in the spirit of John 15:13 ("No one has greater love than this, to lay down one's life for one's friends"). Prayer and fasting were significant features before and after each crusading campaign. It was in this spirit that they massacred the "enemies of Christ" and plundered the lands of the "infidels" and "heathens." As a result, thousands of Muslims, as well as Jews—who were believed to be funding the Muslims and were perpetual scapegoats of Christian frustration—were killed, as were the Christian warriors.

Christianity was now associated with militancy and an entire ethos and vocabulary developed around this experience that continues to shape its mission even today. The good Christian is a "soldier" for Christ and, fortified with the "armor" of faith, is tasked with bringing people to the Lord and "winning" the world over by "defeating" the forces of evil. Christians are urged to develop strategic tactics for "spiritual warfare" in view of occupying unoccupied territories by "deploying" missionaries of evangelism and providing "reinforcements" for purposes of "crusading" campaigns and evangelistic rallies. The Catholic Church even bestowed on its religious leaders titles such as "superior generals" or "mother generals," called their congregations "religious orders," had military orders known as the "Knights," and used a variety of other names associated with militarism. The teaching of "outside the church, no salvation" was no longer just a theological axiom but had now become a political ideology as well. The crusaders converted the "cross of Christ" into a "sword for Christ." Jesus was now the "Lord of lords" and the "King of kings." It was within this new culture of the Crusades that attitudes toward people of other faiths hardened and became even more negative, with numerous caricatures developing about other religions in general and Islam in particular. The notion of *vera religio* (true religion) came into ascendancy and, obviously, Christianity is posited as the only true religion while all others are regarded as false. Some of the more exclusive and condemnatory teachings of the early church were also rehatched and used unsparingly by the Christian leaders during this age. This attitude of self-righteousness became commonplace and was used to bolster the standing of the monarchical papacy or whenever the church and its unity came under threat.

The 1302 papal bull *Unam Sanctam* is a case in point. It was promulgated in the context of a dispute between Pope Boniface VIII and the king of France, Philip the Fair. The pope "resolved" the question about the relationship between the spiritual and temporal authority of the state by appeal to the following: "That there is only one, holy, catholic and apostolic Church we are compelled by faith to believe and hold, and we firmly believe in her and sincerely confess her, outside of whom there is no salvation, nor remission of sins. . . . Furthermore, we declare, state and define that it is absolutely necessary for the salvation of all people that they submit to the Roman Pontiff."[4] Then, in the fifteenth century, the Council of Florence was convoked by Pope Eugene IV in the context of wars in Bohemia and the rise of the Ottoman Empire. There was also the looming challenge to papal authority by the conciliar movement, which advocated that the church's supreme authority resides with an ecumenical council, not the pope. Amid these problems the pope thought it opportune to address Christian unity and encourage the return of the Eastern Churches to the Roman Catholic Church. In the 1442 Bull of Union with the Copts these convictions were included: "[The Holy Roman Church] . . . firmly believes, professes and preaches that 'no one remaining outside the Catholic Church, not only pagans,' but also Jews, heretics and schismatics, can become partakers of eternal life; but they will go to the 'eternal fire prepared for the devil and its angels' [Matt 25:41], unless before the end of their life they are joined [*aggregati*] to it."[5] These sentiments by and large shaped much of the church during the Crusades, especially in its dealings with those falling outside the Christian fold. Embracing the garrison or siege mentality, they helped in preserving the exclusiveness of the Christian faith while keeping at bay any deviation from the church's tradition.

Returning to the impact of the religious wars on the church, it goes without saying that Christian-Muslim relations were at their worst in the age of the Crusades. Many of the stereotypes and myths about Islam, the Holy Qur'an, and the Prophet Muhammad were developed during this period. The religion was painted as demonic and violent and its leaders and followers barbaric and bloodthirsty. Fortunately, however, Christian interaction with Muslims was not confined to the wars. There was also a fertile exchange in the areas of trade, culture, and education. In fact, historians argue that the West benefitted profoundly from these opportunities for cross-fertilization, especially in the areas of scientific, philosophical, and artistic learning. A number of the classical manuscripts that were found in libraries under Muslim rule were translated from Greek or Arabic to Latin, enabling the Christian Europeans to rediscover a lot of the important pre-Christian sources of European thought, including the works of philosophers such as Aristotle.

4. Dupuis, *Toward a Christian Theology of Religious Pluralism*, 94.
5. Ibid., 95.

While the sentiments of the church toward Muslims were shaped by the prevailing socio-political climate, there were exceptions of individuals and communities that did not succumb to the torment of fear and prejudice. One that has been highlighted over the years is the witness of St. Francis of Assisi of the early thirteenth century. Famous for his prayer, "Make Me a Channel of Your Peace," he was committed to approaching Islam and the Saracens (as Muslims were known prior to the modern era) peacefully. As a former soldier who had been on to the frontlines with the crusaders, he made the bold and risky move one day of crossing the battle lines in order to visit with the caliph, Sultan Malik al-Kamil, at Damietta in Egypt. On being captured by the enemy forces, Francis was brought before the sultan, whereupon he took the occasion to proclaim to the latter the truth of God as he knew it from the gospels. Impressed by the friar's sincerity and courage, the sultan listened with enthusiasm and asked him to stay on for a few days. He then offered Francis a number of valuable gifts before sending him safely back to his crusading army. While Francis's aim was to preach to and convert the sultan, the method of peace with which he approached the Muslim world was unheard of in the age of the Crusades. This probably captivated the sultan, who, even if not institutionally converted, probably went through a spiritual conversion on account of the event. As for Francis, on his return, he revised the rule of his Franciscan religious community in order to include a special chapter on evangelizing Muslims through the nonviolent and respectful approach. This was truly prophetic in an era when anti-Muslim apologetics was at its height and violence the normative method used in the missionary enterprise.

The Age of Mission

A new era emerged in Christian history beginning in the late fifteenth century, when the Europeans "discovered" new continents. Being the two major navigational and economic powers of the time, Spain and Portugal laid claims over the new lands. The pope drew a north-south dividing line giving Portugal control over Brazil, Africa, and Asia, with Spain taking charge of the Americas and the Philippines. Lacking the necessary resources, the church established the *padroado* (patronage) system whereby the kings of the two countries administered the missions on behalf of the Holy See. This clear-cut marriage of the church and the state saw the goals of the colonial empire as synonymous with the aims of Christian mission. This was happening at around the same time the seven-hundred-year rule of Muslims in Europe was coming to an end, enabling the Europeans to focus their energies elsewhere, in particular the conquest of new territories.

In reflecting on the colonial conquest of the Americas, the Spanish theologians had to justify the *conquista* of the American Indians who, unlike the Muslims, had neither occupied the Holy Land nor posed a threat to Christendom. What gives the *conquistadores* the right to conquer and enslave the natives? Anthropologies that regarded the native peoples as less than human or at least inferior to the European race provided the intellectual and theological justification for the conquest. The use of force was deemed legitimate or even necessary. Some missionaries objected, among them Dominican friar Bartolomé de las Casas, who refused to accept the demeaning caricature of the American Indians and insisted that they be respected as fully human. Because the invaders were after the gold in the New World, he lashed out at the way they treated the natives: "In order to gild a very cruel and harsh tyranny that destroys so many villages and people, solely for the sake of satisfying the greed of men and giving them gold, the latter, who themselves do not know the faith, use the pretext of teaching it to others and thereby deliver up the innocent in order to extract from their blood *the wealth which these men regard as their god.*"[6]

The Spaniards also applied the theories that had been employed during the Crusades to justify their mission, namely, that the unbelief of the infidel natives constituted their sin or even crime against Christianity. They, therefore, saw it as their Christian duty to bring the natives to salvation in Christ as it is for their own sake. The Dominican Francisco de Vitoria challenged this line of reasoning by asserting that unbelief is not so much a sin as it is a punishment or consequence of original sin. So, the invaders have no right to impute guilt to the natives. Against the argument that the Gospel had already been preached by the missionaries and yet the natives refused to accept it, de Vitoria responded that the

6. Robert Ellsberg, "Las Casas' Discovery: What the 'Protector of the Indians' Found in America," *America: The Jesuit Review* (November 5, 2012), https://www.americamagazine.org/issue/las-casas-discovery; emphasis in original.

way the Gospel is presented matters. It cannot be presented by force or with a sword hanging over the native's head. This is de Vitoria's take on the matter:

> It is not sufficiently clear to me that the Christian faith has yet been put before the aborigines and announced to them that they are bound to believe it or commit fresh sin. I say this because (as appears from my second proposition) they are not bound to believe unless the faith be put before them with persuasive demonstration. Now, I hear of no miracles or signs or religious patterns of life; nay, on the contrary, I hear of many scandals and cruel crimes and acts of impiety. Hence, it does not appear that the Christian religion has been preached to them with such sufficient propriety and piety that they are bound to acquiesce in it.[7]

In contrast to the powerful invading army of the Spaniards on the Americas, the Portuguese did not have the finances to pursue mass invasions. Their missions took the form of small groups establishing coastal strongholds in strategic parts of Africa and Asia. What the missionaries encountered in Asia was quite different from that of the Americas. Asia was already very alive with the institutionalized religions and rich scriptural texts well before the arrival of the Christian mission. Lacking the experience of dealing with adherents of other great religious traditions, the missionaries, with the backing of the colonial power, knew only one approach, namely, aggressive and militaristic evangelization. They had to make strenuous efforts to reach out to the natives, whom they regarded as no more than pagans and savages. Bringing the light of the Gospel and filling the minds and hearts of the people with Christ were the professed aims of Christian mission. The rich cultural and religious traditions of the continent were simply ignored and despised. This was generally the modus operandi of the colonial Christian mission to the Far East.

Like everything else, there are exceptions that have become examples. In some instances, the missionaries—especially those to major cities—met with not so much the native tribal class but people from the intellectual and literate class. The Jesuits who were the main missionaries

7. As cited in Sullivan, *Salvation outside the Church?*, 72.

to these locations had a more optimistic anthropology and were generally positively disposed to the non-Western cultures. They employed a different missiological approach and focused their efforts on the accommodation of the Christian faith to the local cultures. Mateo Ricci is the principal protagonist of this method and, upon his arrival at the Portuguese settlement of Macau toward the end of the sixteenth century, immersed himself in the study of the language and cultures of the people, as well as of the Confucian classics and the Chinese religions. In preaching about Christianity he sought points of convergence between how the Chinese worshiped and the Christian faith. He translated the biblical term for God into the Chinese term *Tianzhu* (Lord of Heaven), which is commonly used in Chinese folk religion. Later, the Jesuits also adapted by using the terms *Tian* (Heaven) and *Shangdi* (Supreme Emperor). Ricci advised that the Chinese practice of ancestral veneration and other Chinese imperial rites and rituals were not so much religious as civil or socio-political rites and so did not contradict Catholic beliefs. The other missionaries, such as the Dominicans, Franciscans, and Augustinians, who were mostly ministering to the ordinary working-class Chinese in the villages and witnessed a lot of the folk practices, disagreed and advocated that ancestral veneration was superstitious and idolatrous and should be forbidden. This resulted in the Chinese Rites Controversy, culminating in Pope Clement XI issuing the papal bull *Ex illa die* in 1715 condemning the Chinese rites. The condemnation was reaffirmed in 1742 by Pope Benedict XIV's papal bull *Ex quo singulari*. This papal suppression was to stay in place for almost two hundred years, until 1939 when Pope Pius XII ordered the Sacred Congregation for the Propagation of the Faith to relax the ban and allow Catholics to participate in what the church now confirms are civil practices.

The beginnings of the age of mission also saw Western Christianity going through the Protestant Reformation and the Catholic Church's response in the form of the Council of Trent. Doctrinally, the council made no changes on the matter of those outside of the Christian faith since the Protestant reformers were as insistent as the Catholic tradition that salvation comes from Christ and only through the church. But the council did make two statements that left open how the doctrine of "outside the church, no salvation" is to be understood. First, it appealed to Hebrews 11:6 ("And without faith it is impossible to please God, for whoever would approach him must believe that he exists and that he rewards those who seek him"), where faith is taken to mean belief in God's existence and not so much the explicit faith in Christ. Second, the council recognized the viability of what is known as the baptism of desire (*voto*) for salvation. That means salvation is granted also for those who wished for it even as they are not explicitly baptized into the church. So, this enabled the missionaries to be more flexible about the conversion of those in Asia and Africa where the people do have faith in God but have not been evangelized about the knowledge of Christ. Robert Bellarmine, who taught Ricci at the Jesuit Roman College, helped in the articulation of this teaching: "I reply that the saying 'Outside the Church no one is saved,' should be understood of those who belong to the Church neither in reality nor in desire, just as theologians commonly speak about baptism. Because catechumens, even though not in the church *re* (in reality), are in the church *voto* (by desire), and in that way can be saved."[8]

The Age of Dialogue

The twentieth century saw "dialogue" as the new catchword in the social and political spheres as well as in many other disciplines of studies. Philosophical theories of dialogue emerged from thinkers such as Martin Buber and educationists such as Paulo Freire. All point to the need and urgency for engagement across party lines for the purpose of fostering better understandings between radically different viewpoints and entities. The advent of postmodernist thought and its abhorrence of uniformity, universality, and absoluteness or even of objective reality meant that Christianity had the new task of discerning its identity, revisioning its mission, and reviewing its relationship with other religions. The shift in the understanding of the structure of reality and of truth itself resulted in exclusivist and monologic attitudes making way for approaches that are more dynamic, conditional, and dialogical. The classicist and absolutist views in metaphysics, epistemology, missiology, soteriology, and many other branches of theology and philosophy were gradually replaced by the more mutual, relational, and dialogical views. The advent of biblical criticism, historical consciousness, hermeneutics, the sociology of knowl-

8. Ibid., 88.

edge, developmental psychology, and other fields of study contributed significantly to this paradigm shift.

It is by no means a coincidence that this shift was accompanied by the fall of the European-cum-Christian Empire and the birth of a new world order. Independent nation-states and the resurgence of religions other than Christianity are only a small part of what was to become a new consciousness. This consciousness saw the relativization of knowledge, including religious knowledge and faith, making dialogue with other faiths and religions imperative. This need is concurrent with the surge of information in the world about religion in general and the world's religions in particular. The mass movements of peoples across continents, especially those from East to West and South to North, meant that the previously homogenous Christian Europe became more multicultural and multireligious. There was no escape from realizing that other religions not only exist but are here to stay and that they have their own intricate symbol systems and institutions. While previously it might have been possible to adamantly hold on to the view that one's own religion is the only true one or the most superior of all, the new era of dialogue renders such notions almost illusory. If anything, there is the realization that many of the adherents of these other religions are good, loving, and holy people, not so much despite, but precisely because of their religions.

In the face of this new reality, Christians have been almost forced to accept, even if reluctantly, that Christianity is but one among many competing religious traditions in the world. Appreciating this new context makes it difficult to continue with the assertions that Christians are the only ones who will be saved and that people of other religions are doomed to eternal hellfire. In fact, even asking if salvation is possible for those who have not embraced the Christian faith is deemed inappropriate. Instead, Christians should be asking how Christianity fits in to the divine economy of God's salvation in the world of many religions and how Christians can be in dialogue with their adherents in order to discover God's truth together. To be sure, in the light of the new reality of religious pluralism, Christianity's theology and relationship with other religions need to be revisited especially in exploring how scripture, history, theology, and mission are understood. Numerous theological questions are raised with regard to these in the new age of dialogue.

In thinking about scriptures, for example, questions need to be asked as to whether the Bible is the only Word of God, or could there be others? Also, how is one to understand the authority of scripture and its application in religiously plural contexts? If Christians use biblical texts to assess or pass judgments on other religions, then should not the same courtesy be extended to their religious neighbors, inviting them to judge Christianity on the basis of their own holy writings? Christians have also to be mindful that not all religions have written scriptures, and, even among those that have, they do not confer similar divine authority on their scriptures. Moreover, the practice of citing scriptural texts as justification or mandate for one's beliefs or actions is in the main alien to those who are not Christians. This leads to the next issue of history. That the Bible has endowed theological significance on the people of Israel means nothing to those who do not accept its authority. More important, why should the Jewish people be regarded as God's chosen people and Christians the people of God while people from other parts of the world are not afforded such status? Do people in India or China who are not Christian or the unbaptized first peoples in Australia and the Americas not mean anything in the eyes of the just and loving God of all? Are they able to make similar claims to divine election or are they simply to be regarded as not people of God?

In the new age of dialogue, questions also need to be raised about the theological enterprise itself. Do the scriptures and teachings of the other religions feature at all in the activity of Christian theology? Does God reveal only to Christians or do persons of other religions also have a contributing role in the discernment of God's will for humankind? Can we still talk about theology as such or should we always premise it by saying it is merely Christian theology and has no relevance whatsoever to those who are not Christian? Or should Christians integrate the scriptures and reflections of their religious neighbors in their own theological reflections on the world, on God, and on God's relationship with humankind? This leads us to the controversial subject of mission. How is the theology of mission understood in religiously plural societies? Do Christians still insist on *missio ad gentes* (mission to the nations) or should they be moving toward *missio inter gentes* (mission with the nations), that is, mission engaged in together and in partnership with their religious neighbors? Can Christian mission still be a one-way proclamation in view of bringing the other to one's fold or should there be another way of proclaiming the coming of God's kingdom on earth?

These are but some of the sticky questions and challenges that the new age of dialogue has brought to the fore. It would not be easy for Christians to fall back on teachings of the church of yesteryears in attending to the new context of engagement with the many cultures and religions of the world. Moreover, Christianity is in this dialogue today as one among equals, which makes the challenge difficult but interesting and certainly life-giving. What results from this dialogue between the religions will shape the Christian tradition as it moves forward together with the other religious traditions in this world that is becoming more connected, on the one hand, but also more divisive and fractured, on the other. The world is certainly in need of peace, harmony, and healing, and all the world's religions have a role to play in ensuring that.

Conclusion

The church has had a rich history of theological discussion on the place of those who are not Christians in the divine economy of God's salvation. If in the early centuries the concerns were with apostasy and heresy and in encouraging Christians to remain faithful to the faith, the issues today are about Christianity's relationship with the world of other religions. While many have resorted to using the doctrinal formulas of the early church in addressing the concerns of religious pluralism today, others are calling for more contextualized approaches. To be sure, Christians will not be able to discern the most appropriate response on their own. They will need to be discovering this in dialogue with their brothers and sisters of other religions. This is what the signs of the times invite Christians to.

Suggestions for Further Reading

Becker, Karl Josef, and Ilaria Morali, eds. *Catholic Engagement with World Religions: A Comprehensive Study*. Maryknoll, NY: Orbis Books, 2010.

D'Costa, Gavin, ed. *The Catholic Church and the World Religions: A Theological and Phenomenological Account*. London: T & T Clark, 2011.

Dupuis, Jacques. *Christianity and the Religions: From Confrontation to Dialogue*. Maryknoll, NY: Orbis Books, 2002.

Kärkkäinen, Veli-Matti. *An Introduction to the Theology of Religions: Biblical, Historical and Contemporary Perspectives*. Downers Grove, IL: InterVarsity Press, 2003.

Plantinga, Richard J., ed. *Christianity and Plurality: Classic and Contemporary Readings*. Oxford: Blackwell Publishers, 1999.

6

Vatican II Christianity and Interfaith Dialogue

Introduction

Whenever I teach a course on the world's religions or on interfaith dialogue I include an assignment where the students will need to visit a place of worship other than their own so that they can witness firsthand how their religious neighbors worship and also engage in real-life interfaith dialogue. In one of these courses a student came to me pleading for an alternative assignment. She said she could not fulfill the assignment as her mother forbids her to do so. Her mother feels it is sinful for her Catholic daughter to be stepping foot into a Muslim mosque or a Buddhist temple or a Sikh gurdwara. I quickly googled the words "Pope John Paul II" and "mosque" and showed her the image of the eighty-one-year-old pontiff removing his shoes and entering the historic Umayyad mosque in Damascus, accompanied by Syria's leading Muslim cleric, Sheikh Ahmad Kuftaro.

This chapter looks at the revolution in the Catholic Church that was inaugurated by the Second Vatican Council. It will first discuss the convocation of the council by Pope John XXIII and the dynamics that brought it to fruition. Attention will be given to how the topic of the church's relations with other religions emerged and how the statements made about interfaith dialogue evolved during the course of the council. The chapter will then examine the significance of some of these teachings, especially in relation to what it means to be church in pluralistic contexts. It will also look at how the renewal that the Second Vatican Council spearheaded has been implemented under the popes of the post–Vatican II church.

All the papacies since the 1960s will be surveyed, paying attention to the contributions made to the ministry of interfaith dialogue during the leadership of each of the popes. A specific theme or name of a church document will be highlighted for each of the papacies, identifying each of the popes with an explicit focus.

Pope John XXIII: *Aggiornamento*

Following the death of Pope Pius XII in 1958, Pope John XXIII was elected to the papacy and, within the first one hundred days of his reign, announced on January 25, 1959, that a worldwide, or ecumenical, council for the universal church would be convoked. The bishops, especially those staffing the Vatican curia or administrative offices, were taken by surprise. The church, as they saw it, was doing fine, with record numbers attending Mass and a uniform liturgical life throughout the world. It also had many missionaries serving in the missions and the theologians were all safely under the control of the hierarchy. Moreover, there was no looming crisis coming from either within or without the church to warrant an ecumenical council. The most recent council, Vatican I (1869–1870), was called amid the threat of modernity, facilitated by the Enlightenment, the industrial revolution, and advances in science. The previous one was the Council of Trent (1545–1563), called as part of the Catholic Counter-Reformation movement responding to the challenges posed by the Protestant reformers. But no such threat confronted the church in the mid-twentieth century. The curial bishops could not understand why the pope was calling for the council.

Pope John XXIII, however, wanted a council for the church to undergo what in Italian is called an *aggiornamento* (bringing up to date) so as to enable the church to refresh itself and catch up with the progress made in the modern world. While the church was relatively stable, a lot was going on in society that raised questions for Christianity and religion in general. Despite the social and political transitions and upheavals, John XXIII had a general optimism about the world. He envisioned not so much a church that places itself above or against or away from the world but one that is situated within the modern world, at once evangelizing it as well as being evangelized by it. He rebutted the bishops and cardinals who had a pessimistic worldview and who were also against the idea of the council. In his opening address to the council on October 11, 1962, he had this to say:

> In the daily exercise of our pastoral office, we sometimes have to listen, much to our regret, to voices of persons who, though burning with zeal, are not endowed with too much sense of discretion or measure. In these modern times they can see nothing but prevarication and ruin. They say that our era, in comparison with past eras, is getting worse, and they behave as though they had learned nothing from history, which is, none the less, the teacher of life. They behave as though at the time of former Councils everything was a full triumph for the Christian idea and life and for proper religious liberty. We feel we must disagree with those prophets of gloom, who are always forecasting disaster, as though the end of the world were at hand.[1]

Prior to his election to the highest office of the Catholic Church, John XXIII had served as nuncio in France and delegate to Bulgaria, Greece, and Turkey. He thus had firsthand experience with both the Eastern Orthodox Churches as well as with Muslims and Jews, including those who were victims of the Holocaust. While the preparations for the council were underway, John XXIII established the Secretariat for Promoting Christian Unity on June 5, 1960, and made it one of the council's preparatory commissions. His trusted friend Cardinal Augustin Bea was appointed to head the secretariat, which was also charged with the responsibility for inviting other churches and world communions to send observers to the council. A week later, the French Jewish historian Jules Isaac, whose family was put to death during the Holocaust, had an audience with the pope. He presented his intensive research on the roots of Christian anti-Semitism and asked the pope to initiate substantive change in the church's attitude toward Jews at the upcoming council. Pope John XXIII directed Isaac to meet with Cardinal Bea and instructed the latter to include the "Jewish question" into the council's agenda.

For Pope John XXIII, the most urgent call of the council was for the church to keep up to date with the changed circumstances of the world, be more concerned with the suffering of its people, and renew Christian

---

1. "Pope John's Opening Speech to the Council," *Vatican II: The Voice of the Church* (St. Peter's Basilica, October 11, 1962), http://vatican2voice.org/91docs/opening_speech.htm.

teachings or practices where they were outdated. Moreover, he saw the council as a "new Pentecost" where the church would renew itself completely and be in the service of promoting Christian unity, as well as the unity of the entire human community. He called for a conscientious reading of the "signs of the times" so that Catholics may appreciate the actual facts and realities of the contemporary world and adapt church thinking and methods appropriately. The following quotation is attributed to Pope John XXIII on his deathbed on May 24, 1963:

> Today more than ever . . . we are called to serve man as such, and not merely Catholics; to defend above all and everywhere the rights of the human person, and not merely those of the Catholic Church. Today's world, the needs made plain in the last fifty years and a deeper understanding of doctrine have brought us to a new situation. . . . It is not that the Gospel has changed, it is that we have begun to understand it better. Those who have lived as long as I have . . . were enabled to compare different cultures and traditions, and know that the moment has come to discern the signs of the times, to seize the opportunity and to look far ahead.[2]

Pope Paul VI: *Ecclesiam Suam*

Pope Paul VI succeeded John XXIII in June 1963, in between the first and second sessions of the Second Vatican Council, which met between September and December each year from 1962 to 1965. He carefully saw the council through to its completion and the delicate task of implementing the decisions and recommendations made by the conciliar bishops. This was to be the most revolutionary exercise for the church since the Council of Trent and affected practically every aspect of church life. At the opening of the second session of the council in September 1963, which was the first time Paul VI was attending it as pope, he gave a one-hour address where he identified the council's main objectives: "For reasons of brevity and better understanding we enumerate here those objectives in four points: the knowledge, or—if you prefer—the awareness of the

---

2. Bishop Remi J. De Roo, "Discerning the Signs of the Times," *Vatican II: The Voice of the Church* (2002), http://vatican2voice.org/2need/deroo.htm.

Church; its reform; the bringing together of all Christians in unity; the dialogue of the Church with the contemporary world."[3] He stressed the importance of the church being missionary and open to the world and to engage especially in dialogue with other believers as well as with those who do not adhere to any faiths. He promised he would elaborate on these themes in a follow-up inaugural encyclical.

This took the form of his first encyclical, titled *Ecclesiam Suam* (ES), issued on August 6, 1964.[4] It was as much a blueprint for his pontificate as for the council, which was still going on. He began by spelling out what *Ecclesiam Suam* intends: "The aim of this encyclical will be to demonstrate with increasing clarity how vital it is for the world, and how greatly desired by the Catholic Church, that the two should meet together, and get to know and love one another" (ES 3). He then identified three principal policies of his pontificate: (1) that the church engage in a deeper scrutiny of itself to investigate its doctrines and practices more thoroughly (ES 18–40); (2) that members of the church renew themselves, correct their faults, and strive for perfection (ES 41–57); and (3) that the church establish positive relations with the surrounding world in which it lives and works (ES 58–119). As is obvious, the three policies are by no means equal in weight as the final policy—the one on dialogue and engagement with the world at large—occupies more than half the length of the document.

This third and longest section of the document is titled simply "Dialogue." The word "dialogue," in fact, appears eighty-one times, resulting in *Ecclesiam Suam* being known as the dialogue document and Paul VI, the dialogue pope. It is actually the first time the word "dialogue" was used in a church document. Dialogue, as we know, can happen only where there is a reciprocal relationship. That *Ecclesiam Suam* insists that "the Church must enter into dialogue with the world in which it lives" (ES 65) means there is respect for the world at large. While the church has something to

---

3. Opening General Congregation September 29, 1963, "Pope Paul Sets Agenda as Council's Second Session Opens," *Vatican II, 50 Years Ago Today* (September 29, 2013), https://vaticaniiat50.wordpress.com/2013/09/29/pope-paul-sets-agenda -as-councils-second-session-opens/.

4. Pope Paul VI, *Ecclesiam Suam: On the Church* (August 6, 1964), http://w2. vatican.va/content/paul-vi/en/encyclicals/documents/hf_p-vi_enc_06081964 _ecclesiam.html.

say to the world, it is implied that the world too has something to teach the church. Paul VI maps out the forms of dialogue that the church has to be engaged in through the use of four concentric circles, beginning with the outer circle, the most encompassing: (1) the entire human race, the world, including those who profess no religion (ES 97–106); (2) worshipers of the one God, the Jews, the Muslims, and followers of the great Afro-Asiatic religions (ES 107–8); (3) Christians of other denominations in ecumenical dialogue (ES 109–12); and (4) members of the Catholic community in an internal dialogue within the church (ES 113–16).

While *Ecclesiam Suam* was Paul VI's major contribution to Vatican II Christianity's attitude toward interfaith dialogue, another contribution took the form of the 1975 apostolic exhortation *Evangelii Nuntiandi,*[5] the fruits of the Synod on Evangelization that was held the year before. The importance of a reciprocal relationship with the world outside of the church was reiterated in the document: "The Church is an evangelizer, but she begins by being evangelized herself" (EN 15). In *Evangelii Nuntiandi,* Paul VI states unequivocally that the principal method of evangelization is through the witness of Christian truths and values: "As we said recently to a group of lay people, 'Modern man listens more willingly to witnesses than to teachers, and if he does listen to teachers, it is because they are witnesses' " (EN 41). In keeping with the theology of the Second Vatican Council, he emphasizes the church's respect for the other religions but also underlines that they await their fulfillment in the Gospel of Christ:

> The Church respects and esteems these non-Christian religions because they are the living expression of the soul of vast groups of people. They carry within them the echo of thousands of years of searching for God, a quest which is incomplete but often made with great sincerity and righteousness of heart. They possess an impressive patrimony of deeply religious texts. They have taught generations of people how to pray. They are all impregnated with innumerable "seeds of the Word" and can constitute a true "preparation for the Gospel," to quote a felicitous term used by the Second Vatican Council and borrowed from Eusebius of Caesarea. (EN 53)

5. Pope Paul VI, *Evangelii Nuntiandi* (December 8, 1975), http://w2.vatican.va/content/paul-vi/en/apost_exhortations/documents/hf_p-vi_exh_19751208_evangelii-nuntiandi.html.

Nostra Aetate and Other Conciliar Documents

The Christian theology of fulfillment of other religions was clearly articulated in the official documents of the Second Vatican Council. The one document that addresses this theme in particular and interfaith dialogue in general is *Nostra Aetate* (Declaration on the Relation of the Church to Non-Christian Religions). Though the shortest of all the council documents (consisting of just over one thousand words in five articles), its impact on the church has been tremendous, especially in shaping Catholicism's attitude toward those who adhere to other religions. Its import is better appreciated if read alongside other documents such as *Lumen Gentium* (Dogmatic Constitution on the Church), *Gaudium et Spes* (Pastoral Constitution on the Church in the Modern World), *Dignitatis Humanae* (Declaration on Religious Freedom), *Unitatis Redintegratio* (Decree on Ecumenism), and also *Ad Gentes* (Decree on the Mission Activity of the Church). These documents together provide the vision for the Catholic Church's engagement with the world outside of it, also known as its mission *ad extra*.

When Cardinal Bea and the commissions were preparing for Vatican II they did not anticipate a document such as *Nostra Aetate*. As mentioned earlier, the plan was to address Christian teachings only on Judaism. The issue of the "Jewish question" was to be inserted into the document on ecumenism or the promotion of Christian unity. A general statement on religious freedom for everyone else was also supposed to constitute part of the ecumenism document. When the bishops from the Middle East who lived in Muslim-majority nations were aware of this impending statement about the Jews, they raised concerns that it could be perceived as the Catholic Church taking sides in the Arab-Israeli tension that was brewing in the 1960s. The draft on the Jews was revised to include a positive statement about Muslims and the religion of Islam. When the bishops from Asia heard about this development they too raised concerns that this might be perceived as the Catholic Church's appreciation for only the Abrahamic faiths to the exclusion of the other religions. The draft was revised again to include aspects of Hinduism and Buddhism and also the traditional religions. The end result of these discussions over four years was that the church's relationship with all the other religions would be addressed in an independent document called *Nostra Aetate* and that the theme of religious freedom would constitute yet another independent document called *Dignitatis Humanae*. *Nostra Aetate* was finally approved by the council fathers on October 28, 1965, with 2,221 voting in its favor and only eighty-eight voting against. This vote has to be appreciated in the context of the approval of *Lumen Gentium* (LG)[6] a year earlier, on November 21, 1964, as a statement within it provides the doctrinal base for understanding the church's attitude toward other religions:

> Finally, those who have not yet accepted the Gospel are related to the people of God in various ways. There is, first, that people to whom the covenants and promises were made, and from whom Christ was born in the flesh. . . . But the plan of salvation also includes those who acknowledge the Creator, first among whom are the Muslims: they profess to hold the faith of Abraham, and together with us they adore the one, merciful God, who will judge humanity on the last day. Nor is God remote from those who in shadows and images seek the unknown God, since he gives to everyone life and breath and all things and since the Saviour wills everyone to be saved. Those who, through no fault of their own, do not know the Gospel of Christ or his church, but who nevertheless seek God with a sincere heart, and, moved by grace, try in their actions to do his will as they know it through the dictates of conscience—these too may attain eternal salvation. . . . Whatever of good or truth is found amongst them is considered by the church to be a preparation for the Gospel. (LG 16)

Nostra Aetate (NA)[7] begins by affirming the unity of humanity, in their origin as well as in their final destiny, while at the same time appreciating the fact of religious plurality (NA 1). Article 2 discusses in broad sweeps what would now be known as the indigenous religions and then identifies by name the religions of Hinduism and Buddhism, spelling out the essential dimensions of each of these traditions. It then states unequivocally that "the Catholic Church rejects nothing of what is true and holy in these religions. It has a high regard for the manner of life and conduct, the precepts and doctrines which, although differing in

6. *Lumen Gentium: Dogmatic Constitution on the Church* (November 21, 1964), in *Vatican Council II: The Basic Sixteen Documents*, ed. Austin Flannery (Collegeville, MN: Liturgical Press, 2014).

7. *Nostra Aetate: Declaration on the Relation of the Church to Non-Christian Religions* (October 28, 1965), in Flannery, *Vatican Council II*.

many ways from its own teaching, nevertheless often reflect a ray of that truth which enlightens all men and women" (NA 2). Article 3 addresses the religion of Islam, singling out areas in its teachings and practices that coincide with Catholicism, and concludes by acknowledging the centuries of hostilities between the two religions, but it "pleads with all to forget the past, and urges that a sincere effort be made to achieve mutual understanding; for the benefit of all, let them together preserve and promote peace, liberty, social justice and moral values" (NA 3).

The fourth article is disproportionately much longer than all the other articles since it was the original impetus for what ended up as *Nostra Aetate.* It acknowledges the spiritual bond between the church and the Jewish religion, especially the church's indebtedness to Abraham's stock for the revelation of Hebrew Scriptures. It then avers that even if it is true that it is "the Jewish authorities and those who followed their lead [who] pressed for the death of Christ, neither all Jews indiscriminately at that time, nor Jews today, can be charged with the crimes committed during his passion." It then adds that "it is true that the church is the new people of God, yet the Jews should not be spoken of as rejected or accursed as if this followed from holy scriptures." As such, it "deplores all hatreds, persecutions, [and] displays of anti-semitism levelled at any time and from any source against the Jews" (NA 4).

What is revolutionary about *Nostra Aetate* and the other documents of Vatican II is that for the first time in the church's history the other religions are mentioned in a positive light. They are even acknowledged as containing elements of salvation, leading to the call for Catholics to be engaged in "discussion and collaboration with members of other religions . . . [so as to] acknowledge, preserve and encourage the spiritual and moral truths found among non-Christians, together with their social life and culture" (NA 2). Moreover, "the church reproves, as foreign to the mind of Christ, any discrimination against people or any harassment of them on the basis of their race, color, condition of life or religion" (NA 5).

Pope John Paul II: Assisi World Day of Prayer

Pope John Paul II was elected to the papacy in October 1978, following the sudden death of Pope John Paul I, who served as pope for only thirty-three days after succeeding Pope Paul VI, who died in August 1978. If

Paul VI is identified as the pope who first introduced dialogue into the vocabulary of the church, John Paul II is often identified as the pope who actually engaged in the ministry of interfaith dialogue on a global scale. Included in his 1979 inaugural papal encyclical *Redemptoris Hominis* (RH)[8] is the following statement, which offers a glimpse of his attitude toward religions other than Christianity:

> What we have just said must also be applied—although in another way and with the due differences—to activity for coming closer together with the representatives of the non-Christian religions, an activity expressed through dialogue, contacts, prayer in common, investigation of the treasures of human spirituality, in which, as we know well, the members of these religions also are not lacking. Does it not sometimes happen that the firm belief of the followers of the non-Christian religions—a belief that is also an effect of the Spirit of truth operating outside the visible confines of the Mystical Body—can make Christians ashamed at being often themselves so disposed to doubt concerning the truths revealed by God and proclaimed by the Church and so prone to relax moral principles and open the way to ethical permissiveness. (RH 6)

Thanks to enhanced travel and communication, John Paul II became known as the globetrotting or pilgrim pope who made 104 international trips, visiting 129 countries during his twenty-seven-year papacy. Whenever he visited a country where the majority of the population adheres to a religion other than Christianity, he would include in his itinerary not only a meeting with the religious leaders but also a visit to a place of worship of that religion. Thus, he became the first pope to visit a Buddhist temple in Thailand in 1984, to enter Rome's Great Synagogue in 1986, to wear the Hindu *tilaka* (sacred sign on one's forehead) in India in 1986, to pray at the Western Wall of Jerusalem in 2000, and to enter a Muslim mosque in Syria in 2001. He is also the first pope to call for an assembly of the world's religious leaders to pray for peace. This World Day of Prayer for Peace was held in Assisi, Italy, on October 27, 1986, and saw the participation of more than 120 representatives of different religions and Christian denominations who spent the day in fasting and

8. Pope John Paul II, *Redemptoris Hominis* (March 4, 1979), http://w2.vatican.va/content/john-paul-ii/en/encyclicals/documents/hf_jp-ii_enc_04031979_redemptor-hominis.html.

prayer. Though mainly symbolic gestures, these activities speak to John Paul II's respect for the other religions. The World Day of Prayer for Peace was a gesture so radical that the event was even boycotted by some very high-level curial officials who were worried that the pope had put the other religions on the same level as the Christian faith.

In his long reign as pope, John Paul II obviously not only engaged in the ministry of interfaith dialogue but also taught a lot on the matter. His numerous apostolic teachings and papal encyclicals speak to many aspects of church life, especially on issues of justice and peace and personal morality. The encyclical that has the most relevance to interfaith dialogue is the 1990 *Redemptoris Missio*, subtitled "On the Permanent Validity of the Church's Missionary Mandate." Two other Vatican documents were issued during John Paul II's papacy that have much to say about the church's relationship with other religions: (1) the 1984 document Reflections and Orientations on Dialogue and Mission: The Attitude of the Church towards the Followers of Other Religions (referred to as "Dialogue and Mission") and (2) the 1991 document Dialogue and Proclamation: Reflection and Orientations on Interreligious Dialogue and the Proclamation of the Gospel of Jesus Christ (referred to as "Dialogue and Proclamation"). The former is the fruit of a study by the Secretariat for Non-Christians to commemorate the twentieth anniversary of both the secretariat's founding and also the document *Ecclesiam Suam*, while the latter is the product of a collaborative study between the same secretariat (renamed Pontifical Council for Interreligious Dialogue in 1988) and the Congregation for the Evangelization of Peoples (previously known as the Sacred Congregation for the Propagation of the Faith or simply *Propaganda Fide*) to commemorate the twenty-fifth anniversary of *Nostra Aetate*. A synthetic summary of these three documents—*Redemptoris Missio* (RM),[9] Dialogue and Mission (DM),[10]

---

9. Pope John Paul II, *Redemptoris Missio: On the Permanent Validity of the Church's Missionary Mandate* (December 7, 1990), http://w2.vatican.va/content/john-paul-ii /en/encyclicals/documents/hf_jp-ii_enc_07121990_redemptoris-missio.html.

10. Secretariat for Non-Christians, *The Attitude of the Church towards the Followers of Other Religions: Reflections and Orientations on Dialogue and Mission* (May 10, 1984), http://www.pcinterreligious.org/dialogue-and-mission_75.html.

and Dialogue and Proclamation (DP)[11]—read in the light of the other documents of Vatican II offers three highlights of Vatican II Christianity's attitude toward interfaith dialogue and the theology of other religions.

First, there is a positive evaluation of the religious traditions: "They command our respect because over the centuries they have borne witness to the efforts to find answers 'to those profound mysteries of the human condition' (NA 1) and have given expression to the religious experience and they continue to do so today" (DP 14). Note that this positive evaluation is not just about people of other religions, but about the religions themselves, affirming that they share, together with the Christian religion, a place in God's divine economy of salvation. The Dialogue and Proclamation document elaborates on this:

> *Nostra Aetate* speaks of the presence in these traditions of "a ray of that Truth which enlightens all" (NA 2). *Ad Gentes* recognizes the presence of "seeds of the word," and points to "the riches which a generous God has distributed among the nations" (AG 11). Again, *Lumen Gentium* refers to the good which is "found sown" not only "in minds and hearts," but also "in the rites and customs of peoples" (LG 17). . . . These few references suffice to show that the Council has openly acknowledged the presence of positive values not only in the religious life of individual believers of other religious traditions, but also in the religious traditions to which they belong. (DP 16–17)

Second, in view of this recognition of the divine validity of the other religious traditions, *Redemptoris Missio* posits that "inter-religious dialogue is a part of the Church's evangelizing mission" (RM 55). Furthermore, it is explicit in stating that "each member of the faithful and all Christian communities are called to practice dialogue, although not always to the same degree or in the same way" (RM 57). This is unequivocally mandating that the praxis of interfaith dialogue has to be a constitutive element of Christian living, the actualization of which is a task bestowed on the local church: "Every local church is responsible

11. Pontifical Council for Interreligious Dialogue, *Dialogue and Proclamation: Reflection and Orientations on Interreligious Dialogue and the Proclamation of the Gospel of Jesus Christ* (May 19, 1991), http://www.vatican.va/roman_curia/pontifical _councils/interelg/documents/rc_pc_interelg_doc_19051991_dialogue-and -proclamatio_en.html.

for the totality of mission. Moreover, every Christian, by virtue of his faith and baptism, is called to carry out to some degree the whole mission of the church" (DM 14). Dialogue and Proclamation contends that "the foundation of the Church's commitment to dialogue is not merely anthropological but primarily theological" (DP 38). In other words, dialogue is not just a human or social activity but part of God's calling to all Christians to discover more fully God's plan of salvation. Here is how it explains this:

> To the Church, as the sacrament in which the Kingdom of God is present "in mystery," are related or oriented (*ordinantur*) (cf. LG 16) the members of other religious traditions who, inasmuch as they respond to God's calling as perceived by their conscience, are saved in Jesus Christ and thus already share in some way in the reality which is signified by the Kingdom. The Church's mission is to foster "the Kingdom of our Lord and his Christ" (*Rv* 11:15), at whose service she is placed. Part of her role consists in recognizing that the inchoate reality of this Kingdom can be found also beyond the confines of the Church, for example in the hearts of the followers of other religious traditions, insofar as they live evangelical values and are open to the action of the Spirit. (DP 35)

Finally, *Redemptoris Missio* subscribes to the idea that the praxis of dialogue is "a method and means of mutual knowledge and enrichment" (RM 55) and advises that "those engaged in this dialogue must be consistent with their own religious traditions and convictions, and be open to understanding those of the other party without pretence or closed-mindedness, but with truth, humility and frankness, knowing that dialogue can enrich each side" (RM 56). Authentic dialogue must also reach "a much deeper level, that of the spirit, where exchange and sharing consist in a mutual witness to one's beliefs and a common exploration of one's respective religious convictions" (DP 40). In view of this, the ultimate aim of dialogue is "a deeper conversion of all towards God. . . . In this process of conversion 'the decision may be made to leave one's previous spiritual or religious situation in order to direct oneself towards another'" (DP 41). These teachings of the magisterium of Pope John Paul II are addressed to all people involved in interfaith dialogue, including the Christian participants. This means that Christians must also see dialogue as an occasion for mutual enrichment, where both parties witness to one another and both are led to a deeper conversion, including the possibility of leaving one's religious situation.

Pope Benedict XVI: *Dominus Iesus*

Pope Benedict XVI succeeded Pope John Paul II after the latter's death in April 2005. Prior to that he was Cardinal Josef Ratzinger and had served as John Paul II's prefect of the Sacred Congregation for the Doctrine of the Faith since 1981. That bestowed on him the role of guardian of Catholic teachings and defender of church doctrines, and even though the document *Dominus Iesus* was released during the tenure of John Paul II, it is more associated with Cardinal Ratzinger. In fact, it was Ratzinger himself who presented the "Declaration *Dominus Iesus*: On the Unicity and Salvific Universality of Jesus Christ and the Church"[12] at a press conference in September 2000, signaling its significance for the church at that point in history.

The main aim of *Dominus Iesus*, according to Ratzinger, is to clarify certain aspects of church teachings in the light of the debate on the relationship of Christianity to other religions. The document singles out for mention the dangerous influence of what it alleges are "relativistic" theories advanced to address the phenomenon and fact of religious pluralism. It cautions that the theologies of religious pluralism that have arisen in response to this fact and developed in the context of interfaith dialogue have been bordering on the problem of relativism. To counter them, *Dominus Iesus* reaffirms the doctrines of the uniqueness and universality of Jesus Christ and the church and asserts that they must be upheld in the church's dialogue with other religions. The seriousness of these charges are better appreciated if viewed in the light of the fact that several theologians had been investigated and censured in the 1990s precisely for their views on the theologies of religious pluralism. The following paragraph from *Dominus Iesus* (DI) describes the state of the question and points to the theological issues of concern:

12. Congregation for the Doctrine of the Faith, *Dominus Iesus: On the Unicity and Salvific Universality of Jesus Christ and the Church* (August 6, 2000), http:// www.vatican.va/roman_curia/congregations/cfaith/documents/rc_con_cfaith _doc_20000806_dominus-iesus_en.html.

The Church's constant missionary proclamation is endangered today by relativistic theories which seek to justify religious pluralism, not only *de facto* but also *de iure* (*or in principle*). As a consequence, it is held that certain truths have been superseded; for example, the definitive and complete character of the revelation of Jesus Christ, the nature of Christian faith as compared with that of belief in other religions, the inspired nature of the books of Sacred Scripture, the personal unity between the Eternal Word and Jesus of Nazareth, the unity of the economy of the Incarnate Word and the Holy Spirit, the unicity and salvific universality of the mystery of Jesus Christ, the universal salvific mediation of the Church, the inseparability—while recognizing the distinction—of the kingdom of God, the kingdom of Christ, and the Church, and the subsistence of the one Church of Christ in the Catholic Church. (DI 4)

This is not the place to examine the document in detail, but suffice to say that *Dominus Iesus* was controversial and not too well received both within and without the Catholic Church. If the doctrine of reception states that it is necessary for a teaching to be received by the believing community for it to be valid, one might conclude that some of the more exclusive teachings of *Dominus Iesus* have not been accepted or taken seriously. But the theological exclusivity of the document could help shed light on why, when Pope John Paul II hosted the Assisi World Day of Prayer for Peace in 1986, Cardinal Ratzinger was one of the curial officials who did not support the event. His fear was that it would give the impression that the Catholic Church promotes relativism. He was, of course, acting in his capacity as custodian of the Catholic faith. But, as pope and realizing that he is now the shepherd of the Catholic flock (and so must lead the way in interfaith dialogue as mandated by Vatican II), Pope Benedict XVI did participate in the twenty-fifth anniversary of the Assisi event on October 27, 2011, by leading a pilgrimage of leaders of the other religions and Christian denominations, as well as secularists and humanists, on a train journey from Rome to Assisi where the interfaith encounter took place. Moreover, a year after he became pope, Benedict XVI, against all speculation, visited the Istanbul Blue Mosque in Turkey, where he was pictured standing alongside an imam facing toward Mecca in silent prayer together. He did this respectfully and, following the demeanor of the imam, had his hands crossed on his stomach in classical Muslim style. While the gesture touched many a Muslim heart, some conservative Catholic groups condemned the pope as they regarded his actions heretical and scandalous.

While the three encyclicals promulgated by Pope Benedict XVI made almost no mention of interfaith dialogue, it was under his leadership that the Pontifical Council for Interreligious Dialogue (PCID) collaborated with the World Council of Churches (WCC) and the World Evangelical Alliance (WEA) to produce a joint document titled "Christian Witness in a Multi-Religious World." Among the principles recommended for the practice of all Christians living in multireligious worlds, the following are worth mentioning as they are emphatic that the respectful building of bridges across religions is the Christian duty of our times:

> 10. Renouncing false witness. Christians are to speak sincerely and respectfully; they are to listen in order to learn about and understand others' beliefs and practices, and are encouraged to acknowledge and appreciate what is true and good in them. Any comment or critical approach should be made in a spirit of mutual respect, making sure not to bear false witness concerning other religions.
> 12. Building interreligious relationships. Christians should continue to build relationships of respect and trust with people of different religions so as to facilitate deeper mutual understanding, reconciliation and cooperation for the common good.[13]

Pope Francis: *Evangelii Gaudium*

When Cardinal Jorge Mario Bergoglio was presented as the newly elected pope in March 2013, many Catholics had not heard of him before. He is the first Jesuit pope, the first pope from the global South, and the first pope to opt for the name Francis. The name, in honor of St. Francis of Assisi, is most apt, as it characterizes his attitude of humility, simplicity, openness, and a radical concern for and commitment to the poor. This has been revealed not only in his lifestyle (for example, choosing to reside in the Vatican guesthouse rather than the papal palace) or his choice of words (such as his use of everyday language, even in encyclicals, such as evangelizers taking on the "smell of the sheep," that the confessional

---

13. PCID-WCC-WEA, *Christian Witness in a Multi-Religious World* (January 25–28, 2011), http://www.vatican.va/roman_curia/pontifical_councils/interelg /documents/christian_witness_in_multi-religious_world_english.pdf.

must not be a "torture chamber," or that the church should be more like a "field hospital") but also in his appointment of cardinals or the princes of the church, prioritizing bishops from some of the poorest countries in the world such as Haiti and Burkina Faso and also from the peripheries, such as Myanmar and Tonga.

These activities of Pope Francis reveal an attitude of optimism, love, trust of the world, and also a deep respect for the dignity and freedom of the human person. These concepts come across rather strikingly in his first apostolic exhortation, *Evangelii Gaudium* (EG).[14] As is customary of Vatican documents, the title is actually the first words of the document in Latin, that is, "The Joy of the Gospel." Focused on the joy of proclaiming the Good News, it can be regarded as Pope Francis's personal manifesto for Catholicism today and serves as a map and guide to the church's pastoral mission for contemporary living. In the context of religiously plural societies, *Evangelii Gaudium* teaches that "evangelization also involves the path of dialogue" and this includes the "dialogue with other believers who are not part of the Catholic Church" (EG 238). It then spells out what this entails:

> An attitude of openness in truth and in love must characterize the dialogue with the followers of non-Christian religions, in spite of various obstacles and difficulties, especially forms of fundamentalism on both sides. Interreligious dialogue is a necessary condition for peace in the world, and so it is a duty for Christians as well as other religious communities. This dialogue is in first place a conversation about human existence or simply, as the bishops of India have put it, a matter of "being open to them, sharing their joys and sorrows." In this way we learn to accept others and their different ways of living, thinking and speaking. We can then join one another in taking up the duty of serving justice and peace, which should become a basic principle of all our exchanges. (EG 250)

It is with this attitude of openness in truth and love and in the service of justice and peace that Pope Francis has been showing the way for what being Catholic means in the multireligious world of today. Two examples

---

14. Pope Francis, *Evangelii Gaudium* (November 24, 2013), http://w2.vatican.va/content/francesco/en/apost_exhortations/documents/papa-francesco_esortazione-ap_20131124_evangelii-gaudium.html.

will suffice. First, barely two weeks after his election, he celebrated the Holy Thursday Mass of the Lord's Supper at a juvenile detention center in Rome, where he washed the feet of twelve young detainees of different nationalities and faiths, including at least two Muslims and also two women. Considering that the ritual commemorates the washing of the feet of the twelve apostles by Jesus during the Last Supper, Pope Francis's act can be regarded as radically open and welcoming, especially since the conventional practice is that only men (as representing the apostles) and Catholics have been selected to have their feet washed in the sacred ritual. The second example is the engagement of Pope Francis with the professed atheist Eugenio Scalfari, editor-in-chief of the Italian newspaper *La Repubblica*. A few months after becoming pope, Francis wrote an open response to some of Scalfari's articles on people who don't believe and don't even seek to believe. True to his conciliatory and nonjudgmental style, Francis urged that those who don't believe in God should simply listen to their own conscience, since God's mercy and compassion will reach all persons in whatever state they are in. The letter exchange led to Pope Francis welcoming Scalfari for a personal face-to-face encounter.

This attitude of utter openness and respect for all, including atheists, is really part of Francis's own philosophy and theology of life. In a book that he co-authored with his Argentine compatriot Rabbi Abraham Skorka while still serving as archbishop of Buenos Aires, *On Heaven and Earth*, the future pope had this to say: "Dialogue is born from a respectful attitude toward the other person, from a conviction that the other person has something good to say. It supposes that we can make room in our heart for their point of view, their opinion and their proposals. Dialogue entails a warm reception and not a preemptive condemnation. To dialogue, one must know how to lower the defenses, to open the doors of one's home and to offer warmth."[15] There is evidence that this respectful attitude toward the religious other has rubbed off on the members of the hierarchy and the laity of the church under the leadership of Pope Francis and that the church is moving closer to resembling the vision of Vatican II mapped out for Catholics of the twenty-first century. This is the joy of the Gospel that Francis preaches.

15. Jorge Mario Bergoglio and Abraham Skorka, *On Heaven and Earth: Pope Francis on Faith, Family and the Church in the 21st Century* (New York: Bloomsbury, 2013), xiv.

Conclusion

The Catholic Church has come a long way in its relations with religions other than Christianity, thanks to a great extent to the renewal inaugurated by the Second Vatican Council. That the council was revolutionary is also indicated by the fact that it caused a schism when the French Archbishop Marcel Lefebvre refused to accept its teachings, especially those related to the church's openness to the other religions. For him, it was anathema that the church would validate these other religions and provide them a platform on par with that of the Catholic Church. The last fifty years have seen many other accusations of the same, and popes have even been declared antipopes and heretical for being respectful of religions other than Christianity. All this points to the fact that interfaith dialogue, while touching a raw nerve on the orthodoxy of conventional theology, is really the call of God's Spirit of our times and has the potential for leading Christians to being more faithful to the doctrine of God's universal love and embrace of all humankind.

Suggestions for Further Reading

Chia, Edmund Kee-Fook, ed. *Interfaith Dialogue: Global Perspectives*. New York: Palgrave Macmillan, 2016.

Fitzgerald, Michael L., and John Borelli. *Interfaith Dialogue: A Catholic View*. London: SPCK, 2006.

Gaillardetz, Richard R., and Catherine E. Clifford. *Keys to the Council: Unlocking the Teaching of Vatican II*. Collegeville, MN: Liturgical Press, 2012.

O'Collins, Gerald. *The Second Vatican Council on Other Religions*. Oxford: Oxford University Press, 2015.

O'Malley, John. *What Happened at Vatican II*. Cambridge, MA: Belknap Press of Harvard University Press, 2010.

7

Asian Christianity and Interfaith Dialogue

Introduction

In one of my first classes on Asian Christianity, a student innocently and curiously asked, "Is there such a thing as Asian Christianity? Is not Christianity the same all over the world? If there is an Asian Christianity, does that mean there is also African Christianity and Latin American Christianity as well?" My brief answer to him: "Of course!" I then explained that there are many forms of Christianity, including American Christianity and also European Christianity. The problem, however, is that Euro-American Christianity has been passed down through the ages simply as "Christianity," devoid of any qualifier or adjective. It was treated as if its experience were universal and applicable to everyone. Its spread to the rest of the world was at the expense of the many other local expressions of the Christian faith.

This chapter looks at Asian Christianity, especially how it interacts with the other religions of Asia. It begins with an exploration of the early presence of the other religions in Asia, as well as the precolonial presence of the Christian faith on the continent. This will help in the appreciation of how colonial Christianity was transplanted to Asia. With World War II and the disintegration of the European Empire, the nationalist and independence movements contributed significantly to the quest for Asian indigenous identities. Likewise, local Christians in Asia also began to evolve their own indigenous versions of Christianity to distinguish them from the colonial Christianity that had been passed on to them over five centuries of colonial rule. On the pan-Asian level, the Federation of Asian Bishops' Conferences advanced the thesis of the triple dialogue as central to Asian Christianity. This dialogue emphasizes the fact of the many cultures, many religions, and many poor of Asia. Asian Christianity has thus played a leading role in mapping out a trajectory for the ministry of interfaith dialogue in keeping with Vatican II's *Nostra Aetate*.

Early Presence of Other Religions in Asia

Most, if not all, of the major religions have their origins in Asia. These religious traditions hail from three distinct geographical regions, namely, West Asia, South Asia, and East Asia. They spread to various parts of the continent at different rates and through different circumstances, but mainly in the context of travel along the ancient network of trade routes known as the Silk Road. This gave rise to the religion-with-trade tradition, meaning that those who resided along the trade routes were more likely to switch religions as they had more opportunities for coming into contact with foreign missionaries. The first century CE saw the Hindu faith being carried from the South Asia subcontinent to different parts of Southeast Asia by Hindu priests who accompanied the Indian traders. Within a few centuries Hinduism spread to countries such as Burma, Thailand, Cambodia, and Indonesia, even becoming the state religion in some of these countries at certain periods in history. The first half of the first millennium saw many early kingdoms adopting Hindu texts, theologies, rituals, architectural styles, and forms of social organization. The Hindu tradition's influence across Southeast Asia was concurrent with the spread of Buddhism in many of these kingdoms. The Borobudur temple in the island of Java in Indonesia was built sometime in the ninth century and is regarded as a Hindu-Buddhist temple, influenced by Indian Gupta architecture but featuring Buddhist religious motifs and statues. Similarly, the Angkor Wat temple in Siem Reap, Cambodia, was built in the earlier part of the twelfth century as a dedication to the Hindu god Vishnu, but by the end of the century it had gradually transformed into a Buddhist temple. By then Buddhism had become more widespread in Southeast Asia, replacing Hinduism as the dominant religion by the thirteenth or fourteenth century. Except for the island of Bali in Indonesia, Hinduism lost its mass influence in Southeast Asia although it remained solidly etched in the Indian subcontinent. Today, only India and Nepal have a predominantly Hindu population.

Also having its foundations in India, Buddhism became a major influence in the subcontinent by the third century BCE, especially during the reign of King Ashoka. It then made significant inroads in present-day Sri Lanka and Burma and spread, mainly through traders and travelers, to other Southeast Asian kingdoms such as Thailand, Laos, Vietnam, and Cambodia. By the first or second century CE, the Buddhist tradition was already being practiced by the people in present-day Pakistan, Afghanistan, Iran, and other parts of Central Asia. From there it was brought to China, where it was developed in interaction with the Chinese religions of Taoism and Confucianism. Chinese philosophy coined the term *San Jiao* (three teachings) to refer to the harmonious blend between the three traditions and how they are all integral to the Chinese civilization. The translation of key Buddhist texts into the Chinese language helped in the perpetuation of the religion. From China, Buddhism was introduced to Korea by the fourth century and to Japan by the sixth century. It was later exported to a number of Southeast Asian countries as *San Jiao*, especially through the migration of the Chinese peoples to these nations.

From its origins in the Arab peninsula in the seventh century, Islam rapidly made its way to Southeast Asia through Arab merchants and sailors who built colonies of foreign Muslims in what the Europeans called the Malay Archipelago, an area encompassing present-day Malaysia, Indonesia, Brunei, and the Philippines. The initial communities were not very widespread, but by the twelfth or thirteenth century Islam had established a significant presence in many of these countries. Later, the arrival of the Chinese Muslim traders and the Islamic Sufi mystics in various parts of Southeast Asia helped in the dissemination of the religion among the peoples, resulting in many local converts to the faith. Sufism's openness to the continued practice of pre-Islamic tribal beliefs and customs made the religion more appealing to the locals. This was favorable for the faith, as the majority of the converts to Islam came from the indigenous or tribal communities where the so-called animist beliefs and practices are generally dearly held on to. Today, Islam is the dominant religion in Indonesia, Malaysia, Brunei, Southern Thailand, Southern Philippines, Bangladesh, Pakistan, and most of the West Asian and Central Asian countries. There is also a significant Muslim population in Western China and India.

Christianity in Precolonial Asia

Like other religions, Christianity also had its birth in Asia, specifically in West Asia, more commonly known as the Middle East. So, by right, it should be considered an Asian religion. The reality, however, is that it has been perceived more as a Western religion by most people in Asia, both Christians as well as those who are not Christians. This is probably due to the fact that it moved westward from its birthplace in Palestine and found a new home in Rome and other parts of Europe, from where it spread to the rest of the world, including back to Asia. But, for the first four centuries of Christian history, it was more present in Asia and Africa than elsewhere, with its center of gravity somewhere in Syria.

Tradition has it that the apostle Thomas brought Christianity to Asia when he began preaching in the southwestern coast of India (present-day Kerala). This must have been within twenty to thirty years of the crucifixion and death of Jesus. While the historical certainty of this tradition cannot be definitively ascertained, what is for certain is that there has been a continuous Christian community of Indian Syriac Christians, known as the St. Thomas Christians, who trace their origins to the first century. The tradition also reveals that they interacted positively with their neighbors of the Hindu faith, were duly recognized by the Hindu chieftains, and incorporated a number of practices and customs of Hinduism into their own Christian religious observances. In fact, the community is often described as those who practice Hindu culture, believe in the Christian faith, and worship according to the Syrian rites.

Another tradition of Christianity's early presence in Asia is documented in the eighth-century stone tablet known as the Nestorian Monument. It was discovered in the seventeenth century and records how the Christian monk Alopen and his East Syrian Christian missionaries from Persia reached the Chinese city of present-day Xian in the seventh century. Also known as Nestorian Christians, they brought with them sacred scriptures and Christian images as gifts to the emperor. The emperor, who was himself a great scholar, arranged for the scriptures to be translated, studied them, and decreed that the teachings be disseminated as he found them quite acceptable. The Christians were thus warmly welcomed, with the state supporting them in their preaching of the faith and establishment of churches. Subsequent emperors, however, treated the Christian community quite differently. With time, the Christians began to encounter major opposition from the dominant Buddhist community first and then also the Taoist leaders. That notwithstanding, the Christian community continued to flourish discreetly throughout China. In the ninth century, however, the emperor and local authorities decreed that Christianity and other "foreign cults" were forbidden in the country. The next time

Christianity came into contact with China again was in the thirteenth century when the Italian merchant, explorer, and writer Marco Polo and the Polo family met China's Mongol ruler, Emperor Kublai Khan. The emperor enquired about the Christian faith and then requested the Italian travelers to ask the pope to deploy missionaries and teachers of science and religion to China to educate his people in Western science and Christian beliefs. Only two Dominican friars made the journey to China, but they encountered troubles along the way and so returned to Europe before reaching the Chinese mainland.

While there are other traditions of Christianity's early presence in Asia, by and large no permanent or long-lasting communities were established. The traders and travelers had little interest in remaining in Asia, and so their communities disappeared and, along with them, Christianity. The locals simply regarded them as temporary residents who left little impact on the way of life of the Asian communities. This, however, was to change with the advent of European colonialism.

Colonial Christianity in Asia

Western imperialism in Asia began in the fifteenth century with the search for new trade routes from Europe to China. With the advent of early modern warfare in what the Europeans call the age of discovery or the age of exploration, the Western powers were able to invade and conquer much of Asia with little difficulty. By the early sixteenth century the European colonial administration had already begun establishing colonies in Asia. The Portuguese were the first, in their conquest of Goa, India (1510), and Melaka, Malaysia (1511); Spanish rule in the Philippines began with its conquest of Cebu (1565) and Manila (1571); Dutch colonialism of Indonesia began in the seventeenth century; the British conquered Burma and Malaysia in the eighteenth century; and in the nineteenth century France moved in to Vietnam while the Americans established the Philippines as their colony. It was during these five centuries of colonial rule in Asia that the establishment of Christian communities took place on a substantial scale.

Most of the churches in Asia today trace their history back to the colonial era. The Christian faith was brought to Asia as missionaries were often co-opted to accompany the military and the merchants to serve as chaplains, not only to the traders and soldiers, but to their families as well. In time, when settlements were established, the missionaries began to reach out to and evangelize the local population as well. The various colonial powers had differing policies about the proselytization of the locals they encountered. The Portuguese and Spanish were very missionary oriented while the British and Americans were less aggressive. The policies notwithstanding, because Christianity was a latecomer on the Asian religious scene, the inroads made were not as substantive as in the Americas. By the sixteenth century most local communities in Asia were already entrenched in their adherence to one of the major religious traditions such as Buddhism, Hinduism, Confucianism, Taoism, or Islam. Converts to Christianity came mainly from the tribal communities or those who adhered to the indigenous religious traditions.

In view of intense rivalry between the European colonial powers, the different missionary movements were able to establish churches in colonies belonging only or mainly to their own countries. Likewise, the intense rivalry between different Christian denominations in Europe meant that the Catholic-Protestant conflicts were also largely transplanted into Asia. Some colonial administrations went to the extent of segregating Asian territories by denominations. Thus, the Dutch colony of Indonesia had Dutch Protestantism as the dominant form of Christianity in its many islands. French Catholicism was pervasive in its colonies, for example, Laos, Cambodia, and Vietnam, while Spanish Catholicism invaded most of the Philippines. It also became the practice of local administrators to ensure that the denominational segregations were maintained at the local levels by allowing only one or two denominations to establish themselves in particular cities, villages, or islands. So, where there is already a Presbyterian church in operation in a city, one can expect that a Lutheran church would not be invited in. Likewise, if a Catholic school is already running successfully on an island, chances are the Methodists were asked to build their schools elsewhere. This was all part of the divide-and-rule policy that was practiced by the imperial governments throughout Asia.

Because churches in Asia were modeled after their mother churches in Europe, they never really developed their own individual local identities during the colonial era. In fact, the European outlook and ethos of the local Christians gave rise to the perception that they had not only been converted to Christianity but to Western culture as well. It comes as no surprise, then, that Christianity was regarded as a foreign religion in Asia, a label that unfortunately continues to persist even today. In the Malay and Indonesian languages it is sometimes known as *agama orang putih* (literally, the white person's religion), the same way English is known as the white person's language. Besides the reality of its association with the European colonial rulers who transposed the faith to Asia, there is also the reality that Christian doctrines continue to be presented and taught by means of Greco-Roman thought patterns and Christian rituals continue to be expressed in Western garb. This has reinforced the image of Christianity's foreignness, as has the many church buildings in Asia that have been styled after Romanesque, Baroque, or Gothic architecture instead of employing local art forms.

Another reality is that the churches continue to have greater association with the West than with institutions of Asia. They are generally reliant on Western norms and governance patterns and submit to Western authority, be it in Rome, Geneva, New York, or Salt Lake City. Dependence on the West for support and to finance their development and ministries also serves to amplify Christianity's Western image. What exacerbates the perception is that local Christian communities have sometimes been established in seclusion and away from the locals of other religions, resulting in the development of geographical ghettos that, in turn, can foster exclusive mind-sets. All of these realities contribute to the perception that Christianity is alien to Asia and is but a remnant of colonialism. This was the legacy that colonial Christianity left behind and that the churches in Asia are still struggling to shed today.

Independence and the Quest for Indigenous Identities

The Second World War is often regarded as a watershed moment for the peoples of the many colonized countries in Asia. It opened their eyes to another perspective of Western imperialism in general and the Christian tradition in particular. This was a war that impacted many Asian countries, bringing countless hardship and suffering to many people. Even as it began as a tribal quarrel between European nations, millions of young men from the "colonies" in Asia and Africa were drafted to fight in a war against people and governments that they had no quarrel with. Many of those from Asia adhered to religions other than Christianity and were generally left helpless in the battlefields with no chaplains of their own tradition accompanying them in their hour of need or when nearing death. They and their families and others in Asia could only look in horror when "Christian nations" such as Germany and the United States engaged in horrendous crimes such as the Holocaust and the atomic bombing of helpless civilians living peacefully in Hiroshima and Nagasaki. If the great Christian faith the European missionaries had been preaching to them could not contain such acts of terrorism and mass destruction, what does it say of its credibility and efficacy? Why export it to Asia, then?

Another aspect of World War II that impacted the perception of Asians toward imperialism in general was the role of the Japanese, especially in their occupation of vast lands across Asia. While many Asians suffered immensely when their own countries were colonized and subjugated by the Japanese Imperial Army, they could not help but notice something very different in the Japanese colonization. Unlike the European colonizers, the Japanese colonizers were fellow five-foot-tall brown-skinned Asians, who were neither gigantic in stature nor foreign in appearance. That they could not only stand up to the Western Allied forces but also brutally beat up and drive away the European soldiers raised questions about the myth of European invincibility and superiority. When the Japanese surrendered in 1945, the local nationalist revolutionaries in many Asian countries turned into independence movement advocates, campaigning for self-rule rather than a return to Western colonial rule. There was no way to stop the spirit and momentum for self-governance. Within one or two decades several dozen European colonies in both Africa and Asia were liberated from their colonial masters and became independent nation-states.

With independence, the native social and political leaders found themselves charged with the task of nation building. Establishing a national identity entails not only the quest for one's local and indigenous identities but also identifying and extending the resources responsible for shaping them. The Asian religious traditions feature significantly among these resources. Most people in Asia turn to their religion for spiritual support in attending to the challenges of daily living. Religion ranks highly in determining the well-being of Asian societies. The various nations in postcolonial Asia, therefore, saw the renewal and resurgence of the Asian religions, as they were deemed integral to the construction of their own national identities. This happened all across Asia, resulting in the Asian religious traditions being brought into the consciousness of the global communities. Thus, the world saw, for example, the rise of Buddhism in Sri Lanka and Thailand, Hinduism in India and Nepal, and Islam in Bangladesh and Indonesia. In some instances this resurgence swung the pendulum to the extreme (as a form of catharsis against the many years of oppression and suppression during the colonial era), resulting in the more fundamentalist forms and manifestations of these religious traditions coming to the fore. This continues today, and it will be a while more before the catharsis simmers.

In the unstinting quest for their own national and indigenous identities, the native political leaders and government officials sought to minimize or totally eliminate the role and growth of all elements associated with colonial rule. Christianity was viewed as one of these elements on account of its being considered a Western religion. Moreover, the perception was that the churches in Asia did not really play an active part in the nationalist quest for independence since they had been the beneficiaries of colonial rule. Because of this Christians were sometimes viewed with contempt and suspicion by their compatriots of other faiths. Therefore, the process of decolonization also meant the process of de-Christianization. This began with the expulsion of Western Christian missionaries from many countries in Asia. Further steps included curbing the influence of Christian schools, hospitals, and other social agencies on society and erecting barriers to the development and the general propagation of the Christian faith. Laws and structures in a number of countries of postcolonial Asia generally favored the rights and well-being of the religious majority, and because Christians are minorities in most countries they were generally discriminated against. Some countries even saw the active persecution of the Christian community, who, now bereft of colonial protection, were left to their own devices.

With the status and privileges afforded to Christianity during the colonial era removed, the local Christian community embarked on a process of renewal on their own in order to re-create Christianity's image and to find a place for it in the new independent nations of Asia. If their compatriots were in search of an indigenous national identity, the local Christians in Asia were in search of their own ecclesial and theological identities. If in the colonial era Christianity merely established a church *in* Asia, the aim of the postcolonial quest was to enable it to become truly a church *of* Asia. Asian Christians dreamed of the day they could rightfully claim to be at once truly Christian as well as truly Asian. Among the more significant issues that had to be addressed in this quest was Christianity's relationship with other religions. This was by no means an abstract theological issue to be discussed but one that had significant consequences on the lives of Asian Christians. Not only do most Christians in Asia have roots in these other religions, many also have family members (spouses, parents, and children) who continue to adhere to them. While in the past they were informed by a theology that speculated that all of their loved ones were destined to hell unless they were baptized, the quest for a truly Asian Christianity opened up new frontiers for a theology that was not only less derogatory toward other religions but also enabled them to be viewed in a more positive light.

Advent of Asian Christianity

As is obvious from the preceding discussion, the most important issue to attend to in Christianity's quest for an Asian identity is to shed its foreign image. To that end, the postcolonial church in Asia realized that it had to work on an authentic process of contextualizing the faith so as to enable it to be more recognizable and acceptable to the peoples of Asia. Contextualization (variously referred to as inculturation, indigenization, or localization) simply means enabling Christianity to fit in to the context and resonate more with Asian sensibilities. The first step usually taken in the contextualization process is to translate Christian Scriptures, church teachings, and prayers to the local language. This is then followed by some degree of adaptation of the basic terms, doctrines, and practices of the Christian faith to the indigenous worldview so that they could be expressed through local concepts, images, and culturally specific symbols. These steps have generally been taken by the Western missionaries during the colonial era. More well-known exemplars of this method of adaption are Mateo Ricci in China, Roberto de Nobili in India, and Alexander de Rhodes in Vietnam. But these first steps remain lacking because the critical issues of the church's identity, especially how it relates with its surrounding contexts and cultures, are not adequately addressed. A more authentic process of contextualization would need to entail the total transformation of the life of the Christian community and especially how the Gospel of Christ is brought to the people, ensuring that these are expressed in ways that are more respectful of the Asian community and are harmonious with its values and ethos. An illustration may help to shed light on why this is crucial.

Think of colonial Christianity as something like a helicopter descending on an Asian colony. Its foreignness stands out, as does its grandeur and power. It might adapt itself. The colonial missionaries in the helicopter, once they descend, might adapt themselves by speaking in local languages and presenting their teachings in idioms understandable to the native peoples. With the backing of the imperial powers the colonial church believed it would not only survive but also thrive on Asian soil. But five hundred years of colonial Christianity proves otherwise. It remains a tiny minority in Asia, which means it is generally not well accepted. What needs to be addressed, instead, is the basic structure of the vehicle and the manner in which it descended on Asia. While descending, the helicopter Christianity's first act was to blow away everything that was on the ground so that a clear landing pad was provided for the European Church to land. No concern was given to the elements on the ground or to what they had to offer. Colonial Christianity had no time for the heathen cultures and pagan religions. They were to be wiped out to enable the Christian faith to be transplanted onto Asian soil, where it was expected to take root and bear the same fruits it bore right across the European continent in the first millennium and the Americas in the second. There was almost no sensitivity to how the local population felt about the imposition on them of this foreign culture and religion called Christianity. This was basically the attitude and theology that motivated the missionaries in their mission to the continent of Asia during the colonial era.

A deeper and more authentic process of contextualization begins by taking seriously the world of Asia, in particular the plurality of its cultures, the diversity of its religions, and the distress of its poor. It would look more like a Christianity that comes to Asia as a bullock-cart. This is a vehicle very much indigenous to Asia and represents a church that is at once truly native and homegrown as well as modest and humble. Coming not from above but from below and in touch with Asian soil, the bullock-cart church resonates more with its peoples, religions, and cultures. This form of Christianity is certainly more acceptable and less threatening to the local population. It does not need the support of any external power to sustain it, for its witness and message ensure that the Good News of Jesus Christ is spread far and wide. Just as it is necessary for the bullock-cart to be in continuous contact with the ground, the church too has to be in continuous contact with the peoples and religions of Asia. It is precisely in the contact, and the friction that is generated, that the mission of the bullock-cart church is enabled to move forward. This means that an authentically contextualized Christianity in Asia has to be in contact and dialogue with its cultures, its religions, and its peoples, especially the poor. Dialogue is as much for the purpose of enabling the church to become more authentically local as it is for the purpose of enabling the peoples of Asia to better acquaint themselves with the postcolonial church. Through this process of dialogue Asian Christianity could hopefully become more appreciated by Asians and even be regarded as one of Asia's own religions.

The Asian Church and the Triple Dialogue

Many Asian Christian theologians and institutions have reflected on what a truly contextualized postcolonial Asian Christianity would look like. The most constructive work has been done by the Federation of Asian Bishops' Conferences (FABC), which is itself very much the fruit of this authentic contextualization. Conceived during the period of the Second Vatican Council, the FABC was finally instituted in 1972, following the apostolic visit of Pope Paul VI to Manila, Philippines, in 1970. It is made up of all the national episcopal conferences in Asia, representing almost thirty countries, and is the only pan-Asian institution that can rightfully speak on behalf of the Catholic Church and for the 120-plus million Catholics in Asia. Since its foundation, it has had twelve plenary assemblies and has run many programs, congresses, bishops' institutes, and consultations. Each of these events usually culminates in an official statement of the bishops, and it is through them that we can discern the bishops' thinking and theology on specific issues of church life. Because the bishops are in FABC representing their dioceses and because all the dioceses in Asia together make up the Asian Church, the theologies revealed in these statements can rightly be classified as Asian theology. The most important theological contribution of Asian theology is its insistence that being church in Asia entails the triple dialogue of the church with the cultures, the religions, and the poor of Asia. The triple dialogue is employed in the way theology is done in Asia, and it is also the way the church engages in its mission. In short, it is the way of being church in Asia.

Dialogue with the Cultures of Asia

At its very first plenary assembly, held in Taipei, Taiwan, in 1974, the bishops unanimously spelled out what the Asian church ought to look like. First, they proclaimed, it has to be the local church that is preaching the Gospel in Asia. The church in Asia can no longer be the European Church and should not even look like it, much less serve as its branch office or extension. Gone is the era when the local church was merely a recipient of missionary expansion. In the postcolonial and postmissionary era the local church has to be its own agent and subject of mission. Only when Christian mission is performed by the local church will the message and life of Jesus reach the minds and hearts of the peoples of Asia. The primary focus of the bishops therefore is the building up of a local church, one that not only is constituted by native Christians but also embraces the native values, ethos, and cultures of Asia. This can be accomplished only through an engagement or dialogue of the church with the rich cultural traditions of Asia.

The local church will have to enable the message of the Good News to reach the peoples in Asia through means and ways that are familiar to them, much like how the bullock-cart engages with its surroundings. The many centuries of cultural estrangement during the colonial and missionary phase has made this all the more necessary. Local Christians will therefore have to witness to Christ through how they live, especially in the way they relate with others who are not of the Christian faith. The local Christian community has to live in a positive relationship with peoples of other cultures and religions and not in isolation from them. It should seek to build bonds of friendship and communion with all the peoples of Asia. This will bring them a step closer to the ultimate thrust of contextualization, which is the building of a truly local church. The Asian bishops use the term "inculturation" to describe this process. The final statement of the First FABC Plenary Assembly prescribes the following:

> The local Church is a church incarnate in a people, a church indigenous and inculturated. And this means concretely a church in continuous, humble and loving dialogue with the living traditions, the cultures, the religions—in brief, with all the life-realities of the people in whose midst it has sunk its roots deeply and whose history and life it gladly makes its own. It seeks to share in whatever truly belongs to that people: its meanings and its values, its aspirations, its thoughts and its language,

its songs and its artistry—even frailties and failings it assumes, so that they too may be healed.[1]

Dialogue with the Religions of Asia

Second, because the Asian religions are an integral aspect of the Asian cultures, the process of inculturating Christianity must also involve the dialogue with the Asian religions. The Asian bishops are very clear that this is essential, as the majority of the people in Asia adhere to religions other than Christianity. The only countries in Asia where Christians are in the majority are the Philippines and East Timor. All others have Christians in the minority, and, in some cases, such as Bangladesh, Cambodia, or Thailand, they make up less than 1 percent of the population. So, the task of authentic contextualization of the Asian Church must involve a dialogue with the great religious traditions of Asia. Also called interreligious dialogue, the bishops specify what the dialogue with other religions entails:

> In this dialogue we accept them as significant and positive elements in the economy of God's design of salvation. In them we recognize and respect profound spiritual and ethical meanings and values. Over many centuries they have been the treasury of the religious experience of our ancestors, from which our contemporaries do not cease to draw light and strength. They have been (and continue to be) the authentic expression of the noblest longings of their hearts, and the home of their contemplation and prayer. They have helped to give shape to the histories and cultures of our nations.[2]

Given the role played by the other religions in the lives of the peoples, the Asian bishops then asked, albeit rhetorically, "How then can we not give them [the religions] reverence and honor? And how can we not acknowledge that God has drawn our peoples to Himself through them?"[3] The Asian bishops insist that it is only through dialogue that the

1. Gaudencio Rosales and C. G. Arévalo, eds., *For All the Peoples of Asia: Federation of Asian Bishops' Conferences*, Documents from 1970 to 1991, vol. 1 (Quezon City, Philippines: Claretian Publications, 1997), 14.
2. Ibid.
3. Ibid.

church will be able to discover in the other religions the "seeds of the Word" of God. Furthermore, dialogue will enable the church to discover the essential thrusts of Asian spirituality in general, helping the church to express its own faith in more authentic ways. In other words, it is through dialogue that the church can learn what it means to be Christian in multireligious Asia. Dialogue, therefore, is for the purpose of learning more about how the other religions nourish the lives of their believers and to discover the place of the church in the rich mosaic of religious traditions in Asia.

Dialogue with the Poor of Asia

Third, in the context of Asia, inculturation is accomplished primarily through the church's involvement with its people. Because the majority of the population in most countries in Asia is very poor, especially those suffering under the yoke of oppression, the priority of the church has to be its active engagement with the many poor of Asia. This is what the Asian bishops refer to when they advocate engaging in dialogue with the poor of Asia. They spell this out in their statement:

> A local church in dialogue with its people, in so many countries in Asia, means dialogue with the poor. For most of Asia is made up of multitudes of the poor. Poor, not in human values, qualities, nor in human potential. But poor, in that they are deprived of access to material goods and resources which they need to create a truly human life for themselves. Deprived, because they live under oppression, that is, under social, economic and political structures which have injustice built into them.[4]

There are two interrelated dimensions to this dialogue, namely, that the church speaks out against the structures that dehumanize the poor in Asia and takes the side of the many poor, in particular those who are oppressed. This means it is necessary for the Christian community to have a more comprehensive understanding of the issues and causes related to poverty and injustice. The aim of Christian mission, then, is to work toward social transformation so that the poor in Asia are no longer bur-

4. Ibid., 15.

dened by the structural evils that the powerful and those responsible have put in place. Also necessary is the conscientization of those in positions of privilege and power so that they too are converted to the values of God's kingdom in their dealing with all peoples, especially the poor in Asia.

Another goal of Christian mission is to enable the church, the disciples of Christ, to be evangelized and motivated enough so that they can be working not only *for* the poor but *with* them as well. This is in order to enable all peoples of God to live the fullness of life that Jesus came to give. This is essentially what proclaiming Jesus Christ in Asia means as being in solidarity with the poor is itself a Gospel response to the message of God's kingdom. Standing in solidarity with the poor is also especially crucial for the church in Asia because it was the Christian West that committed much of the injustice of conquest, plunder, and domination on the non-Christian East during the colonial era. As this has left many countries in Asia divided and poor, the Asian Church must share in the responsibility, together with the former colonial powers, for alleviating the suffering of the poor in Asia. The engagement or dialogue with the poor therefore is an integral element of being church in postcolonial Asia. It is the Asian way of discipleship in the living Christ. The Christian disciple who participates in this ministry with the poor is reminded by Jesus who said that "just as you did it to one of the least of these who are members of my family, you did it to me" (Matt 25:40).

Asian Theses on Interreligious Dialogue

The triple dialogue that the Asian bishops recommend has served as a blueprint for what it means to be church in Asia and for how the church ought to be pursuing its missionary activity in the context of the many ancient and rich religious and wisdom traditions of the continent. What is unique about the Asian Church is its tiny but vibrant Christian community with an immensely rich experience of engagement and dialogue with the other religions. Over the years it has learned ways in which the Gospel is to be preached to people who are already very content with their own religion and have no interest in becoming Christian, as well as how to negotiate between the social and political forces that have no interest in seeing the growth of Christianity. While being Christian has been challenging in these circumstances, it has also been a gift that most

Christians in other continents have little experience of. Realizing that this is its unique gift and vocation, the Asian bishops' Theological Advisory Commission (later renamed Office of Theological Concerns) has been consciously developing a comprehensive theology on interfaith dialogue for the Asian Church, taking as a starting point its contextual realities and also the teachings of the Second Vatican Council, especially the document on the church's relationship with other religions, *Nostra Aetate*.

In an in-depth multiyear study on this matter and through the publication of "Theses on Interreligious Dialogue: An Essay in Pastoral Theological Reflection," the Theological Advisory Commission suggests that it is the firsthand experience of the Asian bishops with persons of other religions that has led them to adopting a rather positive appreciation of the role of other religions in God's divine plan and economy of salvation. This appreciation has as its basis the theological conviction that there is only one plan of salvation for all of humanity and that no one is excluded from this divine plan. It is therefore incumbent on Christians not only to discern how God's saving activity is in operation and made manifest in the other religions but, more important, to conscientiously discern where and how Christianity fits in to God's universal plan of salvation. In other words, the other religions do not revolve around Christianity, but Christianity has to find its place in the orbit of the world of many religions. What follows are the seven theses that the Asian bishops' Theological Advisory Commission developed.[5]

The first thesis is that the religions (including Christianity) of Asia are integral to the growth and development of the continent. They provide a common and complementary moral and religious foundation for this development and are at the forefront of the struggle of the people toward liberation and wholeness. They have a prophetic role to play in society and in facilitating communion between peoples and in arresting conflicts. They can do this better if they collaborate with one another, and this can happen only if there is dialogue between the religions.

The second thesis is that because the other religions are acknowledged as part of God's design of salvation, Christians have to engage with them as a fundamental element of the mission of the church. This is especially

---

5. Theological Advisory Commission of the FABC, "Theses on the Local Church: A Theological Reflection in the Asian Context," in *FABC Papers*, no. 60 (Hong Kong: FABC, 1991), http://www.fabc.org/offices/csec/ocsec_fabc_papers.html.

important given Christianity's minority status in many countries in Asia, and it is incumbent on the church to be in collaboration with the other religions. In view of their being a "little flock," Christians are to see it as their vocation to play a catalyzing role in facilitating interreligious dialogue between the adherents of the other major religions and in their witness to the Spirit of God drawing all peoples to unity.

The third thesis is that the Christian faith in the Trinity, which believes that God is a mystery of communion in interpersonal dialogue, demands that Christians are actively engaged with adherents of other religions in a common pilgrimage of all peoples toward communion in the Trinity. The Christian belief that the universal salvific will of God leads all peoples to a unity implies that dialogue is necessary for Christians to grow into the fullness of the divine life. Dialogue enables them to participate more fully in the spiritual quests of all persons in their pursuit of Truth.

The fourth thesis is that interreligious dialogue is a relational activity between believers and not institutions. It is an engagement between believers who are rooted in their respective faiths but at the same time open to the beliefs of the religious other. Through dialogue they share with one another their experience of, vision of, and reflection on how the Spirit is working among them. This helps the parties grow toward mutual understanding and enrichment and toward committing themselves to working for the common good. Interreligious dialogue is a journey they embark on together to promote communion of minds and hearts.

The fifth thesis is that interreligious dialogue involves both individuals as well as communities. But preparation has to be made for the communities to remove their prejudices about the other's religion and to be able to embrace a spiritual perspective that enables them to engage with their dialogue partners nonjudgmentally. It then moves gradually to deeper levels of engagement and the deepening of each community's religious experience. These communions could find expression through the praxis of common prayer, reading of scriptural texts, celebration of festivals, and events that transform the respective communities. The focus of these dialogues is the building up of a new human community.

The sixth thesis states that both dialogue and proclamation are integral dimensions of the church's mission of evangelization. They are both necessary and are dialectical and complementary to the single but complex mission of the Christian faith. It is in dialogue that Christians witness to their faith. Likewise, they are also witnessed to by their dialogue partner on the faith of the other religions. Proclamation and dialogue are to be held in mutual relationship and cannot be reduced one to the other, so as not to rob proclamation of its specific meaning or instrumentalize dialogue.

The seventh thesis states that interreligious dialogue is the task of the local church, which is always involved in the life and struggles of the peoples, especially the poor. Because the majority of Asia's poor adhere to religions other than Christianity and because the other religions are also engaged in the liberation of the poor, Christians have to dialogue with persons of other religions in fulfilling their mission and in developing a local church. Interreligious dialogue, inculturation, and the quest for justice and liberation, therefore, are all mutually involving ministries of the singular mission of the church. They have to be held together and go hand-in-hand in the building up of an authentic contextualized Asian Christianity.

Conclusion

Asian Christianity has been blessed with having to discover its mission on earth as a co-pilgrim with the other ancient religious traditions in Asia. In so doing, it has developed new ways of appreciating what it means to be church and also what the Christian mission is in the context of the religiously plural Asia. Developing toward being a local church in Asia with a spirituality, theology, liturgy, and church structures that are meaningful and relevant to the Asian context, Asian Christianity has had to experiment and create and, in the process, learn from its mistakes. The task is still a long ways from being complete. But in the meantime, it has successfully developed some tentative theological trajectories for the local churches to traverse as well as to explore in order to find its place in the divine economy of God's salvation in the world of many religions.

Suggestions for Further Reading

Ariarajah, Wesley. *Not without My Neighbour: Issues in Interfaith Relations.* Geneva: World Council of Churches, 1999.

Chia, Edmund Kee-Fook. *Edward Schillebeeckx and Interreligious Dialogue: Perspectives from Asian Theology*. Eugene, OR: Pickwick Publications, 2015.

For All the Peoples of Asia: Federation of Asian Bishops' Conferences Documents. 5 vols. Quezon City, Philippines: Claretian, 1997, 1997, 2002, 2007, 2014.

Phan, Peter C. *Christianities in Asia*. Hoboken, NJ: Wiley-Blackwell, 2010.

Pieris, Aloysius. *An Asian Theology of Liberation*. Quezon City: Claretian, 1989.

PART 3

THEOLOGIES AND PRAXES

8

Global Movement for Christian Unity

Introduction

Mary and Sally came from different parts of the country to begin college studies. Having found each other on the first day, they became almost inseparable, going everywhere together and doing everything together. The college's Christian Fellowship Center became their focal point, and they played leadership roles in many of its activities. Because the Christian community was small, there was only one fellowship that served all the Christian students who belong to different denominations. Thus, Catholics were engaged in Bible sharing with Methodists, and Lutherans were breaking bread with Pentecostals. Things went on smoothly until the semester break, when the students returned home. Mary's parents were horrified to find out that she was no longer attending a Roman Catholic Church on Sundays but instead was going to a Baptist service at Sally's church.

This chapter explores the dynamics of intra-Christian dialogue, that is, the relationship between the different Christian denominations. It begins with an overview of why and how Christianity split into many churches over the centuries. This scandal of Christian division calls for an ecumenical vision that invites the churches to strive for the unity that Christ prayed for in his disciples. The origins and evolution of the modern ecumenical movement will then be studied, as will the reasons for the initial cautious participation of the Roman Catholic Church. With the Second Vatican Council and its teachings on ecumenism, however, the Catholic Church has come to the fore and made Christian unity one of its priorities. The impact of these teachings and the challenges in implementing them will be looked at, especially from the perspectives of the local churches. The call for the ecumenical movement to embrace the wider ecumenism of dialogue with the other religious communities will also be highlighted.

The Scandal of Christian Division

There are hundreds, if not thousands, of different Christian denominations in the world today. There are so many churches that some people wish that Christianity would return to being the one single united church inspired by Jesus Christ. It probably will never happen; moreover, there never was a time in history when there was only one single united church. This is because Christianity did not really begin from a single church but from numerous Christian centers, each under the leadership of one or several of the early disciples of Jesus. These leaders and their followers had very different experiences and understandings of the significance of Jesus. The Jewish Christians, for example, had a radically different view of Jesus from the Gentile Christians, but both groups continued to flourish, mostly independently of one another. Of course, things came to a head at times, as evidenced by the account related in Acts 15 when the Council of Jerusalem had to intervene to exempt Gentile Christians from the Law of Moses. But the Mosaic Law and practices were not condemned, as Jewish Christians continued with its adherence; it was merely not universalized. The Council of Jerusalem, sometimes regarded as the very first ecumenical or worldwide council, upheld the ideal of pluralism in the ecclesial or church traditions.

With the rapid spread of the Christian movement outside of Palestine into Asia Minor, northern Africa, Arabia, Greece, and Macedonia, it would be expected that the followers were not teaching the same thing, following the same practices, singing the same hymns, or telling the same story about Jesus in every city or to everybody. So, diversity was the trademark of Christianity from its very beginning. The Christianity practiced in Antioch or Damascus was probably quite different from the one practiced in Malta or Ethiopia, as each community adopted or adapted from the practices and beliefs of their own local cultures and contexts. Despite the diversity, the different churches did have something in common. They collectively shared in the faith in Jesus Christ as God and Savior. In that sense, they were one united church. That Jesus is Lord and Messiah who is fully divine and fully human was the confession of all Christians; it still is today. This central christological faith became the litmus test of orthodoxy. Those who refused to abide by it, such as the Ebionites and Gnostics, were termed heretics and excommunicated primarily because of their heterodox views.

The initial pluralistic vision of the church, however, was lost in the course of history. With the identification of Christianity with the Roman Empire in the fourth century, uniformity was insisted upon, not only in matters of beliefs and doctrines, but also in ecclesial structures and organization. While this contributed to the political stability of the empire, it was at the expense of the needs of Christian communities that felt they should be adapting to new local contexts. The prophetic innovations of leaders who felt prompted by God's Spirit were also not tolerated. Unfortunately, some of those who challenged the status quo simply had no choice but to eventually separate from the mainstream church, following the decisions of ecumenical councils. The ecumenical councils of the fourth and fifth centuries are well known today for the doctrinal formulations arising from the christological debates. But they significantly rocked the Eastern Church, causing those who sided with the Antiochean School—led by Nestorius, who denied the divinity of Jesus—to separate from the predominant Alexandrian School. That was the first major official split within the church. The second major separation was also a result of theological controversies, this time in the opposite direction, with what has come to be known as the Monophysite group rejecting the humanity of Christ. It culminated in the separation of the Oriental Orthodox Communion from the dominant Eastern Church. The third separation, this time between the whole Eastern Church and the entire Western Church, was due more to politics than to doctrine. Differences in language, culture, liturgy, and theology—which characterized the rivalry between Rome and Constantinople—were contributing factors to the Great Schism, the ultimate and final straw of which was the issue of papal jurisdiction. The fourth division was severe, and its effect on the Western Church is still felt quite widely today. This was the sixteenth-century Protestant Reformation sparked by corrupt practices such as the sale of indulgences, nepotism, and questionable devotional practices. From then on, more and more splinter groups emerged within both Protestantism and, albeit to a lesser extent, the Catholic Church. Through it all each new group believes itself as the true church of Christ, as being the "one, holy, catholic, and apostolic" church, and considers the others as deviant and having lost their way.

As can be seen above, the many divisions in Christian history are due to a variety of factors. While the initial breakaways occurred because of doctrinal controversies, the other splits were due to many other reasons. These splits happened on account of theology, such as differences in understanding the Bible, Christian uniqueness, and salvation; organizational concerns such as the role of the laity or women, the structure of the church and leadership, or the components of church services; factors that have to do with culture, language, politics, and economics; or even the misuse of authority and funds or simply personality clashes. Obviously, this is not the Good News that Jesus preached and constitutes the major scandal of Christian division that the contemporary leaders of the various churches have to deal with today.

Ecumenism and the Vision of Ecclesial Unity

In light of the above causes of Christian disunity, it would be an illusion to believe that there will come a time when all the differences will be forgotten and a single united church of Christ established. Nor will it be possible to reduce all the differences in favor of one community, be it Catholic, Orthodox, or Protestant. Christian diversity is the very nature of the church and has been since the time of the New Testament. It is in the diversity that the catholicity of the church is expressed. Thus, Christian unity should not be conceived of in terms of the reunification of all the diverse expressions of church life today. Rather, it should be united precisely in its pluriformity and not so much in its uniformity. But even this unity in pluriformity is challenging. It calls for every church to relinquish its claim to being the truest expression of Christianity in favor of working toward a unity expressed in their moving closer toward the center of the Christian faith, namely, Jesus Christ. This is premised on the faith that if all the churches move toward Christ the center, they will hopefully be moving closer to one another in brotherly and sisterly love. Despite what each church community believes, it is probably accurate to assert that no single ecclesial community is the perfect representative of Christ on earth; each is growing in faithfulness. In the process of growth they can learn from and share with one another what it means and takes to be moving in faithfulness to Christ. This is essentially what the quest for Christian unity entails.

The movement toward Christian unity usually cites the Gospel of John to urge that the prayer of Jesus—"that they may be one, as we are one, . . . so that the world may know that you have sent me and have loved them even as you have loved me" (John 17:22-23)—can one day be realized. This prayer of Jesus for his initial disciples is still relevant for the Christian disciples of the contemporary times. The phrase "that they may all be one," in fact, has been used quite often in ecumenical gatherings and is even chosen to serve as motto of some unified ecclesial entities. Another biblical verse often used in ecumenical circles comes from one of Paul's epistles where he begs his followers in Ephesus to live a good life and ensure that they do whatever is in their means "to maintain the unity of the Spirit in the bond of peace" (Eph 4:3). Paul provides the theological justification for this unity: "There is one body and one Spirit, just as you were called to the one hope of your calling, one Lord, one faith, one baptism, one God and Father of all, who is above all and through all and in all" (Eph 4:4-6). In other words, Christian unity is supposed to be a reality already. It is a gift that Christians simply have to make visible. The goal of the churches today is to work together in order to actualize and make visible this gift of Christian unity. These biblical verses have shaped and inspired the various Christian communities in their efforts of promoting better relationships between the different denominations.

Historically, ecumenism (from the Greek word *oikoumene,* literally meaning "the inhabited world") was used to denote the great ecumenical councils convened under the auspices of the Roman emperors. These councils, beginning with Nicaea in 325, brought together bishops from what was thought to be the whole inhabited world to deliberate on Christian teachings and doctrines for the purpose of fostering a united Christianity for the sake of a united Roman Empire. Today, however, the term "ecumenism" is used primarily to refer to efforts taken to promote relationships and collaborative ventures across different Christian denominations and ecclesial communities in view of uniting the whole Christian world. While complete reconciliation and full unity is hoped and prayed for, the little steps taken by each church in building bridges of friendship and trust with other churches and in breaking down enmity and prejudices are what matters most at the moment.

The Modern Ecumenical Movement

These little steps that each local Christian community takes build on a huge step taken at Edinburgh in 1910 when the first World Missionary Conference was held. The event is often considered to be the watershed for the modern ecumenical movement as it brought together Christians from many different mainly Protestant churches to deliberate on how they can be more united in their activities in mission territories. The conference was very much the fruit of years of friendship and cooperative ventures among the Christian missionaries, especially those working in Asia and Africa. These ventures included partnerships in ministries such as Bible translations, health care, and education, and the fellowships occurred by way of socializing in pubs or libraries with their compatriots of other Christian churches. To be sure, relationships developed and these then led to conversations about forging better partnerships for the purpose of mission.

While the partnerships were being developed in Asia and Africa, North Atlantic interdenominational activities had also been actively developing. Beginning first as informal movements among young people, they eventually led to the formation of the Young Men's Christian Association (YMCA) and the Young Women's Christian Association (YWCA) in England during the early nineteenth century. The Christians who joined the associations did so independently and not as representatives of their churches, and so denominational issues never arose. It was only after the First World War that Christian unity was included in the organizations' aims. Toward the end of the nineteenth century the World Student Christian Federation was founded, bringing together autonomous national student Christian movements under the leadership of key leaders such as John Mott and Nathan Söderblom. They were to later become major figures at the Edinburgh 1910 conference. Mott, who was an American YMCA leader, chaired the Edinburgh conference.

While the 1910 Edinburgh conference is now known as an ecumenical conference, its initial aims were to discuss ways in which missionaries could be equipped with more effective methods and to address the problem of interdenominational competition in the mission fields. To be sure, it was more missionary in its objectives than ecumenical. The aim of Christian unity was actually in the service of mission and evangelism. While the division between the different denominations was detrimental to authentic Christian witness in the mission territories, the scandal of disunity also severely impacted the mother churches in Europe and North

America. Unity in the mission fields, therefore, was hoped for in view of it pointing the way toward the possibility of healing the Christian disunity in the Euro-American homelands.

At the end of Edinburgh 1910, a continuation committee was appointed that eventually became the International Missionary Council in 1921. At around the same time European Christians were busy with projects on behalf of justice and peace, especially as a response to the chaos in the aftermath of World War I. Söderblom, who had become a bishop of the Swedish Lutheran Church, and other Christian leaders hosted the Universal Christian Conference on Life and Work in 1925 in Stockholm to address issues of international relations and social and economic life. The Life and Work movement focuses on the practical collaboration of the different churches in ensuring that the Christian faith is brought to bear on the social, political, and economic dimensions of societies. On the theological front, Anglican Bishop Charles Brent of the US Episcopal Church took to the stage to urge cooperation in the study of the roots of Christian division. This resulted in the establishment of the Faith and Order Movement, and its first international conference was held in Lausanne in 1927. The Faith and Order movement focuses on theologically exploring doctrinal issues in view of working toward a consensus among the member churches.

The biggest step taken by the ecumenical movement occurred when over one hundred church leaders voted in 1937 and 1938 for the establishment of the World Council of Churches. Its inauguration, however, was delayed by the Second World War. Finally, in 1948, the council became a reality with the Life and Work and the Faith and Order movements joining with many churches to found the World Council of Churches. Its first assembly was held in 1948 in Amsterdam. In 1961 the International Missionary Council also joined the World Council of Churches, and the World Council of Christian Education did the same ten years later. Since then the ministries of the respective streams have been organized under the auspices of the World Council of Churches.

Catholicism's Cautious Approach to Ecumenism

The Roman Catholic Church dealt with the ecumenical issue in its own way. Its efforts in the nineteenth and early twentieth centuries were based primarily on the ecclesiology of a "return" of the other Christians to the

Holy Roman Catholic Church and their acceptance of papal authority and primacy, as well as the teachings of the Catholic faith. In 1908, the Catholic Church, on its own, introduced the Octave of Christian Unity, urging Catholics to pray for unity (read: return) among the churches. The week begins on January 18 (feast of the Chair of Saint Peter) and ends on January 25 (feast of the Conversion of Saint Paul). The observance was renamed Universal Week of Prayer for Christian Unity in 1935. With the founding of the World Council of Churches in 1948 it became more universally adopted by the different denominations around the world, even as the dates of the observance may differ. Churches in the southern hemisphere, where January is summer vacation, usually observe this Week of Prayer for Christian Unity around Pentecost.

Understandably, the Roman Catholic Church was not a participant in the Edinburgh 1910 Conference or the formation of the World Council of Churches. In fact, the 1917 Code of Canon Law actually forbids Catholics to assist or participate in the activities of the other Christian churches. When Bishop Brent met with Pope Benedict XV in 1919 to invite the Roman Catholic Church to send participants to the Faith and Order movement, the pope declined. But he did promise to pray for the initiative and added that "if the congress is practicable, the participants may, by God's grace, see the light and become reunited to the visible head of the church, by whom they would be received with open arms."[1] The Vatican offices similarly declined when invited to send Catholic participants to the first Life and Work conference in 1925. In the following decades the Vatican blocked all attempts by Catholics to participate in the activities of the ecumenical movement.

But with the issuance of the 1949 document *Ecclesia Sancta* by the Holy Office of the Roman Curia, a cautious openness to the spirit of ecumenism began to develop, putting an end to the spirit of fear and suspicion. While Catholics were still cautioned about ecumenical activities, special approval was given to some Catholic experts and theologians to engage in dialogue with their fellow Christians from other denominations. Augustinian priest George Tavard was an unofficial participant at the Second Assembly of the World Council of Churches in 1954. The Vatican appointed him as its official Catholic observer at the Faith and

---

1. Tom F. Stransky, "Roman Catholic Church and Ecumenism," in *Dictionary of the Ecumenical Movement*, 2nd ed. (Geneva: World Council of Churches, 2002), 997.

Order Commission conference in Montreal in 1963. He was also invited to serve as *peritus* at the Second Vatican Council. Two Jesuit priests, John Courtney Murray and Gustave Weigel, were also officially approved to attend the Conference on Faith and Order in Oberlin, Ohio, in 1957. They were to become ecumenical giants within the Catholic Church and contributed significantly to the discourse on church unity, especially during the Second Vatican Council and also in North America. For Murray, the ecumenical agenda was something to which he himself was gradually converted. He notes:

> The men of my generation have been converts to ecumenism; we were not brought up as ecumenists. Now we have to see to it that theological students are, as it were, born ecumenists. Moreover, even at the moment, not to speak of the past, ecumenism appears as a dimension added to theology from without. We have to see to it that ecumenism becomes a quality inherent in theology, as it is an impulse intrinsic to Christian faith itself. We have to develop a new style of theology and a new style of theologian.[2]

These little steps taken by church officials and theologians in the 1950s more or less marked the beginnings of the pursuit of ecumenical theology within the Catholic Church prior to the Second Vatican Council. Other theological giants in the field include Abbe Ferdinand Portal, CM, Yves Congar, OP, and Paul Couturier, all of whose works were precursors to the Catholic Church taking the gigantic leap of faith of embracing ecumenism as a central ecclesial concern at the Second Vatican Council.

Vatican II's Embrace of Ecumenism

Like many other issues in Catholicism, it was the Second Vatican Council that really opened up the Catholic Church to the modern ecumenical movement. It was by no means a coincidence that Pope John XXIII chose to announce his intention of convoking a universal ecumenical council on

2. J. Leon Hooper, ed., *Bridging the Sacred and the Secular: Selected Writings of John Courtney Murray* (Washington, DC: Georgetown University, 1994), 331. Murray's text was published in 1932.

January 25, 1959, the feast of the Conversion of Saint Paul and the end of the Week of Prayer for Christian Unity. The pope was explicit that the topic of ecumenism should be included in the discussion of the world's bishops. His experience as papal nuncio to Turkey (with Muslims) and Bulgaria (with Orthodox Christians) probably played a role in his understanding of the church and its rightful place in the wider world. Having worked with cultural and religious traditions other than Catholicism, he saw the importance of the church engaging with other Christian communities. One of the first steps Pope John XXIII took was to establish the Secretariat for Promoting Christian Unity in 1960 (elevated to Pontifical Council status in 1988) to enable the Catholic Church to begin serious conversations with the other Christian communities around the ecumenical agenda. A significant contribution of the secretariat was its role in identifying and inviting key leaders from the major Orthodox, Protestant, Anglican, and Reformed Churches and Church Communions to participate in the council as observers. This was an unprecedented move in church history. By the time the council came to an end in 1965, nearly one hundred of these Christians from the other churches, who were previously known by the derogatory terms "schismatics" and "heretics" but now were called "our separated brethren," had participated in the Second Vatican Council.

It is useful to point out that some of these ecumenical observers had already been actively involved in the Faith and Order Commission. As the Secretariat for Promoting Christian Unity played a critical role in the preparation of various Vatican II documents, such as the documents on ecumenism (*Unitatis Redintegratio*), on religions other than Christianity (*Nostra Aetate*), on religious liberty (*Dignitatis Humanae*), and on divine revelation (*Dei Verbum*), the input and influence of the observers from the other Christian churches on the council was obvious. Though they had no voice during the official sessions, it is not difficult to imagine that the interactions and discussions during coffee breaks and after-session debates would include issues that the ecumenical movement was addressing or had already attended to. Some of the more important and relevant ideas naturally found their way into the Vatican II documents. A number of ideas from the Faith and Order's 1963 statement on scripture and tradition, for example, can be found replicated in Vatican II's 1965 document *Dei Verbum*.

Aside from texts and documents, gestures are as important in assessing the Roman Catholic Church's commitment to the ecumenical agenda.

One such gesture, which clearly highlighted ecumenism as the way of the Second Vatican Council was delivered at the end of the council. Cardinal Franz König, archbishop of Vienna and council father, recounts:

> I will never forget the solemn ecumenical service in St Peter's on 7 December 1965 which marked the end of the council. I was one of a small group on the altar with Pope Paul VI. After asking the representative of the Ecumenical Patriarch of Constantinople to join him there, the Pope announced that the Papal Bull of 1054, which had declared the Great Schism between the Western and Eastern Church, was now null and void. I can still hear the thundering burst of spontaneous applause with which this announcement was greeted. For me this highlight signaled that the impulses set off by the council were already at work. The crucial process of reception, that all-important part of any church council, which can take several generations, had begun. It continues today.[3]

Catholic Documents and the Ecumenical Vision

The 1964 decree *Unitatis Redintegratio* (UR) was the council's official statement on ecumenism. Since then a number of documents have been promulgated to promote the Roman Catholic Church's commitment to Christian unity. In 1967, the *Directory Concerning Ecumenical Matters, Part I* was published; the second part followed in 1970 as *Ecumenism in Higher Education*. In view of the development in the church since the publication of the two-part Ecumenical Directory and especially with the publication of the 1983 new *Code of Canon Law* for the Latin Church, the 1990 *Code of Canons of the Eastern Churches*, and *The Catechism of the Catholic Church* in 1993, a new and updated ecumenical directory was deemed necessary. Hence, in 1993, the *Directory for the Application of Principles and Norms on Ecumenism* was published. Then, in 1995, Pope John Paul II issued an encyclical specifically addressing the call for Christian unity titled *Ut Unum Sint*, and in that same year *The Ecumenical Dimension in the Formation of Those Engaged in Pastoral*

3. Cardinal Franz König, "It Must Be the Holy Spirit," *Tablet* (December 21–28, 2002), http://www.bc.edu/content/dam/files/research_sites/cjl/texts/cjrelations/resources/articles/konig.htm.

Work was published in conjunction with the plenary meeting of the Pontifical Council for Promoting Christian Unity. All of these documents serve as guides to Catholics in their engagement with Christians of other denominations.

Unitatis Redintegratio begins by declaring that "the restoration of unity among all Christians is one of the principal concerns of the Second Vatican Council" (UR 1).[4] It goes on to state that even as Christ founded only one single united church of God, it is unfortunate that Christians over the centuries have separated from one another: "Such division openly contradicts the will of Christ, scandalizes the world, and damages the sacred cause of preaching the Gospel to every creature" (UR 1). Despite the reality of Christian division, the Second Vatican Council believes that real communion is possible among all Christians. The basis for this confidence is the one faith and baptism that all Christians share in Jesus Christ, the Lord and Savior, their commitment to the triune God, and that it is the communities of Christians, not just individual Christians, who are responding to the call for the restoration of Christian unity. The Catholic Church, therefore, accepts that all those who have been properly baptized "are put in some, though imperfect, communion with the Catholic Church" (UR 3) or exists only in different gradations among the churches. Moreover, it is also the conviction of the council that "all who have been justified by faith in baptism are incorporated into Christ; they therefore have a right to be called Christians, and with good reason are accepted as sisters and brothers in the Lord by the children of the Catholic Church" (UR 3).

The Catholic Church's acceptance of their separated brothers and sisters is premised on the principle that "some, even very many, of the significant elements and endowments which together go to build up and give life to the church itself, can exist outside the visible boundaries of the Catholic Church" (UR 3). In other words, the Holy Spirit has been working within the other Christian churches, and Catholics have much to learn and could benefit from associating with members of these other denominations. How they understand the Bible, how they live the life of grace, how they experience faith, hope, and charity, and how they worship

4. *Unitatis Redintegratio: Decree on Ecumenism* (November 21, 1964), in *Vatican Council II: The Basic Sixteen Documents*, ed. Austin Flannery (Collegeville, MN: Liturgical Press, 2014).

are some elements that can enrich Catholics. It is the council's belief that "the Spirit of Christ has not refrained from using [the other churches] as means of salvation which derive their efficacy from the very fullness of grace and truth entrusted to the Catholic Church" (UR 3).

To that end it would be important for Catholics to "become familiar with the outlook of the separated churches and communities" (UR 9). There is no shortcut to this but for Catholics to take the trouble to faithfully study what their separated brethren believe in and how they practice their Christian faith. As Catholics, we "need to acquire a more adequate understanding of the respective doctrines of the separated communities, their history, their spiritual and liturgical life, their religious psychology and cultural background" (UR 9). The diligent investigation of these elements enables Catholics to expand their horizons so as to better appreciate the beliefs and practices of their separated brothers and sisters. More important than just plain study would be the actual encounter in the flesh of Catholics with Christians of other denominations "where each can treat with the other on an equal footing. . . . From such dialogue will emerge still more clearly what the situation of the Catholic church really is. In this way, too, we will better understand the outlook of our separated sisters and brothers and more aptly present our own belief" (UR 9). The fruits of these studies and encounters should not be underestimated. Its benefits are not only to the Catholic, but "everyone gains a truer knowledge and more just appreciation of the teaching and religious life of both communions" (UR 4). Dialogue implies that the Catholic also needs to share with the other what the Catholic Church teaches and how Catholics practice their faith. This witnessing component of dialogue means that the Catholic needs to be well-versed in the theologies of their own Catholic faith. Ecumenical dialogues are therefore means by which Catholics can learn not only about the religious worldview of their separated brothers and sisters but can also clarify and deepen their very own Catholic worldview as well.

Besides mutual witnessing in the Catholic's encounter with other Christians, "these communions engage more intensively and more cooperatively in fulfilling those duties toward the common good of humanity which are demanded by every christian conscience" (UR 4). In short, the encounters between Christians of different churches have a way of leading them beyond their parochial denominational concerns in support of each other in their outreach to the wider community and to care for the common good of humanity. The impetus for reconciliation and unity between Christians is ultimately oriented toward the reconciliation and unity of the entire human race: "that they may all be one. As you, Father, are in me and I am in you, may they also be in us, so that the world may believe that you have sent me" (John 17:21). The church of Jesus Christ serves as light and hope for the rest of the world: "The church, then, God's only flock, like a standard lifted on high for the nations to see, ministers the Gospel of peace to all humankind, as it makes its pilgrim way in hope toward its goal, the homeland above" (UR 2). Thus, the Second Vatican Council "exhorts all the catholic faithful to recognize the signs of the times and to take an active and intelligent part in the work of ecumenism" (UR 4). It is hoped that "as the obstacles to perfect ecclesiastical communion are gradually overcome, all Christians will be gathered, in a common celebration of the Eucharist, into the unity of the one and only church, which Christ bestowed on his church from the beginning" (UR 4).

Fruits and Challenges of Ecumenism

The effectiveness of the teachings of the Second Vatican Council on ecumenism is best discerned by looking at how they have been received by the churches at the national, diocesan, and local levels. A consultation organized by the Pontifical Council for Promoting Christian Unity in November 2004 to commemorate the fortieth anniversary of *Unitatis Redintegratio* reviewed and assessed the progress made by the worldwide ecclesial community in the area of ecumenism. Many signs point to Catholics everywhere having generally embraced the call to Christian unity. Attitudes of triumphalism, suspicion, polemics, and condemnation have largely given way to respect, acceptance, and even admiration of the other Christian denominations. Prior to Vatican II, even stepping foot into another Christian church was almost unthinkable, but today interdenominational marriages, joint liturgical celebrations, and actively collaborating with other Christians to host civic, local, and national celebrations have become commonplace. Most dioceses are actively involved in not merely organizing the Week of Prayer for Christian Unity but also in organizing them ecumenically with their partners of other Christian churches. A number of Catholics are also involved in the practice of "spiritual ecumenism," which *Unitatis Redintegratio* calls "the soul of the whole ecumenical movement" (UR 8). Through prayers, retreats, Bible studies, faith sharing, pilgrimages, and participation in programs such as the Taizé ecumenical monastic order, they pursue their sense of Christian holiness together with their brothers and sisters of other denominations. Likewise, Catholics in partnership with their separated brothers and sisters have been organizing conferences based on the principle of "receptive ecumenism," which focuses on what each person can learn or receive from their ecumenical partner. These new forms of academic partnerships have become routine in many parts of the world. Besides, there is also widespread exchange of resources, sharing of church buildings, and, in some regions and countries, the establishment of ecumenical formation programs and active collaboration in theological education, including instituting theological consortia of Catholic and Protestant seminaries.

At the organizational level, most episcopal conferences around the world have a department or commission for promoting Christian unity. Some have members who are themselves specially trained in the theology of ecumenism. If before Vatican II the Roman Catholic Church was not a member of any National Council of Churches, today about seventy of the 120 National Council of Churches worldwide have Catholic membership. The Catholic episcopal conference of countries mainly in Europe, Africa, Oceania, and the Caribbean are the ones participating in the National Council of Churches, which is each nation's umbrella organization for Christians of all denominations. Since 1968 the Vatican has been appointing about a dozen Catholic theologians to be official members of the Faith and Order Commission. It has also established a joint working group between the Catholic Church and the World Council of Churches, sends Catholics as observers to various ecumenical gatherings, and invites fraternal delegates of other churches or ecclesial communities to participate in major events of the Catholic Church, such as the synod of bishops. The following churches and world communions are listed as partners engaged with the Catholic Church in international theological dialogues: Orthodox Churches of the Byzantine Tradition, Oriental Orthodox Churches, Assyrian Church of the East, the International Old Catholic Bishops' Conference of the Union of Utrecht, Anglican Communion, Lutheran World Federation, World Methodist Council, World Alliance of Reformed Churches, Baptist World Alliance, Disciples of Christ, Pentecostal Churches, Mennonite World Conference, and World

Evangelical Alliance. Both bilateral and multilateral dialogues have been engaged in by the Catholic Church over the years.

Despite much that has been accomplished in the ministry of ecumenism, there is also much more that needs to be done. Some of the challenges and stumbling blocks to ecumenism are structural and some personal. One of the main problems posed structurally is the size of the Catholic Church. Consisting of more than 1.2 billion members, or half of the Christian population in the world, it is obvious why the Catholic Church is not a member of the World Council of Churches, which is a fellowship of over three hundred member churches representing just a little more than half a billion Christians. Membership would mean that the one Catholic representative will be speaking for more people than all the Protestant representatives combined. As someone once put it, "It is like a full-grown elephant sitting down at the table with a bunch of rabbits." That also accounts for why there are still many countries around the world where the Catholic Church is not a member of the National Council of Churches. Most of these are countries where the number of Catholics exceed the membership of all the Protestant churches put together. Where it is not in the majority, the Catholic Church has usually sought membership with the country's National Council of Churches.

This brings us to the next issue, namely, the difference between the Catholic Church and the World Council of Churches. The former is by definition a confessional entity while the latter is by nature an ecumenical body. In other words, the raison d'être of the World Council of Churches is to enhance the ties between different Christian communities while the same cannot be said about the Catholic Church, except that ecumenism has arisen as one of its many major concerns since the Second Vatican Council. The World Council of Churches' primary contact point with the Catholic Church, as represented by the Vatican, is the Pontifical Council for the Promotion of Christian Unity, which is but one among dozens of dicasteries operating within the Roman Curia. Thus, when the secretary general of the World Council of Churches wishes to meet the Roman Catholic Church's counterpart, it is the president of the Pontifical Council for the Promotion of Christian Unity who is met and not the pope or the secretary of state. The implications of this are significant. The Pontifical Council for the Promotion of Christian Unity can speak only for its own office and not for the entire Catholic Church. The World Council of Churches, on the other hand, if it decides on something, commits

its whole organization, not merely a single department or desk, to that decision. With such an arrangement, it appears that the carts are being reversed. The lack of equitable structures between the two world Christian institutions is a real and serious issue confronting ecumenism on the world stage. That aside, there are also many other Christian communities that are not represented in the ecumenical movement. The participation of the Evangelicals and the Pentecostals on a more active basis would be welcome. Until then, the ecumenical movement still has much work to do if it wishes to come closer to approximating Jesus' prayer that they may all be one.

The New or Wider Ecumenism

As mentioned earlier, the gospel verse of John 17:21 has played a central role in the ecumenical world. The part of the verse that reads "that they may all be one" focuses on the importance of Christian unity, while the part that reads "so that the world may believe" focuses on the impact of this unity on the world at large. Just as the nation of Israel is the light to the nations, Christian unity serves as the sign of God's care and blessings for all the peoples in the world. That the movement toward Christian unity is called "ecumenical" means that the ultimate concern is the entire inhabited world, that is, all its people. In other words, while enhancing interdenominational relationships serves as its immediate aim, the ecumenical movement's final goal is expressed through its concern for the needs and suffering of the peoples of this world, including those who are not Christian. The movement is fully ecumenical when it takes care of not only its *ad intra* Christian needs but also the *ad extra* problems and challenges of the world at large. The Christian community has a role to play in facilitating the salvation or wholeness of all the earth's inhabitants and also of the entire created world. Ironically, this service to the larger community can sometimes become precisely the forum and avenue for uniting the different Christian denominations, especially where the doctrinal differences between them are so severe that reconciliation on the basis of beliefs is almost impossible. The oft-used slogan of "doctrine divides, but service unites" informs this optimism.

Thus, Christian unity must have at its fore the alleviation of the suffering, especially of those who are poor and oppressed, and the promotion of peace, justice, and the integrity of creation. This service to the wider community is part of the Christian movement's participation in the *missio Dei* (God's mission), which is to enable all peoples to live life in all its fullness (John 10:10). In fulfilling the *missio Dei*, Christians realize that they are not the only ones attempting to bring about a better world and that their neighbors of other religious traditions are also very much engaged in the same mission. Besides, the problems of this world are so enormous that Christians alone will never be able to resolve them without the participation and cooperation of peoples of other religions. The Christian community therefore needs the help and assistance of the other religious communities if they desire to be truly ecumenical (world) in scope. This is the new or wider ecumenism that they are called to: to be in dialogue and partnership with their brothers and sisters of other religions.

In an ecumenical statement issued jointly by the Pontifical Council for Interreligious Dialogue of the Catholic Church, the World Council of Churches' Program on Interreligious Dialogue and Cooperation, and also the World Evangelical Alliance, titled *Christian Witness in a Multi-Religious World: Recommendations for Conduct*, the three major worldwide Christian bodies posit (under the topic of "A Basis for Christian Witness") that "Christian witness in a pluralistic world includes engaging in dialogue with people of different religions and cultures (cf. Acts 17:22-28)." The eighth principle of the document specifically spells out the nature of this engagement: "Christians are called to commit themselves to work with all people in mutual respect, promoting together justice, peace and the common good. Interreligious cooperation is an essential dimension of such commitment." This is the ecumenical agenda of the twenty-first century.

Conclusion

The wider ecumenism is the new ecumenism that all Christians are invited to participate in. Of course, this is not to suggest that Christian ecumenism is irrelevant. On the contrary, it is still very much needed. In the contemporary world, where many conflicts and tensions have roots in religious differences, reaching out to peoples of other religions to build partnerships to address the common challenges of humanity will serve as a clear sign that Christians take seriously the prayer of Jesus "that they may all be one. As you, Father, are in me and I am in you, may they also be in us, so that the world may believe that you have sent me" (John 17:21).

Suggestions for Further Reading

Koshy, Ninan, ed. *A History of the Ecumenical Movement in Asia.* Vol. 1. Hong Kong: World Student Christian Federation, 2004.

Lossky, Nicholas, et al. *Dictionary of the Ecumenical Movement.* 2nd ed. Geneva: World Council of Churches, 2002.

Gros, Jeffrey, Eamon McManus, and Ann Riggs. *Introduction to Ecumenism.* New York: Paulist Press, 1998.

Pathil, Kuncheria. *Models in Ecumenical Dialogue.* Bangalore: Dharmaram, 1981.

Radano, John A., ed. *Celebrating a Century of Ecumenism: Exploring the Achievements of International Dialogue.* Geneva: World Council of Churches, 2012.

9

Contemporary Theologies of
Religious Pluralism

Introduction

I still remember that during my first years of theological studies the authors I came across had names that sounded foreign to me, and their theologies didn't resonate much with my Asian psyche either. It didn't make any difference whether I was reading a text from Athanasius or Aquinas, Schleiermacher or Barth. I found it difficult to identify with any of them as they were all, as I later came across the phrase, no more than "dead white men." I would never have imagined then that a theological treatise or book of theology could actually be written by someone I might one day get to physically see or talk to. It was therefore quite a treat when, as a young scholar, I was able to not only meet with but also wine and dine with some of the big-name theologians of our times. Since encountering them in the flesh, when I read something written by them the text tends to come alive and I actually "hear" it as if the author is speaking to me in real life, complete with intonation, accent, smile, and humor!

This chapter discusses contemporary theologies of religious pluralism. As religious diversity has only recently come into global consciousness, the theologies that have arisen to deal with it are also relatively young. The pioneering figures in this field are twentieth-century scholars, many of whom are still very much alive: they are by no means dead, only white, or only men! The chapter will explore very briefly the thinking of eight scholars whom I have had the privilege not only to meet but also to become friends with, all of whom I deeply admire and respect. They are well-known as Christian theologians advocating a pluralistic approach to other religions. They no longer ask if other religions are true, as they have been presuming that in all of their writings. While every single one of them has written many volumes of books on practically every area of Christian theology, this chapter will explore only one or two aspects of each scholar's works for the purpose of delineating the various dimensions that could be attended to when discussing Christian theologies of religious pluralism.

Raimon Panikkar: Intrareligious Dialogue

Often regarded as a pioneer of interfaith dialogue, Raimon Panikkar's life itself is an illustration of this dialogue. Born in Barcelona of a Hindu Indian father and a Roman Catholic Spanish mother, Panikkar subsequently became a Catholic priest, theologian, and scholar of the Indian religions. One of his earliest works on interfaith dialogue is his book *The Unknown Christ of Hinduism,* where he proposes that "Christ" is the universal symbol of the divine-human unity. Moreover, Christ is also not the monopoly of Christianity as, according to St. Paul, it is "the name that is above every name" (Phil 2:9).[1] But his most famous quote, found in the book *The Intrareligious Dialogue*, is "I 'left' as a Christian, I 'found' myself a Hindu, and I 'return' a Buddhist, without having ceased to be Christian."[2] This describes his leaving Europe for India, immersing himself in Hinduism and Buddhism, and then returning to Europe and still remaining Christian. He speaks of these encounters with other religions as touching two levels: one external and in the main doctrinal (called interreligious dialogue) and the other internal and stirring one's whole self to ask deep questions (called intrareligious dialogue). It is this internal intrareligious dialogue that Panikkar suggests takes place at the core of our being in a quest for the truth of salvation. This dialogue entails, on the one hand, a willingness to question our own belief systems and, on the other, openness to learning from the religious other. It also

1. Raimon Panikkar, *The Unknown Christ of Hinduism: Towards an Ecumenical Christophany* (London: Darton, Longman & Todd, 1964).

2. Raimon Panikkar, *The Intrareligious Dialogue* (Mahwah, NJ: Paulist Press, 1978), 40.

entails accepting that what we learn can challenge us to a conversion that risks upsetting our own tradition. This is undoubtedly a bold and religious act because it is inviting us to look toward the transcendent, our tradition, and also the world of the religious other for the truth of the mysteries of life. Intrareligious dialogue, in helping us discover our own and the other's tradition, contributes directly and indirectly to bringing the different religious traditions together in a mutual dialogue on the mystery of God's salvific intent for all of humankind.

Panikkar proposes five attitudes that our personal intrareligious dialogue can embrace:

(1) *Exclusivism*: We believe that only our religion is true and all others are false. This attitude inspires dedication, as we are convinced that we are on God's side and adhering to a universal and absolute truth. Nevertheless, it breeds intolerance, assumes that truth is purely logical and conceptual, and does not recognize that truth can be multifaceted. Moreover, we fail to appreciate that even if our own tradition does contain the fullness of truth we may not be interpreting this truth appropriately.

(2) *Inclusivism*: We believe our own religion is true while acknowledging truth in the other religions as well. But we see ours as including all the truths that are found in the others. In other words, ours is the truest while others are true only to the extent that their truths are found in ours, the supra-religion. This attitude enables all other religions to exist and does not condemn them as wrong since they will eventually be assimilated into our own or will serve as preparation for their believers' encounter with Christ.

(3) *Parallelism*: We believe ours to be the right path while fully cognizant that other people also believe the same about their own religion. This is the conviction that the various religions run parallel to one another without any one being superior to the others, trusting that all will meet at the end of the human pilgrimage. Our task is therefore to deepen everyone's adherence to their own religion, avoiding muddy syncretism and eclecticism by keeping the boundaries between the religious traditions clear.

(4) *Interpenetration*: We realize that the different religions share a lot in common, are complementary, and also challenge one another. This attitude inspires mutual confidence and encourages us to engage with

the religious other in dialogue. This can contribute to mutual enrichment within a synthesis where the values of the other can be integrated into our own beliefs and tradition and vice versa.

(5) *Pluralism*: This is an attitude that stands between unrelated plurality and a monolithic unity. This implies that, on the one hand, we are displeased with the contemporary reality where the religions are separate from one another without any relationship between them whatsoever and, on the other, that we do not support the thesis of one universal religion or that any single religion should triumph over the rest. Such an attitude facilitates dialogue between peoples of different religions in order to bridge the gaps of mutual ignorance that each has about the other's tradition.

Paul Knitter: No Other Name?

The five intrareligious attitudes above have been expounded on differently, especially by means of other models. One cogent model is that presented by the Catholic theologian Paul Knitter, professor emeritus of world religions and culture at Union Theological Seminary in New York City after a long teaching career at Xavier University in Cincinnati. He came to fame with his landmark book *No Other Name?*, which reviewed the different models Christians employ in attending to the fact of religious pluralism. He later set out revising the book but, in view of the changes to the religious landscape, ended with a totally new book titled *Introducing Theologies of Religions*.[3] The question mark after the *No Other Name* title distinguishes it from many other books by the same title. Unlike other authors, Knitter raises the question as to whether Christians can still hold on to the doctrine that there is indeed no other name under heaven by which peoples of religions other than Christianity can be saved without embracing Jesus or without being baptized into the church (Acts 4:12). He reviews four models for dealing with this question, at times even identifying them with particular Christian denominations.

---

3. Paul F. Knitter, *No Other Name? A Critical Survey of Christian Attitudes toward World Religions* (Maryknoll, NY: Orbis Books, 1985); Paul F. Knitter, *Introducing Theologies of Religions* (Maryknoll, NY: Orbis Books, 2002).

First, the *exclusivism* model is generally identified with the conservative Evangelical Churches, with Karl Barth as its main representative. Its starting point is that there is one God, that this God was revealed to the world in Jesus Christ, and that it is only God, through Christ, who can save humankind. Thus, there can be only one true religion, and the Christian's mission is to replace all the others with Christianity. This model is ecclesiocentric (church-centered), as baptism into the church is believed to be necessary for salvation.

Second, the *inclusivism* model is identified with both the mainline Protestant Churches as well as the Roman Catholic Church. It acknowledges that God's revelation can also be found within other religions but does not admit that salvation is possible independent of Christ. Beginning with the conviction that God wills the salvation of all, it allows that other religions do mediate the salvation of their followers but that it is actually through Christ (whether those who are saved know it or not) that this salvation is made possible. Christianity does not replace the other religions but fulfills them. Karl Rahner's theory of the anonymous Christian is the best representative of this. This model is Christocentric (Christ-centered), as it believes that ultimately Christ, and not so much the church, is necessary for salvation. Obviously, Christ's salvific act stretches beyond the boundaries of the church.

Knitter then conflates the parallelism, interpenetration, and pluralism attitudes of Panikkar into two main models. His third, the *theocentric* model, considers not so much Christ but God as the means of salvation. The various religions, including Christianity, are pathways to God, the one and only absolute. While there are similarities between the religions, they are also very different ways of reaching God. Pluralism it is! Moreover, no one religion can claim superiority over the others, and so every person actually experiences both revelation and salvation in and through their own religion. Acknowledging that there are many true religions, this model promotes mutual respect and invites the religious adherents to engage with one another in dialogue. It is theocentric (centered on God), based on the conviction that we are ultimately saved by the one God of the universe who is the same God of the many true religions.

Finally, the *soteriocentric* model is a variation of the theocentric model and attempts to respond to the criticism that not all the religions have a belief in God. Plunging beneath the surface similarities of the different religions we find that, even if there is a belief in God, who God is and what God is like differ significantly from one religion to another. The soteriocentric (from the Greek word *soter*, which means "savior") model proposes that at the core of every religion is the vision of liberation or salvation for the suffering masses. Salvation (from the Latin word *salus*, which means "wholeness") is the universal aim of the various religions. This model's focus therefore is on how the different religions can and must work together to alleviate the people's suffering and facilitate the liberation of humankind and that of the earth. These are steps the various religions have to take in view of ushering in the reign or kingdom of God. This model, centered on action and praxis, focuses on the ethical dimension of the faith.

John Hick: The Pluralistic Hypothesis

The British Presbyterian philosopher John Hick is perhaps the foremost scholar who has radically embraced the theocentric and pluralist approach to other religions. Coming initially from a conservative and even fundamentalist Christian background, he underwent a personal conversion when he moved to Birmingham in the 1960s and found himself working and even living with many neighbors who adhered to religions other than Christianity. His firsthand experiences of interacting with them and worshiping in their houses of worship led him to develop what he calls the "pluralistic hypothesis" as the ideal approach in apprehending the religiously ambiguous world. He expounds on this in numerous publications, more directly in *God and the Universe of Faith,* which explores the issue of religious language and God-talk as representing how the world's religions interpret the same divine reality, and *An Interpretation of Religion,* which offers the most comprehensive presentation of his theory of religion in the context of pluralism.[4]

Epistemologically, Hick questions the traditional Christian definition of faith as intellectual assent to propositional truths. Instead, he considers faith as our response to religious experience as mediated through our own human experience of the world and interpreted through our *a*

---

4. John Hick, *God and the Universe of Faith: Essays in the Philosophy of Religion* (London: Macmillan, 1973); John Hick, *An Interpretation of Religion: Human Responses to the Transcendent* (New Haven, CT: Yale University Press, 1989).

priori knowledge and structures of consciousness. Hick's starting point is Immanuel Kant's distinction between the noumenal and the phenomenal, which he uses as the premise to postulate his pluralistic hypothesis. While the former refers to, in German, the *Ding an sich* (thing in itself), which is not completely knowable through the human mind and sensation, the latter is how the thing or reality is experienced by human beings through their culturally and historically conditioned lenses and worldviews. When speaking about God (whom Hick calls the Real) or the absolute, ultimate, and transcendent reality, Hick makes a distinction between the noumenal ineffable Real *an sich* and the phenomenal subjective Real that is experienced by human beings. The world's religious traditions are expressing the latter, that is, at the phenomenal level, when describing God as Yahweh, the Trinity, *Allah*, *Shangdi*, *Ik Onkar*, *Krishna*, and *Vishnu*, as that is the only way the Real *an sich* can be defined and perceived by finite human beings. The parable of the three blind persons touching the elephant is often used to illustrate this. The first touches the leg and describes the elephant as a tree trunk; the second touches the trunk and describes the elephant as a large snake; the third touches the elephant's side and describes it as a great wall. While all of them are correct from where they are standing and how they are "seeing," no one person has the complete picture of what the elephant is or is even capable of realizing it at all. As long as they are contingent beings, the phenomenal level is the only way they can perceive as well as express reality, including the Ultimate Reality.

In line with this hypothesis, all the teachings, doctrines, and even truth claims about God and religious faith are really perceptions and pronouncements at the phenomenal level. They point to the noumenal, the God *an sich*, but they are not the really Real. This is another way of saying that our knowledge of God and our religious truth claims are limited, in view of the finiteness of our human condition, and that they are also shaped by cultural and historical forces and so should by no means be considered absolute. That accounts for why there is so much diversity between the religions, and conflicting truth claims should be understood as incompatible only at the phenomenal level. It is in this context that Hick rejects the claims to the absoluteness of Christ and the Christian faith. He calls for a paradigm shift, or Copernican revolution, in how Christians appreciate the world of many religions. Positing that, just as Copernicus maintained that the sun and planets do not revolve around the earth, Christianity must also assume that other religions and their adherents are not centered on Christ or Christian salvation. True to the theocentric model, he argues that all the religions, including Christianity, revolve around God, the Real *an sich*. This hypothesis has led him to review all areas of theology, including the doctrines of the incarnation, salvation, the Trinity, and so on. A controversial book that he edited is *The Myth of God Incarnate,* which challenges the way Christians interpret the doctrine of the incarnation.[5] Hick submits that many of Christianity's absolute claims, because they are on the phenomenal level, have to be understood not so much as metaphysical claims but as metaphorical or mythological in tenor.

Peter Phan: Being Religious Interreligiously

One theologian for whom religious pluralism is not only a theological hypothesis but very much a lived reality from the time of his birth is the Vietnamese American Catholic priest Peter Phan. Phan fled his home country as a young adult and arrived in the United States as a refugee when the communists invaded Saigon in the 1970s. Regarded as the foremost Asian American Catholic theologian, he completed a three-volume work on Asian theology, titled *Christianity with an Asian Face*, *In Our Own Tongues*, and *Being Religious Interreligiously*.[6] It is in the third volume that he addresses head-on some of the challenges that religious pluralism and interfaith dialogue pose to the Christian faith in the context of postmodernity. Within a year of its publication, the Vatican's Congregation for the Doctrine of the Faith (CDF) informed Phan that the book was being investigated because it contained serious ambiguities and doctrinal problems. He was presented with a document outlining areas that needed correction and a set of questions that he was to respond to. Correspondence between Phan and the CDF, as well as with the Committee on

5. John Hick, ed., *The Myth of God Incarnate* (Philadelphia: Westminster, 1977).

6. Peter C. Phan, *Christianity with an Asian Face: Asian American Theology in the Making* (Maryknoll, NY: Orbis Books, 2003); Peter C. Phan, *In Our Own Tongues: Perspectives from Asia on Mission and Inculturation* (Maryknoll, NY: Orbis Books, 2003); Peter C. Phan, *Being Religious Interreligiously: Asian Perspectives on Interfaith Dialogue* (Maryknoll, NY: Orbis Books, 2004).

Doctrine of the United States Conference of Catholic Bishops, went on for two years but concluded with no resolution.

Finally, in 2017, Phan produced *The Joy of Religious Pluralism,* a book-length response to the set of questions given him by the CDF more than a dozen years earlier.[7] One might note that Phan's investigation began under the papacy of Pope Benedict XVI but his book-length response was published following Pope Francis's 2013 apostolic exhortation *Evangelii Gaudium* (The Joy of the Gospel) and his 2016 postsynodal apostolic exhortation *Amoris Laetitia* (The Joy of Love). Phan's *The Joy of Religious Pluralism* offers a response to the four basic concerns and questions raised by the CDF: (1) How is Jesus Christ unique and what does the universality of his salvific mission mean? (2) What is the salvific significance of religions other than Christianity? (3) How is the church unique and what is its role as instrument of salvation? (4) What is the mission of the church in the context of religious pluralism?

Instead of responding directly to the questions, Phan sets out to address the question of theological method. He argues that a lot of the issues raised about his *Being Religious Interreligiously* relate to the question of how he does theology rather than the book's content. Taking the declaration *Dominus Iesus* as an example, Phan notes that the CDF espouses neoscholastic methodology, which takes God's revelation as starting point. The document proceeds deductively (top-down) and insists that any act of theology has to begin with the faith of the church as taught by the church's magisterium. These teachings are then substantiated by verses from the Bible and the tradition of the church in a method called proof-texting. This gives primacy to magisterial teachings over the teachings of Jesus as found in the biblical texts, which are practically used to confirm church teachings. For Phan, theology, as inspired by the Second Vatican Council, is done inductively, taking the "signs of the times" and the experience of the people as starting points for reflection. These are then reflected against the teachings of the church and scripture, taking into account that the church's magisterium refers to the multiple magisteria that are in the service of the global church. These are (1) the episcopal magisterium of the bishops in union with the pope; (2) the magisterium of the theologians, who promote the understanding of the faith; (3) the

7. Peter C. Phan, *The Joy of Religious Pluralism: A Personal Journey* (Maryknoll, NY: Orbis Books, 2017).

magisterium of the laity or the *sensus fidelium* (instinct of the faithful); (4) the magisterium of the poor, the inheritors of the kingdom of God (Matt 5:3); and (5) the magisterium of the believers of other religions, along with the wisdom of their tradition and sacred scripture. Phan's conviction is that theological differences are rooted in theological methodologies: "Disputes about particular doctrines will ultimately turn into disputes about *how* those doctrines should be derived from the sources of the faith of the community (which method?) and by *whom* (which magisterium?)."[8]

Aside from exploring the issue of theological method, Phan also discusses the foundations supporting the Christian beliefs about Jesus Christ, those who are not Christians, the church, and its mission. The foundation stone, he avers, is none other than the theology of the Holy Spirit, the third person of the Trinity. Like Jesus the Son, the Holy Spirit fulfills the one divine plan of salvation of God the Father. The one economy of salvation entails that the two agents or "hands" of God act in their own time, space, and way. Thus, the Son and the Holy Spirit, as the two "hands" of the one Divinity, act independently but complementarily and in mutual dependence of each other. As such, it is the Holy Spirit, as agent of God, who was at work before and after the incarnation of Jesus of Nazareth, especially in the lives of those who did not accept Jesus as Lord and Savior. It is this same spirit, acting as the Divine agent, who is mainly at work in religions other than Christianity. This pneumatological understanding is used by Phan to serve as basis for his response to the questions about Christ, church, mission, and other religions. He does this not so much by disputing the theologies arrived at by the neoscholastic tradition but by providing alternative ways for appreciating the teachings and doctrines. In particular, he showcases other methods and theologies that have been circulating in Asia since Vatican II, especially those advanced by the Federation of Asian Bishops' Conferences.

Kwok Pui-Lan: Discovering the Bible in the Nonbiblical World

Another thinker who theologizes from the Asian perspective and who also focuses on methodological issues in theology is Kwok Pui-Lan.

---

8. Ibid., 46.

Having grown up as a Chinese in the British colony of Hong Kong and converting from the Chinese folk religions to the Anglican tradition in her teens, Kwok furthered her studies in North America in the 1980s. She has since taught in various institutions, primarily at the Episcopal Divinity School in Cambridge, Massachusetts. A past president of the American Academy of Religion, Kwok is regarded as the foremost Asian American woman theologian and has published significant work on feminist theology, postcolonial theology, and biblical hermeneutics. Her *Discovering the Bible in the Non-Biblical World* offers a new approach to the task of biblical hermeneutics.[9] She begins with the reminder that Asia is unique in that, unlike Africa and the Americas, the European missionaries to Asia encountered not only a population that was already very religious but one that also had its own corpus of scriptural texts and a long tradition of hermeneutics, commentaries, and exegesis on the *Analects*, *Tao Te Ching*, *Bhagavad Gita*, and many other sacred books. Kwok therefore argues for a more dialogical and multidimensional reading of Christian Scriptures, including the use of multi- and interreligious hermeneutics. In multiscriptural contexts there is a need to rethink how sacred authority associated with the Bible is understood. Biblical claims to truth, Kwok contends, are less determined by appeal to theories of inspiration than by its liberative effects. The extent to which a scriptural text inspires action on behalf of justice and peace and the liberation especially of the most vulnerable in society is the extent to which it is seen as true and truly the Word of God. This obviously means that questions are raised if indeed the Bible is the only revelation of God's Word. Scholars rooted in Asian pluralism, and the experience of multiple religions, find it difficult to deny the authenticity and authority of the other wisdom traditions. Elsewhere, Kwok refers to this through the concept of polydoxy, which "debunks the myth of the superiority of one God, one creed, and one church, and holds multiple traditions and perspectives together when looking at God and reality."[10]

Kwok also suggests that scripture is not necessarily looked on by Asians the way it might be in the West since there is an overall suspicion

9. Kwok Pui-Lan, *Discovering the Bible in the Non-Biblical World* (Maryknoll, NY: Orbis Books, 1995).

10. Kwok Pui-Lan, *Globalization, Gender, and Peacebuilding: The Future of Interfaith Dialogue* (Mahwah, NJ: Paulist Press, 2012), 77.

about text in general. Zen Buddhism warns against relying on words and letters at the expense of direct religious experience. There is also a general caution about the limits of human language, and truth is seen as being embodied not so much in a scriptural text but in the everyday lives of people. Moreover, given that most Asians are not educated in the scriptural languages, they depend on translations provided mainly by the early Christian missionaries and bibles produced by their printing presses. As these missionaries are not without their own biases and prejudices, especially with regard to Asian culture, one finds these seeping in to Bible translations as well. For example, when translating the Antichrist term for the dragon-beast found in the book of Revelations, the missionaries used the Chinese character *long*, which refers to the ominous, beneficent mythic animal of historical China and serves as a royal symbol of the emperor. It is obvious that the Western missionaries were preaching, through their translation ministry, that the God of Jesus Christ has come to replace the *long* (dragon) of the Chinese people (Rev 12).

It is in these contexts that Kwok calls for a dialogical approach to biblical hermeneutics. The task of interpreting the Bible in Asia must be connected with Asian spirituality, its traditions, and the life and struggle of the peoples in Asia. It has to also challenge some of the interpretations that have arisen from perspectives that are born out of colonialism, sexism, racism, or ethnocentrism. Dialogical models are not necessarily focused only on the text of scripture but also on the discussion about the written text. The Bible serves more as a "talking book" that invites discussion and helps people reflect on their own situation. It is the community of faith that brings the words of scripture to life. This implies that truth is less dependent on what is within a text than on the multiplicity of voices reflecting on what the text means to their lives as children of God.

Michael Amaladoss: The Asian Jesus

Another Asian pluralist perspective, but this time addressing the topic of Jesus Christ, comes from the Indian theologian Michael Amaladoss. He has been world-renowned since the 1980s, when he served as assistant to the superior general of the Society of Jesus with special responsibilities for evangelization, inculturation, and interfaith dialogue. Amaladoss's *The Asian Jesus* engages these theological themes from the

Asian perspective.[11] It offers another picture of how Christ comes across in Asia, which, not surprisingly, differs significantly from the more dogmatic profile that is presented by the institutional and missionary church. But Amaladoss indicates from the outset that the book does not aim to replace the christological dogmas that were developed by the early church in the context of heresies in the Greco-Roman world. Instead, the book aims to examine the significance of the person and life of Jesus by means of symbols and images. Symbols and images, he argues, are as valuable as dogmas and concepts in understanding Jesus. To privilege abstract conceptual dogmas over evocative symbols and images is to privilege Greek culture and its philosophical tradition. Ultimately, Amaladoss believes, neither dogmas nor symbols can claim to be able to unravel the mystery of divinity.

The Asian Jesus begins with a survey of Jesus in the Bible and in Christian history. Jesus is presented as prophet, messiah, Logos incarnate, Lord, high priest, Word of God, King of kings, crucified one, liberator, and so on. The book then examines the same from the perspective of Asians who adhere to other religions. Jesus is looked on as moral teacher, *avatar* (incarnation of a deity), *satyagrahi* (seeker of truth), *advaitin* (someone in a nondual relationship with God), and *bodhisattva* (a compassionate, altruistic individual who delays entry into nirvana in order to assist humankind further). The book then investigates images of Jesus that arise in the context of the cultural and religious pluralism of contemporary Asia. Specifically, it discusses images such as Jesus, the sage; Jesus, the way; Jesus, the *guru* (teacher); Jesus, the *satyagrahi*; Jesus, the *avatar*; Jesus, the servant; Jesus, the compassionate; Jesus, the dancer; and Jesus, the pilgrim. It is important to note that all of these symbols and images are rooted in both the Christian faith and the Asian cultural and religious traditions. They are images that are not particular to any one religion although more widely used in some than in Christianity. The primary motivation of Amaladoss is to point to their relevance for Asian Christians by highlighting how the same images can actually be found in the biblical and Christian tradition. His aim is not so much to engage in a comparison of how the different religions employ the images or symbols, except to note that similarities and differences do exist. For sure, he does not compare them on the philosophical or theological levels and does not in any way attempt to prove that Jesus is the one and only or the most superior sage or way or *guru* or *satyagrahi* or pilgrim.

11. Michael Amaladoss, *The Asian Jesus* (Maryknoll, NY: Orbis Books, 2006).

Symbols and images, Amaladoss is convinced, are able to provoke thought and reflection better than doctrines and concepts. They invite us to draw connections with similar images used with reference to other religious figures so as to better understand the meaning, life, and message of Jesus. This serves a twofold purpose. First, it enables Asian Christians to appreciate the other religions and see in them common elements shared with the Christian faith. Second, it enables peoples of other religions to appreciate that Jesus Christ is not exclusive to Christians and has meaning and relevance to their own life of faith as well, without the need for them to become Christian. It is in this way that the Asian Church preaches that Jesus Christ has universal relevance for the peoples of Asia and that his message of salvation cannot be confined within the Christian community but ought to have an impact on the adherents of the other religions as well.

Edward Schillebeeckx: No Salvation outside the World

The soteriocentric approach to religious pluralism focuses on ethics and salvific action. The ethical dimension and the place of other religions in relation to the Christian faith are taken up more specifically by the Dominican priest Edward Schillebeeckx. Born in Belgium, Schillebeeckx came to prominence in the Netherlands through his work as theological consultant to the Dutch bishops, especially during the Second Vatican Council. His most famous contribution to the world of theology is his christological trilogy, the first on the topic of *Jesus*, the second on *Christ*, and the third on *Church*.[12] It is in the third book that the issue of religious pluralism was elaborated on. In *Church: The Human Story of God*, Schillebeeckx looks at what it means to be church in an increasingly secular and pluralistic world. He does this by expanding the church's horizons so that Christians see their mission as *in* the world rather than *for* the church. He begins his reflection by turning the age-old adage *extra ecclesiam nulla salus* (outside the church, no salvation) to *extra mundum nulla salus* (outside the world, no salvation). He assumes that salvation is achieved in

---

12. Edward Schillebeeckx, *Jesus: An Experiment in Christology* (New York: Collins and Crossroad, 1979); Edward Schillebeeckx, *Christ: The Christian Experience in the Modern World* (London: SCM Press, 1980); Edward Schillebeeckx, *Church: The Human Story of God* (New York: Crossroad Publications, 1990).

and through the world, wherein the various religions are the ordinary sites for most people to become aware of God's saving action in history. Schillebeeckx asserts that the religions, including Christianity, are sacraments of God's salvation in the world. He is therefore explicit that religions other than Christianity are as much vehicles of God's salvific acts and ways of salvation. He points to the Second Vatican Council's document *Nostra Aetate*, which reminds us that men and women look to different religions for the message of salvation. It follows that those who belong to religions other than Christianity find salvation not so much despite their religion but precisely in and through it. Schillebeeckx believes that the different religions, including Christianity, must allow themselves to be challenged by each other and that no single religion can claim monopoly to or exhaust the whole meaning of truth. As historical particularities, religions are relative in relation to God and to one another. They have to be brought into a critical correlation and confrontation with each other, so as to better discern truth from that which is untrue.

Hence, the question is how Christianity can maintain its own uniqueness and at the same time be respectful of other religions. It is in view of this that Schillebeeckx deems it important that we explore anew Christianity's self-definition, including its claims to uniqueness and universality. This is for the purpose of putting Christianity in its place while at the same time giving it its rightful place. To begin, Schillebeeckx affirms that all religions are unique in and of themselves. Each manifests a different face of God, the God who is totally other, even as Christians believe that God has appeared in Jesus of Nazareth. Christianity's distinctiveness is revealed in the human person of Jesus, the historical expression of God's universal love and saving message as presented to Christians in the gospels. On the basis of his own historical and hermeneutical investigations, Schillebeeckx proposes that the distinctiveness, uniqueness, and foundation of Christianity lie in the message of Jesus and especially in his praxis of the kingdom of God. If this message and praxis of Jesus is to see its fruition in God's kingdom, then the career and ministry of Jesus must be continued in his disciples. Without this continuity by the Christian community, the proclamation and praxis of Jesus will remain purely speculative and confessional: "Not everyone who says to me, 'Lord, Lord,' will enter the kingdom of heaven, but only the one who does the will of my Father in heaven" (Matt 7:21). It is incumbent, then, on Christians to do the will of the Father in order to "enable" the kingdom to come. They are reminded of this in the Lord's Prayer: the clause "your kingdom come" is immediately followed by "your will be done on earth." Therefore, "doing" the will of God the Father is imperative if God's offer of salvation in Jesus is to be truly universal. This means that Christians have to be active in continuing the mission of Jesus by following his way of life. Specifically, being in solidarity with the poor and oppressed is a specific task of the Christian disciple's mission. Moreover, as justice and peace are the entitlements of all persons, and not only Christians, this solidarity has to be extended to persons of all religions. This is how the salvation in Jesus can be universalized through Christian praxis. Schillebeeckx is emphatic that the transformation of the world to a higher humanity, to justice and peace, is therefore an essential part of the catholicity or universality of Christian faith.

Aloysius Pieris: No Salvation outside God's Covenant with the Poor

Sri Lankan theologian and Jesuit priest Aloysius Pieris shares a lot with Schillebeeckx, particularly the way he reflects on the essentials of discipleship. Pieris focuses especially on the liberative and praxis dimensions of Christian living in two of his books, *An Asian Theology of Liberation* and *God's Reign for God's Poor*.[13] He shifts the focus of salvation from one based on faith in Christ to the praxis of Christian faith. Like Schillebeeckx, Pieris regards Jesus' baptism by John the Baptist as the first prophetic gesture of Jesus of Nazareth. He discerns four missiological principles from this prophetic act. First, Jesus opted for the ascetic and liberative religiousness of John the Baptist. Second, at the Jordan, Jesus chose to be baptized rather than to baptize, thus joining the ranks of the poor. Third, by submitting himself to baptism, Jesus receives his missionary credentials and authority to preach. Fourth, while losing his identity in baptism, he discovers his authentic selfhood as God's beloved Son, the Messiah. With his identity clarified and authority bestowed, Jesus then set off on his prophetic mission, a journey that saw him, according to Pieris, in defence of the poor and in confrontation with

13. Aloysius Pieris, *An Asian Theology of Liberation* (Quezon City, Philippines: Claretians, 1988); Aloysius Pieris, *God's Reign for God's Poor: A Return to the Jesus Formula* (Kelaniya, Sri Lanka: Tulana Research Centre, 1999).

mammon. It was this, especially his challenge of the ruling religious elites and colonial powers, that led to Jesus' death on the cross. The journey that began at the Jordan in humility was to end on Calvary, not only in humility, but also in shame; the two events are described in the New Testament by the same word, "baptism" (Matt 3:13-15; Mark 10:35-40; Luke 12:50). This leads Pieris to propose that "the baptism of the cross, therefore, is not only the price he paid for preaching the good news, but the basis of *all Christian discipleship* (Mark 8:34)."[14]

Pieris then advocates that the church, as disciples of Jesus, must walk in the footsteps of him who humbled himself in order to serve the poor of his time. The events that took place at Jordan and Calvary are significant markers for Christians of our time, especially in discerning their prophetic role on behalf of the poor. Pieris distinguished between two groups of poor: the first are the poor by circumstance, where poverty is forced on them, and the second are poor by choice, those who choose to embrace poverty voluntarily. Pieris calls those who embrace evangelical voluntary poverty the followers of Jesus; they are the disciples of Christ. The group who are forced into an anti-evangelical poverty and are poor not by choice are the vicars of Christ; they represent Christ who said, "Truly I tell you, just as you did it to one of the least of these who are members of my family, you did it to me" (Matt 25:40). The two groups are necessarily related in that the forced poor (the vicars of Christ) have a right to demand that the followers of Christ (the disciples of Jesus) share in their fate and assist in their helplessness: "As Yahweh's proxy, the poor are authorized by Yahweh, their Covenant Partner, to dictate terms to the non-poor. They are the primordial magisterium. To listen to God (evangelical obedience) is to listen to the poor."[15] It is clear, then, that the poor by circumstance need the intervention of the poor by choice. By the same token, those aspiring to authentic discipleship need the poor they serve. The disciples of Jesus are the proclaimers of God's reign while the vicars are its inheritors. In other words, Pieris asserts, there is "no salvation outside God's covenant with the poor."[16]

This brings us to the question of how the other religions are related to this covenant with the poor. This is a crucial question, especially in Asia

14. Pieris, *An Asian Theology*, 49.
15. Pieris, *God's Reign for God's Poor*, 38.
16. Ibid., 60.

where the church ministers as a tiny minority among adherents of the other great religions of the world, many of whom are also in the service of the poor. They are thus to be regarded as the Christian's partners in the mission of service to the poor. So, following in the footsteps of Jesus, Pieris avers, the church has to submit itself to a baptism by the Jordan of Asia's religiousness. In effect, this means that the church must be extensively immersed in and involved with Asia's other religions and initiated into the pre-Christian traditions under the tutelage of Asia's ancient gurus. In this baptism, the church, like her Master Jesus, has to "sit at the feet of Asian gurus not as an *ecclesia docens* (a teaching Church) but as an *ecclesia discens* (a learning Church), lost among the 'religious poor' of Asia, among the *anawim* who go to their gurus in search of the kingdom of holiness, justice, and peace."[17] Actually, this was what Fr. Aloysius Pieris personally did. Being one of the first Catholics to earn a doctorate in Buddhist philosophy from Sri Lanka, he was still not quite welcome by the Buddhists until he himself was "baptized" in the Jordan of Asia's religion. In his words: "Then one day, garbed in my cassock as a Catholic priest, I took a basket of fruit and flowers and, in the presence of a Buddhist leader, fell prostrate. I worshiped him and asked to be accepted as his pupil. From that day, after this act of humility, I have no problem with Buddhist monks. And now (thank God) they have accepted me as a scholar among them."[18]

Conclusion

Religious pluralism or the reality that contemporary societies are becoming more religiously diverse is a fact that needs no further discussion. How Christianity attends to this fact theologically continues to engender a lot of discussions. Some of these theologies of religions assess the truth or falsity of the other religions against criteria or themes particular to Christianity, such as salvation and uniqueness of Christ or of the church. Others, especially those developed from within the Asian context where

17. Pieris, *An Asian Theology*, 47.

18. Aloysius Pieris, "Two Encounters in My Theological Journey," in *Frontiers in Asian Theology: Emerging Trends*, ed. R. S. Sugirtharajah (Maryknoll, NY: Orbis Books, 1994), 143.

Christianity is a minority religion, have moved beyond theological issues to look at common human concerns. In particular, the soteriocentric approaches to religious pluralism focus on the praxis of the faith and, if they have to make a judgment on other religions, assess its efficacy by its effects: "Thus you will know them by their fruits" (Matt 7:20). How each religion facilitates the salvation and liberation of the people, especially the poor and marginalized, are the prime concerns of these contemporary theologies of religious pluralism.

Suggestions for Further Reading

Hick, John, and Paul Knitter, eds. *The Myth of Christian Uniqueness: Toward a Pluralistic Theology of Religions*. Maryknoll, NY: Orbis Books, 1987.

Panikkar, Raimon. *The Cosmotheandric Experience: Emerging Religious Consciousness*. Translated and edited by Scott Eastham. Maryknoll, NY: Orbis Books, 1983.

Samartha, S. J. *One Christ, Many Religions: Toward a Revised Christology*. Maryknoll, NY: Orbis Books, 1991.

Smith, Wilfred Cantwell. *Toward a World Theology*. Philadelphia: Westminster, 1981.

Swidler, Leonard, ed. *Toward a Universal Theology of Religion*. Maryknoll, NY: Orbis Books, 1987.

10

Interfaith Reasoning, Hermeneutics, Theology, and Worship

Introduction

It was an international Christian-Muslim conference on the theme of globalization and its impact on the religious lives of people. The first day of the conference went well, with great presentations from speakers who were experts in the field. At the end of the day, the steering committee thought that, while the conference was progressing well, it could be enhanced if the Muslims and Christians actually engaged with one another more personally and spiritually rather than mainly on the cognitive level. The committee therefore decided that the days would begin with an interfaith scripture study session where the participants would gather to reflect together on the teachings of their sacred scriptures. A biblical passage would first be read by a Muslim, followed by a Qur'anic text read by a Christian. The rest of the participants were then invited to share their reflections and thoughts arising from either of the two scriptural texts. At the end of the conference nearly everyone remarked that the morning scriptural reflection sessions were the most meaningful part of the four-day event.

While interfaith conferences have become common occurrences around the globe since the mid-twentieth century, what is less common but being experimented with in recent decades is the practice of members of different religions coming together to engage in what has hitherto been in-house religious activities. This chapter looks at some of these newer practices that have come to the fore on account of religious adherents believing that more can be done to build bridges across the religions. It first discusses the exercise of scriptural reasoning, which is essentially the practical activity of reading and studying scriptures together with members of other religions. This will be followed by an examination of the dynamics and implications of cross-textual hermeneutics, a reading methodology promoted among theologians in the multiscriptural context of Asia. Next, how theology can be done by taking seriously the scriptures and theologies of other religions will be discussed in the section on comparative theology. The chapter will conclude with an exposition of how Christians have been coming together with those of other religious traditions for interfaith worship in its different forms.

Scriptural Reasoning

Most religious traditions have a corpus of texts that are deemed sacred and considered scripture by their adherents. The study and meditation of these scriptures are thus religious activities practiced widely, especially among members of the Abrahamic faiths of Judaism, Christianity, and Islam. This practice—of studious contemplation on the Tanakh, New Testament, or Qur'an—enable adherents to better appreciate God's revelation as encapsulated in what each community believes is the Word of God. Christianity has the monastic practice of *lectio divina* (divine reading), a traditional exercise of scriptural reading, meditation, and prayer to enhance one's knowledge of God's Word in order to attain closeness to and communion with God. The Jewish tradition has a movement that arose from the postmodern Jewish philosophy network called textual reasoning, the practice of thinking and studying Jewish texts such as the Tanakh, rabbinic commentaries, and philosophical texts. Traditionally, *lectio divina* and textual reasoning are religious practices engaged in with only members of one's same religion or church or synagogue. But "in the mid 1990s, some Christian friends of members of the Textual Reasoning group sat in on the conversation, and were so attracted by the lively process that they suggested using it as a model for inter-faith conversations. Later, Muslim friends were invited to join the conversation, and 'Scriptural Reasoning' was born."[1] The founders of this international

1. "The History of Scriptural Reasoning," *Scriptural Reasoning*, http://www.scripturalreasoning.org/the-history-of-scriptural-reasoning.html.

group, formed in 1995, include Peter Ochs, David F. Ford, and Daniel W. Hardy. Beginning primarily with members of the Abrahamic faiths, the practice of scriptural reasoning has now extended to include members of the Sikh, Buddhist, Hindu, and Taoist communities.

Scriptural reasoning is an exercise in interfaith dialogue, where, methodologically, its focus is solely on the scriptural texts of the respective dialogue partners. It is not a theoretical paradigm but a practical one. The actual engagement in the practice of reading and studying religious texts together in an interfaith setting is essential for scriptural reasoning. Each participant comes to the scriptural reasoning session committed to contributing actively to the group process. They discuss together a specific theme of interest—for example, how God or creation are presented in the different scriptures or a contemporary social or political issue affecting the community—by reflecting and sharing with one another their understandings of what is taught by their respective scriptures as well as the scriptures of their fellow participants. Each scriptural reasoner reads, interprets, and questions what the different religious texts are saying and are open to listening and learning from how other participants understand and explain them. The aim is not to arrive at any consensus or establish a common ground where all parties can agree but to have a greater understanding of how each tradition interprets a particular life or religious theme on the basis of their scriptures. It is as important to listen to each participant explain his or her own tradition's text as it is to listen to how a participant who is not of the tradition of the text being examined interprets that aspect of scripture. The host of a particular text may be asked to give some initial remarks and explain the background and nuances for a greater appreciation of it but need not have the final say. No one is allowed to dismiss alternative interpretations or to suppress divisive views. Instead, the diversity of interpretations is what makes scriptural reasoning exciting and beneficial even as it is challenging. Differences and even arguments between the traditions are entertained in view of allowing them to be grace occasions for deep learning and in order to facilitate a more informed and healthy disagreement.

There are no fixed patterns or rules that guide scriptural reasoning sessions except that all participants should be allocated equal space and time to speak and to listen. No one person or religious tradition dominates and this is partly ensured by either hosting the sessions in a neutral setting such as a town hall or public library or, if in a house of worship, ensuring that there is a rotation between the different houses of worship. That way, the scriptural reasoners extend and receive hospitality with each participant getting to play host as well as guest, ensuring a certain amount of parity in the leadership, oversight, and ownership of the entire project. Like all other expressions of interfaith dialogue, scriptural reasoning sessions are occasions to promote better relationships between members of the different religious traditions. Friendship is its primary ingredient as well as goal. It is therefore imperative that participants of scriptural reasoning are honest with one another, open to each other's views, and trust that each person is there in good faith and for the common good of the community. This means that no one is allowed to denigrate or even harbor a condescending attitude toward the other or their scriptures even as they are allowed to maintain that their own scripture is truly God's Word. Dogmatic and exclusivist demands about the truth of one's own religion or religious scriptures vis-à-vis their neighbor's religion or scriptures are inappropriate in scriptural reasoning groups. For example, one cannot come to the scriptural reasoning project convinced that one's own scripture is the fulfillment of or have superseded all other scriptures. On the contrary, scriptural reasoners need to be open enough to acknowledge that the Tanakh is God's Word for the Jews, just as the Christian Bible is for Christians and the Qur'an for Muslims. Participants therefore need to take each of the sacred scriptures seriously even if they themselves are not expected to submit to them in faith.

Participants in scriptural reasoning come to the group clearly identifying with their own religious and faith tradition, without having to set aside or bracketing off any aspect of their beliefs and convictions. While not expected to relinquish or compromise on the foundations and principles of their own faith, the process of dialogue and engagement will almost certainly lead the participants to developing a more expansive view of the same. This is what is called learning or conversion, and every participant has to be open to being "converted," not so much to another religion, but to an expanded horizon for appreciating issues of faith and religion. That notwithstanding, they still remain totally committed to their own religious identity and the deepest sources of their faith tradition. Even if not officially sent by their religious community, participants of scriptural reasoning sessions are there representing the religious tradition they identify with. The other participants see them as speaking from and out of that particular religious tradition. When they return to their own home tradition, they are expected to share with those at home about their experience of interfaith scripture studies. In that sense, scriptural reasoners have a responsibility to educate and open the minds and hearts of their fellow believers. This is important since religious differences have too often been a source of divisive ideas and acrimonious actions especially among those who have little or no interactions with people of other religions. Scriptural reasoning is, therefore, by no means merely an in-house activity but has a public function as well. On the one hand, it acts as an antidote to the prejudices that many people have about other faiths and their scriptures. Sometimes, even if a person has absolutely no knowledge whatsoever of what the scriptures of other religions teach, that person easily passes negative judgments on them. In situations like this, scriptural reasoners witness to the positive effects of having positively engaged with those of other religions for the purpose of studying scripture together. That they have become more understanding of the views of their religious neighbors and less antagonistic toward their religions testifies to the value of studying scripture together. On the other hand, scriptural reasoning also witnesses against the contemporary secular liberal culture and politics that often insist that religion has to be privatized and kept out of the public sphere. This is in view of the fact that religion has too often been used and abused by minorities within a variety of religions who hijack it by committing vicious crimes in the name of their religion and scriptures. Scriptural reasoning, by overtly exploring scriptures together, witnesses to the fact that the resources within religion could be garnered rather than marginalized for the benefit of society. It offers alternative interpretations to specific texts within scriptures and informs and transforms attitudes in view of enabling scriptural texts to be used for the common good, including resolving conflict and promoting peace. It is in view of this that the practice of scriptural reasoning has the potential for what in Hebrew is called *tikkun olam*, which literally means healing the world and which all the religions advocate is part of their mission.

Cross-Textual Hermeneutics

While scriptural reasoning arose from within the West, the situation in the East calls for another method in the study of scriptures. As we saw briefly in the previous chapter, discovering the Bible in the nonbiblical world of

Asia can be a major challenge. Not too many people in Asia accept the Bible as divine scripture or Word of God. Two reasons stand out. First, Asia is a continent where other scriptures not only exist but have shaped the lives and minds of the people for centuries and millennia. China and India, in particular, have classics that predate the Bible, which is but a latecomer to the Asian multiscriptural world. These scriptures—of Confucianism, Taoism, Hinduism, Buddhism, and the other religions—have been the basis for the faith of the peoples of Asia long before the advent of Christianity. Second, because the Christian Bible came to form in the Greco-Roman and Latin worlds, it is understood and appreciated rather differently outside of these worlds, more so if the biblical texts are read in translation. In fact, most Christians have access to God's Word only by reading translated versions of the original Greek and Hebrew scriptural texts. In view of these two factors—that Asia is a multiscriptural context and that the Bible is basically read in translation—it is important that Asian Christians attempt to engage in what is called cross-textual hermeneutics. This means that the Bible has to be read in concert with the other native scriptures of Asia. This reading method, championed by the Chinese biblical scholar Archie Lee of Hong Kong, has the potential for mutual correction, as well as mutual enrichment. It enables Asian Christians to appreciate their newly acquired Christian faith vis-à-vis the faith of their ancestors, as well as to appreciate their ancestral native Asian faith in light of the message of the Bible. This effectively means that they are viewing the Bible through Asian eyes, which enables them to see the Bible as reflecting typically Asian concerns.

Because Christianity had accompanied the Western powers into much of Asia during the colonial era, the Christian missionary's perception was that the Asian religio-cultural traditions were equally in need of being colonized. The indigenous religions of Asia were thought of as no more than paganist and idolatrous. This Gospel-against-culture ideology nurtured the Christian's prejudicial views against other religions while at the same time advancing Christianity and its scriptures as the sole authority for missionary activity in Asia. The many other scriptures and classics of Asia were dismissed as inauthentic even before any attempts were made to examine or study them. The aim of Christian mission was to unequivocally discredit the people's faith in their native scriptures in view of promoting the Bible as the divine, universal, timeless, and absolute Word of God.

Not all the missionaries, though, were negatively disposed toward the other religions. Some, on account of encouraging interactions with the followers of other religions, refined their attitude and began considering the Asian religions and their scriptures positively. But, conditioned by their church's fulfillment theologies, they regarded the Asian scriptures as having value only insofar as they serve as preparation for the Gospel of Christ. But this does not mean that the Asian scriptures were granted the same status as that of the Old Testament. This, of course, resulted in questions being raised: "There is a very interesting question often raised by Chinese Christians: Why should Asian Christians adopt the Old Testament as the foundation for their faith and theology when Asians possess sacred texts which might be equally, if not even more, valid and relevant as preparatory to the specific revelation of the New Testament?"[2] To be sure, Asian Christians certainly have a greater affinity to their native scriptures than to the scriptures of the people of Israel. They find it difficult to understand the notion of a closed canon of the Christian Bible, as the Asian religions have generally been receptive of other religions and are able to integrate other scriptures into their own canon of scriptures. Despite the unwelcoming stance of Christianity toward Asian scriptures, Asian Christians were still unable to completely give up the scriptures of their religio-cultural tradition even if they have to be kept secret or hidden from the church: "The whole problematic of Asian hermeneutics is largely that while the newly-acquired Christian Bible began to provide them with a new meaning of life, Asian Christians could not completely sever their connection with their community and its cultural-religious texts, which had nurtured and shaped their lives and continued to sustain and nourish their well-being."[3]

It was not surprising, then, for the early Asian converts to understand Christianity by way of their Asian religions and native scriptures. The religious-symbolic worldview and ethical codes that derive from their ancestral faith were used as templates in the reception of the teachings

2. Archie C. C. Lee, "Scriptural Translations and Cross-Textual Hermeneutics," in *The Oxford Handbook of Christianity in Asia*, ed. Felix Wilfred (Oxford: Oxford University Press, 2014), 122–23.

3. Archie C. C. Lee, "Cross-Textual Hermeneutics and Identity in Multi-Scriptural Asia," in *Christian Theology in Asia*, ed. Sebastian C. H. Kim (Cambridge: Cambridge University Press, 2008), 182–83.

of the newly acquired Christian faith. The Christian missionaries also had to present Christian doctrines employing terms used in the Asian religio-cultural traditions. It was inevitable for the Bible to employ Buddhist concepts, Hindu ideas, Taoist notions, and Confucian terminology in the task of translation. Words used to express religious ideas such as God, heaven, hell, paradise, sin, grace, faith, and salvation had to be borrowed from the scriptures of the local religions if they were to make any sense and be received correctly. Translation, however, is as much an act of interpretation. How, for example, is the biblical God—expressed as *Elohim* or *Yahweh* in the Hebrew Bible, *Theos* in the Greek language, and *Deus* in Latin—translated in the Asian vernacular? The problem is not the lack of terms but the abundance of them. In China, for example, the Supreme Being worshiped by the Chinese goes by names such as *Tian, Shangdi, Tianzhu, Tianzhuan,* and *Shangzhu.* If the theological assumption is that the God of Christianity is a totally new God that the Asian religions know nothing of, then it would be necessary to coin a new term or use a generic one to refer to the divine. Suffice to say that numerous debates took place before an appropriate name was chosen. The Catholic mission of the seventeenth century eventually opted for the term *Tianzhu* (the Lord of Heaven), while the Protestants could not agree on a single term and ended up with accepting both *Shangdi* (the Lord on High) and *Shen* (Gods and Spirits) in the nineteenth century. Even today one can tell if a Bible is a Catholic or Protestant translation simply by looking at how God is named.

Reading the Bible in the vernacular, therefore, means one is also accessing the ideas and teachings of the local Asian scriptures and classics. They are resurrected for no other reason than because the biblical message had no choice but to use Asian terms in the transmission of the Good News of Jesus Christ. Of course, the Bible had to deal with the fact that the Asian religions were basically polytheistic while biblical faith is monotheistic and that Asians believe in a continuum between the divine and the human while Christian belief is that there is a distinctive chasm in the divine-human divide. Cross-textual hermeneutics invite the reader to read the Bible alongside the indigenous sacred texts in order to bring out the fuller and hidden meaning of particular terms and ideas that could have been lost in the translation process. Both the Christian text and the Asian text are assigned equal status, with one offering a critique of the other and vice versa. They are treated as dialogue partners, and the cross-fertilization that occurs enables the Asian reader to integrate how the divine is believed to be involved in the world in the two cultural traditions. This allows the Bible to be enriched and seen as Word of God for the peoples of Asia as well.

Comparative Theology

Besides studying the Bible alongside the scriptures of other religions, it is also becoming increasingly necessary that we do theology alongside the theologies of other religions. This may sound like a radical suggestion, as theology is basically a confessional and sectarian endeavor that takes as presupposition the truths and values taught by one's own religious tradition. Theology is the critical reflection on issues of life and religion that uses the foundation of one's faith from a particular tradition; theological reflection is done within and for a particular community. This is in keeping with Anselm of Canterbury's understanding and definition of theology as "faith seeking understanding." But in the contemporary context where there is conscious awareness of and inevitable interaction between adherents of different religious traditions it makes responsible sense for theology to cross religious boundaries to engage with one another as well. Thus arose the recent discipline of comparative theology, which, according to its leading proponent Francis Clooney, "marks acts of faith seeking understanding which are rooted in a particular faith tradition but which, from that foundation, venture into learning from one or more other faith traditions. This learning is sought for the sake of fresh theological insights that are indebted to the newly encountered tradition/s as well as the home tradition."[4] Unlike comparative religious studies, which stress an objective, religiously detached neutral viewpoint, comparative theology remains strictly a confessional and theological enterprise in that the theologians remain committed to the faith perspective of their home tradition. Its starting point for reflection, in fact, is precisely a commitment to the tradition's scriptures and teaching authority. In other words, comparative theologians do not set aside their religious faith and the beliefs of their home tradition when they consciously go over to another religion in order to learn from its members their understandings of faith from the perspective of that other religious tradition. Thus, Clooney

4. Francis X. Clooney, *Comparative Theology: Deep Learning Across Religious Borders* (Malden, MA: Wiley-Blackwell, 2010), 10.

subtitles his groundbreaking 2010 book *Deep Learning across Religious Borders*. It is the reaching out across religious borders that distinguishes comparative theology from the other traditional confessional theologies.

Needless to say, comparative theology can be done only if one has a positive attitude toward the other religions, relating to them with benevolence and especially with a willingness to learn from them. It also cannot harbor any remnant of triumphalist Christianity: "Comparative theology is an *anti-apologetic programme against the self-aggrandizing and self-immunization of one's own faith*, directed against the degradation of other religions through a hermeneutic of suspicion, which one can study in the exemplary early Christian *Adversus Judaeos* writings, and against the isolationist rhetoric of uniqueness, ignorance and blindness."[5] Instead, comparative theology is premised on the belief that God's revelation to the Christian can also be found outside the church and can be discerned by exploring the faith of our religious neighbors. In other words, if theology is faith seeking understanding, then comparative theologians believe that their intellectual search for God in faith cannot be rationally limited to the boundaries of their tradition alone. This is because the quest for who or what God is or how God relates to the world and the many other questions of ultimate concern is not the purview of Christians alone. All the other religious traditions engage in the same search, and it is this that inspires comparative theologians to reach out in order to learn from them. Comparative theology explores very much the same topics that other forms of confessional theology do, and this includes an analysis of "faith, truth, sin, grace, salvation, community, and worship, both in general and in more specific doctrinal forms, plus an even wider range of vaguer but still fruitful terms such as union or communion, delusion, liberation, humility, devotion, spiritual knowledge, compassion, and healing."[6] But where comparative theology differs is that it extends the exploration by taking seriously the insights and reflections of our neighbors of other religions in view of integrating them into our own.

---

5. Ulrich Winkler, "What Is Comparative Theology?," in *Interreligious Hermeneutics in Pluralistic Europe: Between Texts and People*, ed. David Cheetam (Amsterdam: Rodopi, 2011), 241; emphasis in original.

6. Francis X. Clooney, "Comparative Theology," in *The Oxford Handbook of Systematic Theology*, ed. Kathryn Tanner, John Webster, and Iain Torrance (Oxford: Oxford University Press, 2007), 654.

This means that the comparative theologian must engage in deep learning and serious study, not only of their own tradition, but of the tradition of their neighbor as well. The study of the neighbor's tradition through the reading of their sacred texts and commentaries has to be as intense as the study of one's own tradition. Judgments are withheld until one fully comprehends and appreciates the nuances of the beliefs and practices of both traditions. A comparative analysis is then engaged in with the intention of discerning where some of the beliefs and practices of the respective traditions converge and/or diverge from one another. The analysis can shed light on how central religious symbols of humanity can be reinterpreted so that they are meaningful in religiously pluralistic societies. It can also assist in addressing questions posed by the fact of religious pluralism by offering explicitly theological responses that take into account people's faith. More important, the comparative analysis can provide new insights for a renewed understanding of the Christian's own faith. It helps the Christian to read anew texts from their own tradition, but with new eyes and an expanded vision of truth and religious issues. Comparative theology, therefore, besides promoting mutual understanding and relationship between the different religions and providing a frame of reference for them to interact effectively and function amicably alongside one another, also serves the purpose of strengthening and broadening the Christian's vision of life and faith in general.

Like most other disciplines of theology, comparative theology is primarily an academic exercise of private self-study. It is generally done on one's own time and space without the physical and immediate engagement with the religious other. It is not interfaith dialogue as such, although the activity of interfaith dialogue certainly serves as a beneficial prerequisite that can enhance the practice of comparative theology. But it can count as a form of interior interfaith dialogue: "Yet even if comparative theology is a form of reading, it can also become a form of internal inter-religious dialogue, a learning from the other tradition, questioning it and being questioned by it. . . . If one is taking the other religion seriously, the study itself is accountable to the other, and in both reading and talking, the challenge of the other is present."[7] Thus,

---

7. Francis X. Clooney, "Comparative Theology and Inter-Religious Dialogue," in *The Wiley-Blackwell Companion to Inter-Religious Dialogue*, ed. Catherine Cornille (Chichester, UK: John Wiley & Sons, 2013), 54.

within the process of study, the comparative theologians are responsible and accountable to the communities of both their own tradition as well as their neighbor's, especially in how they analyze and represent the teachings of the respective traditions. The members of both the home and the neighbor's tradition have to be able to generally recognize and accept how their traditions are being presented. This happens when the fruits of the interior dialogue of comparative theology are expressed in the written word as a published reflection. What begins in private no longer remains private but becomes available in the public domain. This allows the work of the comparative theologian to be scrutinized by both members of their own tradition and members of the religious tradition studied. The process, in turn, facilitates interfaith dialogue where the fruits and method of comparative theology can either be challenged or verified. Thus, comparative theology can also be regarded as an expression of interfaith dialogue in its deepest form. Its aim is as much to build bridges and friendships across the religious traditions. The principle of interfaith dialogue that the interlocutors engage the religious other receptively without giving up their own religious identity is also strictly adhered to. The challenge, of course, is in striking a balance between one's commitment and one's openness.

Interfaith Worship

As more and more Christians encounter adherents of other religious traditions in interfaith dialogue, they are also exploring ways in which they can celebrate the liturgy together with their dialogue partners. Thus, there is currently the emerging phenomenon of interfaith worship. The term "worship" is usually used to represent broadly "any ritual symbolizing a relationship to the transcendent dimension of reality and life, . . . not limited to prayer as such, and can include rituals of life and cosmic (natural) cycles, such as healing ceremonies, marriages, and harvest festivals."[8] Participation in worship sessions is therefore normally restricted to those who embrace the faith and subscribe to its creeds as they celebrate and confirm the group's religious identity. But, as with

8. Michael Amaladoss, "Inter-Religious Worship," in *The Wiley-Blackwell Companion to Inter-Religious Dialogue*, 87.

interfaith dialogue, interfaith worship means the crossing of religious boundaries for the purpose of participating in the rituals of a tradition other than one's own. These rituals can be private and informal or they can be public and official. The viability for interfaith participation depends on the "(1) the context in which it occurs, (2) the intention that undergirds the sharing of ritual, (3) the nature of the ritual performed, and (4) the religious communities involved."[9] Interfaith worship can take a variety of forms that are generally distinguished by whether they are individual or social. The former occurs when an individual crosses over to another religion to participate as guest in the rituals of the host tradition. The latter refers to occasions when communities of different religious traditions come together to celebrate in worship, usually in response to or to commemorate a communal event.

Public interfaith worship prayer events generally refer to two qualitatively different modes of prayer expressions. The first refers to events where members of different religious traditions come together for collaborative prayer, but they each take turns to lead and express their prayer. Participants who are members of the tradition leading the prayer will be able to identify with the prayers being said and join in, but the rest, who are not members of the tradition leading the prayer, usually stand by in respectful silence. Even as there is often a common theme that all the prayers are oriented to, there is little or no intermingling of the prayer actions or words used, no coordination between the traditions to ensure a coherent expression of a united prayer, and no presumption that the various parties accept or agree with the content of each other's prayers. The diversity in the prayers is graciously accepted, and the liturgical event is more or less a potpourri of differently sourced religious items brought together and presented in a single prayer event. This mode of interfaith worship is actually more appropriately called multifaith worship, as the members of the different faith communities are together in prayer but praying mainly on their own rather than praying together. The second mode refers to occasions where the prayers used during the interfaith worship sessions are strategically planned so that they are truly

---

9. Marianne Moyaert, "Introduction: Exploring the Phenomenon of Interreligious Ritual Participation," in *Ritual Participation and Interreligious Dialogue Boundaries, Transgressions and Innovations*, ed. Marianne Moyaert and Joris Geldhof (London: Bloomsbury Academic, 2016), 1.

interfaith in flavor. From a multiplicity of resources, a representative committee intentionally develops an innovative prayer event that brings together specific elements from the different religious traditions that are acceptable to all the participants. This will necessarily mean excluding prayer items that are exclusive and deemed insensitive to members of another religion. The Prayer of St. Francis, a universal Hindu chant, a hymn that resonates with all parties, a poem on unity or harmony, a reading from sacred scriptures, and periods of silent meditation could be creatively woven into one synthetic prayer session. This usually results from efforts to ensure a thematic flow in the prayer and some sort of critical interlinking between the different elements that constitute it without compromising or diluting the identities of the different religious traditions represented.

There is a variety of settings in which interfaith worship is appropriate. Public institutions such as schools, hospitals, and prisons are places where this has been introduced, as they have become increasingly multireligious. In multireligious settings it would be deemed inappropriate to be hosting a confessional liturgical event if, for instance, a mass shooting occurs, to celebrate the life of a long-serving deceased principal or director, to commemorate a state anniversary, or to pray for world peace. Interfaith worship events are also often staged to express solidarity if one of the religious communities is unfairly targeted. For example, when a terrorist-related bomb blasts in New York, Paris, or London, unfortunately Muslims living in many cities in the West experience being spat upon, having their headscarves pulled off, or being viciously attacked. In circumstances like these, the different religious communities have come together for interfaith worship to at once pray for the victims of the tragedy as well as protest Islamophobia. With regard to private interfaith worship, the fact that interfaith marriages have been on the rise today means that many more people of different religions but who are related to one another will come together to celebrate liturgically in, for example, life-cycle events of birth, marriage, or death. Another expression of private interfaith worship is when someone believes that crossing over to another religion to experience the tradition's religious rituals enhances their own spiritual growth. Examples are Christians taking on Zen meditation or yoga practices, or going on a pilgrimage to a Buddhist or Shinto shrine or a tomb of an Islamic Sufi saint, or meditating on the sacred scriptures of another tradition to supplement their Christian religious practices.

While interfaith worship has been spontaneously developing as a consequence of enhanced interactions across religious traditions, questions have also been raised about issues of legitimacy. Specifically, how far can guests cross over to participate in the rituals of the host community before transgressing on hospitality? Some traditions are clear about this, such as those who are not Catholics should not participate in the Holy Communion of the Eucharist, and those who are not Muslims should not participate in the official *salah* prayers. This is because these aspects of the rituals are expressions of faith and so presume the participant already accepts the basic beliefs and faith convictions of the host's tradition. The old Latin saying of *lex orandi, lex credendi* (the law of praying is the law of believing) is instructive here: our rituals are an expression of our beliefs. This is why multifaith prayers are generally more acceptable to most religious communities than interfaith prayers. The former simply means we support and stand with other religions in prayer while the latter may refer to the fact that our praying together signifies we already share the same beliefs. This is why Pope John Paul II was emphatic that the 1986 World Day of Prayer for Peace at Assisi that he convened was more in the genre of a multifaith prayer event than an interfaith event. He issued this clarification: "What will take place at Assisi will certainly not be a religious syncretism but a sincere attitude of prayer to God in an atmosphere of mutual respect. For this reason the formula chosen for the gathering at Assisi is: being together in order to pray. Certainly we cannot 'pray together,' namely, to make a common prayer, but we can be present while others pray."[10]

Conclusion

It has to be noted that the different practices discussed above are really a sign of advance in the practice of interfaith dialogue. That Christians have now engaged their religious neighbors in the study of scriptures, doing theology, and common worship is no mean accomplishment for an activity that came to prominence only in the last half century or so. It

10. Pope John Paul II, "To the Faithful in General Audience (Rome, October 22, 1986)," in *Interreligious Dialogue: The Official Teaching of the Catholic Church (1963–1995)*, ed. Francesco Gioia (Boston, MA: Pauline Books & Media, 1997), 341.

is also important to note that the general attitude of openness to learning from our religious neighbor while at the same time being committed to our own faith has permeated the different fields of religious living. This testifies to the importance of being at once rooted in our own tradition while at the same time striving for relationship across religious borders. Rootedness and relatedness, therefore, are key attitudes for interfaith dialogue.

Suggestions for Further Reading

Clooney, Francis X., and Klaus von Stosch, eds. *How to Do Comparative Theology*. Comparative Theology: Thinking across Traditions. New York: Fordham University Press, 2017.

Ford, David F., and C. C. Pecknold, eds. *The Promise of Scriptural Reasoning*. Malden, MA: Wiley-Blackwell, 2006.

Fredericks, James L. *Buddhists and Christians: Through Comparative Theology to Solidarity*. Maryknoll, NY: Orbis Books, 2004.

Ryan, Thomas. *Interreligious Prayer: A Christian Guide*. Mahwah, NJ: Paulist Press, 2008.

Sugirtharajah, R. S., ed. *Voices from the Margin: Interpreting the Bible in the Third World*. Maryknoll, NY: Orbis Books, 2006.

11

Christian-Muslim Dialogue of Theology

Introduction

The professor was a Muslim, and this was a course on Islamic studies. It was the first class in the semester, and he was aware that there were a few of us who were Christians taking the course. He wanted to make sure we were at ease with what he was teaching and so began by pointing to the similarities between Christianity and Islam. He informed us that both descended from Ibrahim (Abraham) and that Muslims have a profound respect for Nabi Isa (Prophet Jesus), who is mentioned by name twenty-five times in the Holy Qur'an. Likewise, the stories of many of the prophets of Hebrew Scriptures are also found in the Qur'an, from Nuh (Noah), Yaqub (Jacob), and Ishak (Isaac); to Musa (Moses), Daud (David), and Sulaiman (Solomon); to Zulkifli (Ezekiel), Zakariya (Zechariah), and Yahya (John). He also told us that Maryam (Mary), the mother of Jesus, is the only woman mentioned by name in the Qur'an and that there is in fact an entire chapter dedicated to her. He thus wanted us to know that Islam teaches very much what Christianity teaches and hoped that Christians and Muslims alike would be open to learning more about Islam. Of course, the majority of the students in the class, who were Muslims, were already quite familiar with what he was saying.

This chapter engages in a Christian-Muslim dialogue of theological discourse and looks explicitly at the Islamic critique of the Christian faith. In particular, the doctrine of original sin and that of redemption through Christ will be discussed, as they represent the central doctrinal problems that Islam has with Christianity. The chapter's approach is to listen attentively to what the Qur'an and Islamic theology teach about these two Christian doctrines and then explore the theological moves called for to make an informed and constructive response. Specifically, attention will be given to what underlies the Islamic critique and especially how Muslims understand the absoluteness of God, in particular the doctrine of monotheism. These reflections will be premised on the conviction that God's Word has been revealed to and apprehended by different religious communities and that they have each grasped this Word in ways that radically differ from one another.

Muslim Questions on Christian Theology

What problems do Muslims have with regard to the Christian doctrines of original sin and redemption through Christ? Most of the questions about these two doctrines are based on how Muslims see Christian Scriptures being interpreted. First, from the first chapters of the Hebrew Bible, Muslim questions have to do with why and how the myth of Adam and Eve has resulted in the Christian doctrine of original sin. This is predicated on questions such as how the progeny of the first parents can inherit their sins, how a newborn is considered already sinful, why God is so unforgiving of the sin of Adam and Eve, and why Christians have such a negative view of human nature. Muslims are raising these questions because, even as the same myth of creation and accounts of the first parents are found in the Qur'an, Islamic theology does not have the equivalent of the doctrine of original sin. The question therefore is this: how are Christians interpreting the creation myth and what are they saying about God and of human nature when reading Christian Scriptures?

Second, from the last chapters of the Christian gospels of the New Testament, Muslim questions relate to why and how the crucifixion and death of Jesus are redemptive of all humankind. These questions arise from trying to grapple with questions about why God would require a repayment for the forgiveness of sins; how the death of an innocent man can wipe away the sins of others, even for generations to come; how a prophet of God can be abandoned to die a horrific death; and how Christians can consider Jesus as Son of God and therefore be in a position to repay God. Here, Muslim concerns are not only with how Christianity has understood or misunderstood Jesus—especially where they differ from the Qur'anic understanding of Jesus—but also with how Christians seem to be conceiving or misconceiving the nature and attributes of God.

Their central concern is that the absoluteness and oneness of God might be compromised.

Islamic Critique of Original Sin

Muslims expound on their difficulties with the doctrine of original sin by appeal to a host of arguments. For instance, some contemporary Muslims appeal to the scientific and commonsense knowledge that human thought and action cannot be transmitted genetically; knowledge cannot be passed through the generations. They insist that it defies common sense to even imagine that it is possible for a child to biologically inherit the sins—or virtues, for that matter—of the parents. Each person is responsible for his or her own actions; no one else can be blamed for them. They then appeal to the Qur'an, which teaches that at the last judgment it is the individual who has to render an account for personal sins and also that no one can shoulder someone else's sins, not even those committed by their own ancestors (Qur'an 52:21; 82:19; 99:6-8).[1] Elsewhere, the Qur'an is even more direct about the unlikelihood of inherited sin by teaching unequivocally that "no bearer of burdens can bear the burden of another" (Qur'an 53:38). Furthermore, appealing to Hebrew Scriptures, Muslims point out that there are verses that have said as much. For instance, the book of Deuteronomy teaches that "Parents shall not be put to death for their children, nor shall children be put to death for their parents" (Deut 24:16) and the prophet Ezekiel has said that "The person who sins shall die. A child shall not suffer for the iniquity of a parent, nor a parent suffer for the iniquity of a child" (Ezek 18:20). As can be seen from the arguments above, it seems obvious to Muslims that there are no scriptural grounds for the Christian doctrine of original sin, and thus it remains a source of major discomfort, especially when reflected against the backdrop of Islamic faith.

Another argument Muslims employ to further their critique is to point out that Adam and his spouse—the Qur'an does not mention her by name—have already been more than punished. After all, they experienced guilt for their actions, had to bear the consequences of their disobedient act, and were eventually thrown out of paradise and banished from the

---

1. *The Quranic Arabic Corpus*, trans. Yusuf Ali, http://corpus.quran.com/.

Garden of Eden. Did this not suffice as punishment for their seemingly measly sin? The Qur'an is also clear that God had accepted their remorse and repentance and forgave them there and then in the Garden of Eden itself (Qur'an 7:23; 2:37). So the doctrine of original sin is really unnecessary in the context of God's gracious forgiveness. In fact, one can even conclude from the Qur'anic account that Islam seems to be focussing not so much on the doctrine of original sin but rather on the doctrine of original forgiveness. God's graciousness, not human depravity, is highlighted. Muslims claim that this is the more important lesson from the myth of creation and the narrative about Adam and his spouse. Thus, with the first parents' sins forgiven, all human beings are subsequently born, according to the Qur'an, in a natural and upright state or *fitrah*. Indeed, Islam rejects the doctrine of original sin and teaches that children are born free from sin. This teaching centers on the vision that human beings are naturally good as they were created by Allah in the state of innocence. An important adjunct to this is that, though good, humans are also essentially weak. They therefore are in need of guidance, which the prophets have provided over the generations. Compared with Christianity, Muslims see Islamic theology as emphasizing the goodness of the human person, whereas they view Christian theology as focused more on its sinful nature. Christians, of course, may or may not agree with this conclusion.

Islamic Critique of Christ's Redemption

This brings us to the second doctrine. Muslims have difficulties with the doctrine of Christian redemption precisely because they do not believe humans are sinful in the first place and in need of any redemption. There are a number of facets to this doctrine, which Muslims find problematic. First, with regard to the sinner: They are unable to appreciate how the sacrifice and death of another can repay the debt of the one who committed the wrongdoing. Just as it is not possible for humans to inherit the sins of the first parents, Muslims believe it is not possible for the sins of humanity to be cancelled by someone else. Reference is made by Muslim theologians to this particular verse found in the book of Psalms of the Hebrew Scriptures: "Truly, no ransom avails for one's life; there is no price one can give to God for it" (Ps 49:7). What is emphasized by Muslims is that the sinner has no choice but to pay for all the sins that they have committed and that there is no passing on the burden to anyone else.

Second, with regard to Jesus: Muslims cannot understand why God allows, much less delivers, an innocent man to die for the guilt and sins of another. Is that not an act of injustice perpetrated by the all-loving and merciful God who is also just and fair? Muslims, of course, do not accept the divinity of Jesus or his divine sonship, but even if they do, they cannot see the logic in him being sent to die. In fact, they view it as even more blasphemous if indeed the eternal God actually died on the cross! But, more important, Muslims cannot accede to the belief that Jesus was sent to die. Because the prophet is specially chosen and sent by Allah, the prophet is never abandoned. For Jesus, or Nabi Isa—the prophet of Allah—to die is tantamount to suggesting that God had abandoned him in the final moments of his earthly existence. This would be an indictment as much on the prophet as on Allah.

This last point is further compounded by the third problem, which is that the Christian gospels actually have records of Jesus' seeming reluctance in this sacrificial act. Verses from the gospels—such as, "My Father, if it is possible, let this cup pass from me; yet not what I want but what you want" (Matt 26:39) and "Eloi, Eloi, lema sabachthani?" (Mark 15:34)—are often used to advance these arguments. Muslims ask: Was Jesus fully an active participant in this redeeming event or was he simply sent against his will to die for the sins of humanity? Again, Islamic prophetology would never allow for the latter conclusion to the prophet's mission. But what is even more critical here for Muslims is the nature of God that this Christian worldview seems to be offering. What kind of God do Christians believe in, especially if this God is willing to not only allow for the death of a prophet but even actively force the prophet to accept such an evil end?

Fourth, if it was indeed true that God had sent Jesus to die for the sins of humankind, why did God take the gift back three days later with the resurrection of Christ? This is baffling to Muslims, as it looks as if the repayment was revoked and so the debt or sin—if it was there in the first place—should remain. It has to be pointed out that Muslims are referring here to the Christian understanding of Christ's resurrection as depicted in the gospels. Underlying the argument is the inconsistency Muslims seem to find within Christian Scriptures: The Christian belief in the resurrection cancels the death of Jesus, and this would mean the cancellation of the so-called debt that was repaid through the death. What dumbfounds Muslims is how Christians can continue to believe in their scriptures despite what they see as glaring contradictions.

Fifth, why is it, if indeed Jesus has already paid in full for the sins of humanity, that the effects of the fall of our first parents still remain, for example, sin, enmity, death, childbirth pains? Does it mean that the debt was not fully accepted? Or, are the so-called effects not really caused by the fall? Whatever it is, Muslims find it hard to appreciate the logic behind the God-Jesus divine repayment scheme. Moreover, there is no empirical evidence to suggest that Christians are any less inclined to sin than those who do not believe in Christ, thus raising questions about what it is that Jesus is purported to have died for. These arguments raise questions not only about the theory that the debt of sin was cancelled by the death of Jesus on the cross but also about how Christians appreciate God's justice and what they understand by sin.

Sixth, why does God not simply forgive the sins of humanity instead of demanding reparation of one man, even if he is the Son of God? Trying to understand the logic of this demand is especially difficult against the teaching of Jesus that it should no longer be about an eye for an eye or a tooth for a tooth (Matt 5:38). Does the almighty God not have the power to simply forgive as Jesus taught, or is there a calculating bloodthirsty streak within the divine that Christians believe in? Or does the Christian vision of faith still include the religious practice of human sacrifice (Gen 22), which the Abrahamic faiths should have long given up?

These are six problems Muslims seem to have with the doctrine of Christian redemption, and, as stated earlier, they are indeed integrally linked to the first problem of the doctrine of original sin. Understandably, doubts over the doctrine of original sin have cast a dark shadow on the doctrine of Christian redemption. Again, this is the Muslim's take on the matter, which Christians may or may not agree with.

Muslim Views on the Crucifixion

If the doctrine of Christian redemption is premised on the doctrine of original sin, the same doctrine of salvation through Jesus Christ is also contingent on the fact of the actual death of Jesus. Thus, the crucifixion of Jesus to his death is essential for Christian belief. This is an even bigger problem for Muslims since the Qur'an presents a somewhat different picture of what actually happened to Jesus of Nazareth. In fact, Muslims dispute not only that Jesus was crucified and died but also what actually happened on the night of his arrest. This arises from one single verse, more specifically only one clause, in the Qur'an, which seems to have denied the accounts of the death of Jesus on the cross as presented by the Christian gospels: "That they said (in boast), 'We killed Christ Jesus the son of Mary, the Messenger of Allah'—but they killed him not, nor crucified him, but so it was made to appear to them" (Qur'an 4:157). There are two versions to understanding the words of the problematic clause *wa-lakin shubbiha lahum* ("but so it was made to appear to them"), which is sometimes also translated as "but so *he* was made to appear to them." The first version is that the crucifixion—it—was apparent to them but it never really happened. The second is that the Jews killed someone else—he—who was made to appear to them to be like Jesus. In any case, this verse has generated a variety of views and speculation by Qur'anic exegetes as to what actually happened. Let us explore only four theories.

The first, and by far the most popular, of the theories is that of substitutionism. Someone else was crucified instead of Jesus. Qur'anic commentators over the years have put forth various possibilities. That it was Judas who was killed has been the most commonly cited, especially with the Arabic translation of the Gospel of Barnabas—which Christians believe is a pseudepigraphal work of the sixteenth century—in the early twentieth century, which suggested the same. Others proffered as candidates for this substitution include Peter, Simon of Cyrene, a young man, a Roman soldier named Titawus, and an associate of the Jews. The second theory is that nobody was crucified and that the crucifixion never actually took place. This is based on the remaining of the verse ("and those who differ therein are full of doubts, with no [certain] knowledge, but only conjecture to follow, for of a surety they killed him not" [Qur'an 4:157]), which implies that even if the Jews wanted to and thought they had crucified Jesus they had not been able to do so. The following verse—"Nay, Allah raised him up unto Himself; and Allah is Exalted in Power" (Qur'an 4:158)—points to what actually happened to Jesus, according to the Qur'an, on that fateful night. Thus, it looks like Muslims believe that God raised Jesus up—not so much from the dead but directly to heaven and before his capture—even before the crucifixion was allowed to take place. A third theory, quite similar to the second, put forward by the rationalists Mutazilites, is that when the religious officials came in search of Jesus he was mysteriously whisked off to heaven. They then pointed to another crucified criminal and spread the news that Jesus had indeed been crucified. For the officials, whose job it was to provide religious guidance to the community, so the theory goes, that deception was better than having the disciples believe in the fact of Jesus' resurrection and ascension into heaven. A fourth theory comes from the Ahmadiyyah sect, founded by Mirza Ghulam Ahmad in the nineteenth century but considered by mainstream Muslims as heterodox. They put forth the swoon theory, where Jesus is believed to have indeed been crucified, but he swooned or fainted on the cross and survived the torment. When his body was handed over to Joseph of Arimathea, it was actually still alive and his disciples saved him when they applied special ointment to his body. He subsequently regained strength and travelled to Kashmir, where he later died of old age.

As can be seen from the various theories above, the Muslim theologian's starting point is that Jesus could not have been killed. Whether it was by substitution, by deception, or through an illusion, the main assertion of the Muslim is that Nabi Isa did not die on the cross. Instead, what happened was that Allah saved him from his enemies and took him up to heaven where he remains. From the teachings of the *Hadith* literature, Muslims further believe that it is Jesus who will come back in the end times in pursuit of the *al-Dajjal* (Antichrist) while restoring peace and order to the world and to all of humanity. These beliefs about Jesus, of course, are premised on faith in the revelation of the Qur'an, resulting in the rejection of the Christian doctrine of redemption through Christ as well as the Christian doctrine of original sin.

Methodological Issues in Theological Dialogue

The discussion above clearly shows that the Islamic critique of the two doctrines of original sin and redemption through Christ does raise serious questions to the Christian faith. But before attempting a response, it would be necessary to outline some methodological guidelines in the interfaith dialogue of theology. Taking seriously the fact that the different religions are integrated and self-sufficient entities, dialogue should entail mutual respect, sharing, and listening. No matter how different the religions are, the dialogical commitment is that we ought to see them as complementary, attempt to find some common ground, and be open to learning from one another. In this respect, it is probably not appropriate if we employ the constructs of our own tradition to interpret the efficacy or evaluate the authenticity of another. If Christians do not wish to have their teachings interpreted against the Qur'anic injunctions and Islamic methods, Muslims will certainly not want the reverse to happen to them either. This is the methodological rule that should be upheld in any dialogue involving one another's theology. It is the golden rule doctrine of "do not unto others what you do not want others to do unto you" (Confucius, *Analects* 15:24).

Specifically, in our discussion on the Muslim's appraisal of original sin and redemption, the Christian might suggest that the problem is because Muslims seem to be interpreting Christian doctrines by taking, as starting point, their own Islamic theology, after which Christian Scriptures are used to substantiate the Muslim's understandings of the doctrines. Of course, the same charge can also be leveled at Christians as they are also inclined to begin with Christian theology when attempting to understand any beliefs and, if needed, will proceed to proof-texting with scriptural sources, including verses from the Bible or the Qur'an or any other sacred texts. It is also obvious that while the Qur'an does have a lot to say about what Christian Scriptures teach, it does not exactly say the same thing. This is because Islam has its own internal logic based on its own epistemology, metaphysics, and hermeneutics. These obviously differ significantly from those of Christianity, which also has its own epistemology, metaphysics, and hermeneutics. These differences between the religions are bound to yield different questions and arrive at different conclusions.

Another methodological error to avoid is the temptation on the part of Christians to examine the Qur'anic injunctions from a historical-critical perspective and allege that the Qur'an itself was somehow influenced by the Docetist and Gnostic views that Christians have long dismissed. In other words it would be methodologically inappropriate to suggest that some of the contradictory Qur'anic views are but borrowings from Christian Scriptures except that they were misinterpreted. Instead, it is necessary that Christians accept that the Qur'an should be read and interpreted on its own terms and not through Christian lens. However different it may be from the biblical accounts, the Qur'anic accounts of the creation myth or of Jesus, son of Mary, has to be appreciated on its own terms.

Similarly, it would be tempting for Muslims to understand the person of Christ and the Christian doctrine of redemption through the lens of

Islam and the Qur'anic accounts. The problem here is that such comparisons often confuse and misinterpret the texts of each other's scriptures and read them as representing historical assertions that have to be accepted by all parties. The reality is that scriptural texts are theological assertions and cannot be regarded as historical and empirical truth. It would be an error therefore to take the assertions of another's sacred text to substantiate the theology of one's tradition, just as it would be an injustice to use the assertions of one's own sacred text to disprove the theology of another tradition. This is not to suggest that we give up our texts; we should not. Instead, we have to take scriptures seriously in what they say but not use one as a criterion to judge the truth or authenticity of the other. As both parties' texts are in the realm of theology, they cannot be juxtaposed against one another as if representing objective historical data.

To be sure, doctrines and beliefs have to be kept within the realm of theology, not history, and treated as faith rather than empirical claims. Faith claims make sense only within one's own community while sounding absurd to those without. They can neither be assessed through empirical means nor deduced through syllogistic or reasoning processes by those who do not share the faith. A commitment to the faith is necessary for the claim to be appreciated. This is doing no more than recapitulating Anselm's definition of theology as *fides quaerens intellectum* (faith seeking understanding). Transposing or imposing one's own faith claims and theological assertions onto another's system and insisting that they be regarded as empirically factual or rationally sound would be unfair at best but could also amount to a gross manipulation of truth. Each faith claim has to be appreciated and evaluated from within its own tradition. Each has its own criteria and standards, with its own verification process performed by those recognized as legitimately qualified to make such assessments.

St. Bonaventure's thesis of the three realms of knowledge is instructive here. He talks about the three modes or three eyes by which we know the world and its realities: (1) the *eye of flesh* refers to our perception of the external world of space, time, and objects, all of which are in the realm of the empirical; (2) the *eye of reason* refers to how we appreciate philosophy, logic, and the mind itself, all of which are in the realm of the intellect and mind; and (3) the *eye of contemplation* refers to our knowledge of transcendent and spiritual realities, all of which are in the realm of faith and contemplation. Theological claims fall within the realm of transcendent realities and are thus appraised with the eye of contemplation and not the eye of flesh or the eye of reason. Thus, the accounts and teachings of one's scriptures and tradition cannot be used as historical or philosophical data to assess the veracity of another tradition through empirical or rational means. That would be a categorical error, which, unfortunately, continues to be committed by a number of people, both Christians and Muslims, who are engaged in the task of the dialogue of theology. It is with these methodological rules in mind that the present chapter will continue the Christian-Muslim dialogue and propose possible means for a mutually enriching engagement on the doctrines of original sin and Christian redemption.

Foundations of Christian Faith

In discussing the doctrines of original sin and Christian redemption, Christians could begin by acknowledging to Muslims from the outset that the former is interpreted through the lens of the latter. We know this for a fact—not only spiritually but also empirically—as even if the Jewish tradition shares the same Adamic myth, mainstream Judaism does not have the doctrine of original sin. In other words it is clear that the doctrine of original sin is a Christian teaching even as its source is a religious myth derived from Jewish Scriptures. The *Catechism of the Catholic Church* (CCC)[2] begins the discussion on the fall of our first parents with these words: "We must therefore approach the question of the origin of evil by fixing the eyes of our faith on him who alone is its conqueror" (CCC 385). The first article of the section dealing specifically with original sin is emphatic that "we must know Christ as the source of grace in order to know Adam as the source of sin" (CCC 388). Thus, appreciating the Christian understanding of original sin would necessarily entail an appreciation of the Christ-event and especially the experience of the early Christians.

This is because Christianity's starting point is the early disciples' encounter with the Nazarene named Jesus and their faith in him. It is their experience of Jesus' life, teaching, ministry, and especially his passion

---

2. *Catechism of the Catholic Church* (Vatican City: Libreria Editrice Vaticana, 1993), http://www.vatican.va/archive/ENG0015/_INDEX.HTM.

and death on the cross that gave rise to what they subsequently taught and that today Christians have access to by reading the Christian Bible and drawing on the apostolic tradition. The early Christians, of course, were also interpreting their experience of Jesus of Nazareth in light of the Hebrew Bible, which was their own sacred scripture. In particular, the horrendous suffering and death of Jesus had to be interpreted in the light of the theology of Christ as Messiah before it began to make sense and empower the disciples. This Jesus whom they had encountered while he walked the Mediterranean and who was crucified and died was the same Jesus whom they were continuing to experience as the risen Christ. The encounter was liberating, leading them to believe, as clearly expressed in the words of the apostle Paul, "Christ died for our sins in accordance with the scriptures" (1 Cor 15:3). Death, however, was not the end as the disciples, under the leadership of Peter, also proclaim his resurrection: "God raised him up, having freed him from death" (Acts 2:24).

It was in the context of this Easter or resurrection faith that the early Christians then went on to interpret other scriptural texts, including the book of Genesis. Attempting to understand their own sinful nature and also the prevalence of sin in the world, the creation myth and especially the fall of Adam and Eve constituted a rich source of theological data for reflection. In the letter to the Romans Paul spells it out this way: "Therefore, just as sin came into the world through one man, and death came through sin, and so death spread to all because all have sinned" (Rom 5:12). But, it must be mentioned hastily, Paul was pointing to this sinfulness in view of presenting the grace Christ had already brought: "For if the many died through the one man's trespass, much more surely have the grace of God and the free gift in the grace of the one man, Jesus Christ, abounded for the many" (Rom 5:15). In other words, Paul's assertion of Romans 5:12 was made with Romans 5:15 in mind. Hence, original sin can be appreciated only if one has faith in the redemption brought about by Christ.

Similarly, it was also in the context of their faith in the living Jesus that theologians of the subsequent centuries continued to offer reflections on the origins of sin and the brokenness of the world. Thus, from the first-century patriarchs such as Clement of Rome and Ignatius of Antioch to the Greek fathers such as Justin Martyr and John Chrysostom to the Latin fathers such as Tertullian and Cyprian of Carthage, Christian theologians postulated a variety of theories on the nature of sin and its origins. They did so in view of bearing witness to the redemption brought about by Christ Jesus, the Lord and Savior of the world (2 Pet 2:20). It is important also to note that these theories and theologies were articulated in the language and cultural frameworks of the time, including the employment of juridical categories.

It was not until Augustine, the bishop of Hippo in the fourth century, that any sustained and systematic development was made on the doctrine of *peccatum originale* (original sin), a term he himself coined. Reflecting on Hebrew Scriptures, especially against the backdrop of his own personal and licentious history, Augustine taught that the primordial sin of Adam and Eve is passed down through the generations by means of the lust and concupiscence involved in the act of procreation. Because all human beings inherit the guilt as well as the punishment incurred in this first Adamic sin, the whole of humanity is condemned. It was the free gift and grace of Christ that enabled some to be reconciled with God and to attain to salvation. This last sentence ought to be foregrounded in any discussion on original sin. Hence, the doctrine's purpose in shining the spotlight on human depravity is really in view of pronouncing the divine grace of goodness and blessing that is already available through Jesus Christ, whom Christians believe as the Son of God.

This, in a snapshot, is how one could proclaim the Christian faith and belief in the doctrines of original sin and redemption through Christ in light of the questions that our Muslim friends ask. Like Islam, the doctrines emphasize God's goodness and salvation rather than divine punishment or human wretchedness. The two doctrines, however, have to be read together. Concentrating on original sin without reference to Christian redemption is grossly misunderstanding the doctrine.

Underlying Concerns of Muslim Questions

As can be seen from the exposition above, the Christian's concern is always centered on Christ, whom Christians believe frees humanity from the bondage of sin. When our Muslim friends raise questions about original sin and Christ's role in redemption they are not questioning the faith dimensions of Christianity but more the scientific possibility or historical viability of such claims. In other words they should not be construed as polemics but more disagreements in the realm of the eye of the flesh and the eye of reason. On the other hand, in their questions one can discern some underlying theological concerns that Muslims share in general. It is important that Christians appreciate these concerns, as they highlight the central tenets of Muslim faith and so can contribute to and enhance Christian-Muslim understandings. It is to these that we shall now turn.

Unlike Christianity, which has as its focus Christ, and Buddhism, which focuses on the teachings of the Buddha, Muslims conceive of Islam as centered not so much on Prophet Muhammad or any particular person but on the one and only God whom they refer to in Arabic as *Allah*. Muslims believe that Islam is the primordial religion of all humankind. It is the religion not of any human founder but of Allah, the transcendent Reality whose absoluteness can be neither compared nor compromised. This is one dimension of faith that Muslims are emphatic about and attempt to safeguard when they raise questions about the Christian doctrines discussed above. How can God, who is so absolute, be affected by the disobedient act of mere creatures such as Adam and his spouse? How can God, who is transcendent but at the same time infinite compassion and mercy, not forgive the sin of our first parents, especially after they repented? Sin, after all, is not all that serious. Except for the sin of apostasy or *shirk* (associating something or someone with Allah), all other sins can easily be forgiven.

To these concerns Christians should unhesitatingly proclaim that Christianity too is unrelenting about the supreme nature of God's transcendence. On that score there is absolutely no divergence. It should also be quickly impressed upon Muslims that, in the God-human relationship, the doctrine of original sin is addressing the human side of the equation and imputing nothing about God. God remains God, unqualified and unaffected. But the Yahwist authors of Genesis 2–3 who wrote the creation myths were trying to make sense of the misery they were experiencing existentially in the world and especially the sinful nature of humankind. This is how contemporary mainstream biblical scholarship understands the myth of Adam and Eve. Thus, the Adamic myth has an anthropological and theological aim, not biological or cosmological. Essential to the theology of original sin is that the brokenness of the world is a result of human sin and by no means intended by God. The doctrine is, therefore, not a scientific or historical assertion about how a particular sin came about but serves as a myth or symbolic narrative to help explain the existential reality of human sinfulness, then and now.

Myths are articulations of faith experience and are not meant to be taken literally as empirical statements. So, there is no question about the genetic inheritance of sin. Moreover, the Christian tradition does not in any way refer to the transmission of guilt. The *Catechism of the Catholic Church* insists that "original sin is called 'sin' only in an analogical sense: it is a sin 'contracted' and not 'committed'—a state and not an act" (CCC 404).

With regard to the doctrine of redemption through Christ, underlying the Muslim's questions are concerns over the understanding of Jesus, on the one hand, and the understanding of God, on the other. But, most of all, their worry is with how Christians have conceptualized the Jesus-God relationship. Because Christian redemption is premised on Jesus as the God-Man, the major concern of Muslims is with the Christian doctrine of the divinity of Jesus. The doctrine is blasphemous to Muslim ears, as the Qur'an has asserted clearly: "They do blaspheme who say: '(Allah) is Christ the son of Mary'" (Qur'an 5:72) and "It is not befitting to (the majesty of) Allah that He should beget a son" (Qur'an 19:35). Islam unequivocally rejects any allusion to Jesus as God or Son of God. The absolute and oneness of God or the doctrine of *tawhid* (monotheism) cannot be compromised: "Say: He is Allah, the One and Only; Allah, the Eternal, Absolute; He begetteth not, nor is He begotten; And there is none like unto Him" (Qur'an 112:1-4).

But it is useful to be reminded here that Islam has no problem with Jesus' unique and special status. Like the Christian Bible, the Qur'an describes him as having a virgin birth, the power to perform miracles, the ability to heal the sick and raise the dead to life, the divine mission to preach to the people of Israel, and a host of other traits characteristic of one chosen by God. This is the portrait of the Muslim Jesus that Christians should be aware of. Jesus is highly revered in the Islamic tradition. Where Islam differs radically from Christianity, however, is what happened between the time of his arrest by the contemporary religious and civil authorities and the time of his ascension into heaven. For Muslims, God would not have forsaken God's chosen prophet (Ps 37:28) and, as we saw earlier, did indeed protect Jesus from the plot of his enemies. This theory is implicitly found in the Qur'an: "And (the unbelievers) plotted and planned, and Allah too planned, and the best of planners is Allah" (Qur'an 3:54). Thus, Muslims are safeguarding God's providence and the uniqueness of the Prophet Jesus—but one who is fully human, like all other prophets—when they raise questions about Jesus' death by crucifixion and the doctrine of redemption.

222 Theologies and Praxes

As a response to these concerns, it would help if Christians refrained from using quotes from the Christian Bible to refute the Qur'anic views of Jesus. It would be an exercise in futility anyway as, according to the Islamic tradition, the Bible as a record of God's Word to Jesus had been tampered with by his followers and so parts of it are erroneous. Besides, both parties' scriptural texts are in the province of religious claims and are therefore transcendent knowledge that can be discerned and accepted only through the contemplative or spiritual eye of faith. Instead, to the charge of what is known as "lesser polytheism," Christians should assert unequivocally that they too believe in only one God, as evidenced in the Nicene Creed, which Christians continue to profess. For Christians, it must be emphasized, God's relation to the world, *ad extra*, is unambiguously unique and one. While firmly entrenched in monotheism, Christians also believe that Jesus is more than just a prophet. They believe that in the human person of Jesus, Christians see the human face of God. It is not as if Christians divinized Jesus but that it was God who revealed God's divine self in the human Jesus. Of course, Christians and Muslims alike would agree that no one can limit God's power; God chooses whatever mode or form to reveal the divine self, be it through human flesh or a scriptural text. If for Muslims God's revelation is through the Qur'an, for Christians, God has been revealed through the human person of Jesus. Moreover, the manner in which Christians proclaim Jesus' divinity does not in any way suggest a multiplicity of God. It is not an empirical or mathematical abstraction; instead, like everything else about God, it is spiritual and beyond simplistic human comprehension. It is accepted in faith that within the Godhead, *ad intra*, or the interior life of God there is Father, Son, and also Holy Spirit. Again, this does not suggest any familial generation whatsoever in God and cannot be understood in the human or carnal sense. Muslims may or may not agree with such explanations, but at least they ought to have a better understanding of what Christians really believe about original sin and Christian redemption.

Conclusion

As can be seen from the discussion above, there are radical differences between faith traditions, not only in their beliefs and practices, but also in the very way these arose. The difference is also fundamentally one of epistemology. Where Muslims see God's revelation as embodied in the Qur'an, Christians see the same as embodied in the human Jesus. These differences, in turn, shape their respective teachings and doctrines, as well as their understandings of each other's religion. It would be almost impossible if not irresponsible to assess the other's faith on the basis of one's own. Instead, the differences and distinctiveness invite us to rise above our egocentric ways of apprehending reality to an appreciation of each other's faith from a spiritual perspective. We are able to benefit from this only if the motivation is to learn and enhance our understanding of not only the other's faith but also our own. Thus, explorations need to focus on not only the similarities but the differences between the faiths as well.

Where might such a contemplation or appreciation lead? How can we eventually make sense of the differences? Essential to any attempt is the need to carefully discern the religious message being advanced, not so much based on the surface-level teachings, but more on what lies as the underlying concerns. At the end of the day Muslims and Christians must go beyond the historical data and scriptural texts of their respective religions and try instead to share in the commonality of faith. If Muslim-Christian dialogue is to be meaningful, it must be convinced that even as Christians and Muslims have followed different roads toward the goal of human fulfillment in God, the goal is one and the roads meet at many points.

Suggestions for Further Reading

Borrmans, Maurice. *Guidelines for Dialogue between Christians and Muslims.* Translated by R. Marston Speight. Mahwah, NJ: Paulist Press, 1981.

Fitzgerald, Michael L., and Robert Caspar. *Signs of Dialogue: Christian Encounter with Muslims.* Zamboanga City, Philippines: Silsilah Publications, 1992.

Michel, Thomas F. *A Christian View of Islam: Essays on Dialogue.* Edited by Irfan A. Omar. Maryknoll, NY: Orbis Books, 2010.

Omar, Irfan A., ed. *A Muslim View of Christianity: Essays on Dialogue by Mahmoud Ayoub.* Maryknoll, NY: Orbis Books, 2007.

Parrinder, Geoffrey. *Jesus in the Qur'an.* Oxford: Oneworld Publications, 1996.

12

Implications and Challenges of Religious Pluralism

Introduction

A Catholic priest visiting the United States was invited to preside at the morning Mass of the parish he was a guest at. It was the first few days of Lent and so during the homily he shared with the parishioners his experience: "When I was growing up in our village in Indonesia I knew it was Lent as mum would get up very early in the morning to prepare a hefty breakfast. We could smell the aroma of the spicy food being cooked from our bedrooms, and she would wake us up just before dawn so we could all have our meal with dad. We then went the whole day with just some snacks but dad would fast completely the entire day, going even without a single sip of water. Just after sunset we would gather at the dining table again and break the day of fasting together with a sumptuous meal." Later, at the breakfast table, the parish priest asked his visitor: "Do you guys fast that way during Lent? At most we abstain from meat and maybe fast on Fridays." The visiting priest replied: "Oh, I forgot to mention that mum is Catholic but dad is Muslim and so we fast the same way in Lent as we do in *Ramadhan*."

This chapter explores the implications and challenges to being Christian in a world that is becoming increasingly multicultural and multireligious. It will examine two phenomena that have arisen especially in the postmodern world and three areas of Christian ministry that have been deeply affected by the fact of religious pluralism. The first phenomenon to be explored is the practice of religious syncretism and the different ways in which people blend different beliefs and practices together as they develop their own spirituality. This will then be followed by a discussion on the phenomenon of multiple religious belonging among Christians who consciously embrace more than one religion at the same time. The challenges the new situation of religious pluralism poses to theological education, especially with regard to interfaith learning, will then be explored. Likewise, how Catholic educational institutions are dealing with religious and cultural pluralism not only within societies but also within their own institutions will also be interrogated. The final theme to be discussed is how the ministry of interfaith dialogue poses serious questions to the traditional understandings of the evangelizing mission of the church.

Religious Syncretism

Every religion considers its worldview, beliefs, and practices as absolutely true and completely self-sufficient. There is no need for an external source to supplement or complement it. Their believers should be able to attain the religious endpoint (be it salvation, union with God, liberation, *nirvana*, or *moksha*) that the religion teaches without the support of any other religious system. So it is generally unthinkable for people to profess more than one religion simultaneously. Not only is it unnecessary, it is also unlikely that people will want to identify with two different socio-religious groups at the same time. While this may be true in theory, the day-to-day reality is something else. Today, it has become perfectly acceptable and not altogether uncommon for people to openly identify with more than one religious tradition. One variation of this phenomenon is classified as religious syncretism, which stands for the blending of two or more religious systems together to establish a new entity that people then embrace as their own. Different circumstances give rise to the syncretistic phenomenon, some of it historical and others cultural. But for those living in today's context, the fact that religious pluralism stares them directly in the face is one reason for the rise of religious syncretism. Catherine Cornille spells this out bluntly: "In a world of seemingly unlimited choice in matters of religious identity and affiliations, the idea of belonging exclusively to one religious tradition or of drawing from only one set of spiritual, symbolic, or ritual resources is no longer self-evident. . . . Why search for answers to the fundamental questions of life in only one religion when so many alternative proposals by time-honored traditions are readily available?"[1]

The phenomenon of religious syncretism expresses itself in varying forms by different groups of people. A first group is represented by those who subscribe to the contemporary, postmodern syncretistic attitude of picking and choosing for themselves very specific religious myths and doctrines as well as techniques and rituals. These are usually selected on the basis that they fit nicely with the person's needs and personality and so are easily integrated into the person's spiritual practice. These practices, usually associated with the New Age movement, are generally eclectic in their spirituality and individualized in their structures. Without denying or demeaning such quests, it might be pointed out that there is the danger of the practice yielding to the consumer mind-set, which treats religion as mere goods to be consumed according to one's desires and will. Sometimes, while people in this group may claim to be practitioners of the beliefs and practices of several religions, they may have no association whatsoever with the community or history of the religious traditions they are borrowing from or embracing. In such cases they can be regarded as those who "believe without belonging." This is the most common form of religious syncretism that has come to the fore of many Western and modernized societies of the twenty-first century.

A second group that the West might classify under the religious syncretism category is represented by those for whom embracing more than one religion comes naturally because it is what most people in their communities do. This is common among peoples in various parts of Asia, where the practice of only one religion is sometimes more the exception rather than the rule. These cultures, in fact, endorse the practice of embracing different religious systems at different junctures of one's life. The Japanese, for example, have a common refrain to characterize their personal religiosity: "Born Shinto, marry Christian, and die Buddhist." They identify themselves with a specific religious tradition at specific moments of their life when specific rites of passage are called for. The Chinese religion is an amalgamation of Confucianism, Taoism, and Buddhism, collectively termed the *San Jiao* (three teachings). These three

---

1. Catherine Cornille, "Introduction: The Dynamics of Multiple Belonging," in *Many Mansions? Multiple Religious Belonging and Christian Identity*, ed. Catherine Cornille (Maryknoll, NY: Orbis Books, 2002), 1.

teachings have, on account of the long history of mutual influence, been considered to be harmoniously integrated with one another so that today one cannot be a Confucian without at the same time embracing some Taoist or Buddhist beliefs and practices. Likewise, it is not uncommon to see Hindus from the Indian subcontinent praying in Krishna Hindu temples, offering devotions to Our Lady of Fatima in a Catholic Church, while also adopting some Buddhist practices all at the same time. The same scenario applies also to those of the indigenous traditions who even after converting to one of the world's religions, such as Christianity, continue with the practices of their former native spiritual tradition. These converts do not give up their indigenous practices, especially those of spirit and ancestor worship, as they see them as complementary to their Christian faith. The examples above are by no means anecdotal but represent the norm of the respective societies and appear perfectly natural to their practitioners. This is because religion is generally regarded as not mutually exclusive to one another but as specialized functions responding to the different needs and situations of people's lives. What in the West is classified as different religions (e.g., Taoism, Confucianism, and Buddhism) are experienced by the practitioners as a single blended coherent entity that has no doctrinal or theological barriers.

A third group that also loosely falls under the category of religious syncretism is represented by those born into interfaith families where their parents have brought them up according to the rituals and practices of both traditions. Like most others who are born into and brought up in the religion of their parents, they probably did not consciously choose to belong to both the traditions or even to either of them. They have, however, grown up becoming naturally accustomed to and at home with the beliefs and practices of both traditions. Moreover, what is important is that they see the practices of both the religious traditions as being in harmony with one another and have, in fact, seamlessly integrated them into their own spiritual life.

Multiple Religious Belonging

Beyond religious syncretism but closely resembling it, there is also the phenomenon known today as multiple religious belonging, sometimes called double religious belonging or multiple religious identities. We are not talking here about adherents of different religions engaging with one another in an interfaith dialogue of spirituality where they experience one another's religious practices while keeping their respective religious identities distinct and intact. We are talking about Christians who consciously commit themselves to another tradition and not only accept but also incorporate some of its teachings and practices into their own spiritual life. For example, a Christian may convincingly accept the Hindu belief in reincarnation as well as engage in the Buddhist practice of *Vipassana* or Zen meditation and fully commit to being a practicing and faithful Christian. Many of these practitioners openly claim they are Hindu-Christian or Buddhist-Christian, while others simply describe themselves as "hyphenated" Christians. They believe it is not only possible but even necessary to accept the teachings and practices of more than one religion, as hybridity enriches rather than confuses their Christian living. For some, embracing another religion is a necessary consequence of a radically enhanced and enlarged vision of their life of faith. This means that they are not delving into another religion because of uncertainty or doubts about their own Christian identity or that they are disillusioned with its institution or ignorant of its teachings. On the contrary, it is precisely because their knowledge has been so deepened that they feel compelled to discover the truths of their Christian faith in another tradition. In other words, it is their firm belief that the revelation and salvation brought about by Jesus can also be found in the other religions that is prompting them in their spiritual quest to look beyond the boundaries of the church to simultaneously embrace another religion.

While the phenomenon of multiple religious belonging seems to be prevalent among adherents of a number of religious traditions, it is problematic specifically for religions that demand an exclusive commitment, in particular the monotheistic faiths of Judaism, Christianity, and Islam. Citing Cornille again, "The more encompassing a religion's claim to efficacy and truth, the more problematic the possibility of multiple religious belonging. Conversely, it thus seems that the idea of belonging to more than one religion can be tolerated only when and where a religion has accepted the complementarity of religions."[2] That accounts for why it is easier for Christians who embrace another religion, say Hinduism,

---

2. Ibid., 2.

to proclaim themselves as hyphenated Christians, i.e., Hindu-Christians. Hinduism has no problem welcoming the Christian even if its tradition is but an adjective or add-on to the Christian's identity and by no means a replacement. Hindus are generally open to accepting the complementarity of religions and so are open to the phenomenon of multiple religious belonging. The reverse, however, is not always true. When Hindus embrace Christianity they are usually expected to renounce their previous religion, since Christianity has no space for more than one commitment. In other words, Christianity expects that the Hindu replaces Hinduism with Christianity and not merely add on elements of Christian practice into the person's Hindu faith and identity. This is because Christianity is by nature an exclusive religion as compared to Hinduism, which is generally more inclusive. Having said that, it is also a reality that religions that are by nature nonexclusive can be transformed into becoming exclusive through socio-political influences, especially in the event of protracted competition with an exclusive religion such as Christianity, as is the case with Hinduism in India or Buddhism in Sri Lanka.

Historically, the practice of double religious belonging was common and almost represented the norm among the Christians of the early church. The immediate disciples of Jesus were all Jews and so were practitioners of the religion of Judaism. That means, as faithful Jews, they continued with their temple worship and, as newborn Christians, they commemorated the Last Supper together at home: "Day by day, as they spent much time together in the temple, they broke bread at home" (Acts 2:46). There was nothing unusual or unnatural about the double religious practices, as they were Jewish Christians. It was only after extended periods of conflict and enmity with their fellow Jews—who accused them of being a deviant sect for believing in Jesus as the Messiah—that the early Christians began to separate themselves completely from their parental Jewish religion. They then evolved into a distinctive religious community independent of Judaism and began shunning its practices as well. Subsequently, as the church grew, most of its converts were Gentiles who had no association with Judaism, and so the problem of dual religious belonging was no longer an issue since the converts were simply expected to renounce their previous pagan religious practices in order to become Christians.

Fast-forward two thousand years and we are now dealing with the phenomenon of multiple religious belonging again as it is being practiced by not a few members of the church rather openly. Reference here is to those who consciously opt for another religion on top of their own Christian faith, mostly after a period of intense searching and reflection. The recognized pioneers of this multiple or dual religious practices are the European missionary monks to Asia. Among the more well-known are the French Benedictine Henri Le Saux, who took on the Indian name Swami (priest) Abhishiktananda, and the English Benedictine Bede Griffiths, who went by the name of Swami Dayananda. They immersed themselves deeply into the study of Hinduism and developed a form of monastic life based on the Indian tradition, even to the extent of adopting the saffron garments of an Indian *sannyasi* (ascetic) for their attire. While living practically as Hindu monks, they remained committed Christians and Catholic priests and, in fact, continued to celebrate the sacrament of the Eucharist. They tended to be looked upon by Hindus as Christian and by the Christians as Hindu. Indeed, they represented Hinduism when engaged in dialogue with Christians and represented Christianity when engaged in dialogue with Hindus. That they were able to do that is because they were firmly rooted in both the Christian and Hindu traditions, were knowledgeable in both their teachings and doctrines, and were committed to bridging the gap between them. This is what is entailed in multiple religious belonging.

Theological Education and Interfaith Learning

If Christians are already engaged in the practice of religious syncretism and multiple religious belonging, those undergoing training to serve the Christian communities should be prepared to at least deal with the basic reality of religious pluralism. This is one of the more pertinent implications for the church's ministries as it strives to find its place in the contemporary world that is becoming increasingly multireligious. Gone are the days when Christian pastors and ministers worked only with their own Christian flock without having anything to do with those outside the boundaries of the church. A parish priest today might have an *imam* (Muslim religious leader) from the mosque across the street coming to enter into a covenantal relationship; a Christian minister serving as a hospital chaplain might have to attend to a sick call from a Buddhist patient or assist in end-of-life care for a member of the Sikh community; a religious education teacher of a Christian school might have Hindu students asking questions about how Jesus is related to the other *avatars* (incarnation of a deity); a Christian social worker of the diocesan justice and peace commission may be asked to collaborate in an interfaith prayer service in support of asylum seekers. Or some members of the pastor's own congregation might be practicing different forms of yoga or Taoist ritual healings or have children in interfaith marriages or be assigned to work in a Muslim-majority nation. It is in view of these realities that every Christian pastor or minister being trained today should be sufficiently equipped with the necessary skills and knowledge to at least understand other religions as well as discuss interfaith issues appropriately. In short, interfaith learning is essential if the Christian minister wishes to be relevant in the contemporary multireligious world and especially if they have a role to play in the public life of their respective societies.

While the contextual realities seem to augur well for the serious engagement with religions other than Christianity, the practical reality is that not all Christian seminaries and schools of theology actually incorporate interfaith learning into their educational curricula. Those that do often place it as an appendix, relegated to an elective or optional course, attended to only after all the required courses have been fulfilled. This is partly because seminaries serve their sponsoring churches, where the immediate need is for trained personnel to take charge of congregations and the related Christian ministries. There are specific needs that are urgent in different contexts. In the global North this often means arresting the decline in church membership or strengthening the church's outreach aimed at attracting the unchurched into their communities. In the global South, especially where Christians are a tiny minority, concerns with protecting their religious rights and very existence often supersede any form of outreach to the religious other for the purpose of mutual learning. It is not surprising, then, to find interfaith learning relegated to the back burner in seminary formation.

In some institutions, however, the study of the world's religions is a required course, especially for those training to become missionaries in countries where religions other than Christianity predominate. Some of these courses are oriented toward helping the missionaries understand the other religion in view of being better adept at proselytizing its members for the purpose of bringing them into the church. But this is not what is meant by interfaith learning, which is aimed at opening the Christian's mind and heart in order to recognize more clearly that God is already present in the other religions. In other words, interfaith learning is meant to encourage Christians to cultivate more positive attitudes toward their neighbors of other faiths and to interact enthusiastically with them despite knowing that they have no intention of becoming Christian. Religious neighbors are then viewed not so much as competitors or targets of the church's evangelism but as partners and co-pilgrims in the journey toward God and God's kingdom. This is a very new ministry, with equally new theological presuppositions. Mutual learning and mutual witnessing are the order of the day. This is where the challenge lies, as not all Christians believe they need to be witnessed to or have anything to learn from their religious neighbors. Suffice it to say that the debate surrounding the need for interfaith education and interfaith dialogue continues. Unlike mission and evangelism, the history of interfaith dialogue is brief, and the benefits and incentives for putting it into motion are often less than obvious.

But this is not to say that nothing whatsoever has been done in the area of interfaith learning in seminaries and theological institutions. There are several models of learning that have been developed by different institutions, and they are generally differentiated by the levels of complexity. The most basic and perhaps most common model is to have a singular course on the world's religions. Some seminaries may have a more focused study on only one of the world's religions, especially if they are located in a context where there is a dominant religion (e.g., Islam in Algeria or Hinduism in Nepal or Buddhism in Myanmar). These courses could include an assignment requiring students to visit a place of worship of the other religion and engage in dialogue and collaboration with its adherents.

A second model is to offer a course such as the "Christian theology of religions," which is essentially an inward look into the Christian faith to examine its attitudes toward the religious outsider. Other courses addressing Christian theological and doctrinal positions with something to say about other religions go by titles such as "theology of interfaith dialogue" or "comparative theology" or "history of interreligious dialogue."

A third model is one that is integral in approach. Instead of creating new courses to be added to the already packed curriculum, this model encourages lecturers to integrate interfaith learning and the study of the world's religions into their existing courses. Some integrate into their core curriculum an aspect of interfaith learning, and some require students to begin the semester with a weekend- or weeklong interfaith immersion program or participate in a weekly field ministry at an institution belonging to religions other than Christianity. Travel programs where theological students go for extended visits to a culture and context that is predominantly Hindu or Muslim or Buddhist have also constituted forms of this integration process. Another form of integration of interfaith learning is where individual lecturers strive to explore aspects of their theological discipline from an interfaith perspective. Thus, the lecturer for the church history course dedicates a session or two to examining the church's positive interactions with the Muslim community during the time of the Crusades or in the colonial era; the liturgy class engages in a comparison between the Christian sacramental system and Hindu rites of passage; the theology professor discusses understandings of Christ from a Confucian or Muslim perspective or the images of God from a polytheistic or nontheistic perspective.

Another way for interfaith learning to be integrated into seminary formation is for the entire program to have an interfaith focus. This takes the integration a step further as all the courses would then be structured from an interfaith perspective. The course on revelation or the course on scriptures, for example, would discuss not only Christian revelation or scriptures but also the Islamic, Buddhist, and Hindu perspectives of the same. The mysticism course would look at Sufism and Kabbalah aside from Christian, Sikh, Jain, and other forms of the mystical tradition. The ethics course would be in the main comparative, as it explores the various aspects of ethics from a truly interfaith perspective.

Finally, perhaps the most radical model for interfaith learning is where the seminary itself becomes interfaith. This is usually brought about by twinning arrangements or mergers between a Christian seminary and one or more formation institution of another religion, such as a Jewish theological seminary or an Islamic college or an institute for Buddhist studies. Where this happens the Christian seminarian is then not only studying about another religion from a lecturer who is of that tradition but also doing so while sitting alongside other seminarians who are members of that tradition as well. Students and lecturers alike will then be benefiting from learning and articulating their views in the presence of their religious neighbors. Aside from the cognitive learning, they also learn to relate to and develop friendships with their classmates of religions other than Christianity. This would be the ideal of interfaith learning, an ideal that probably not many seminaries and Christian theological institutions would be prepared to embrace.

Identity of Catholic Schools in Pluralistic Cultures

Aside from interfaith learning in theological institutions, Catholic education in general has also to deal with the fact of cultural and religious pluralism. Like it or not, Catholic schools and universities are now finding themselves not only immersed in multicultural and multireligious communities but are also becoming multicultural and multireligious within their own institutions. While confession-specific, Catholic educational institutions all over the world are today serving more than just Catholic students or employing only Catholic teachers. Some Catholic schools are even headed by principals who are not Catholic or even Christian. In such contexts, questions about how the school can remain faithfully Catholic—who they are (identity) and what they are supposed to do (mission)—in today's globalized and pluralistic world have often been raised.

A surface-level response would be to focus on the explicit and externals. Now that Catholic people—principals, teachers, and students—can no longer be used as a measure of a school's Catholic identity, attention is somewhat shifted to Catholic things and activities. Hence, the outward display of Catholic signage and symbols, statues and crucifixes, and naming school buildings after saints become important. Likewise, Catholic activities such as school Masses and daily prayers, the singing of Christian songs and religious school anthems, and the celebration of Christian holy days and feast days as well as the teaching of catechism or theology are seen as markers of the school's Catholic identity. It may also be that Catholic identity is measured by the extent the school is of service to the parish. Hence, grade schools are expected to help in the sacramental preparation of the children and in strengthening the *leitourgia* (liturgical) and *koinonia* (communitarian) dimensions of church life, that is, the most basic *ad intra* tasks of the church's mission. High schools build on these to include the *ad extra* tasks such as the *kerygma* (proclamation or preaching) and especially the *diakonia* (service) aspects of being Christian. Colleges and universities do basically more of the same and are tasked with making better Christian disciples of the students.

While the abovementioned structures and programs may be relevant for a Catholic school or university with an enrollment that is still predominantly Catholic, questions need to be raised if many or the most of the students do not affiliate themselves with the Catholic tradition. In such contexts, continuing with such programs is meaningless at best, not to mention how it can serve as a measure of the institution's Catholic identity. Imagine a Catholic university claiming that the provision of daily Mass is part of its Catholic identity and mission but in reality only a handful of its thousands of students attend Mass. This is an especially important issue to address as many students who enroll in a Catholic school or university today do so not so much because of its specifically Catholic practices but simply because it offers an affordable and/ or well-rounded quality education. Testimony to this is the fact that the vision and mission statements of many Catholic educational institutions do not insist on the exclusively Catholic dimension but instead contain variations of the following values: (1) the pursuit of truth and academic excellence; (2) the provision of a total and holistic education; (3) an education that does not negate the religious and faith dimensions; (4) an educational environment that facilitates the building of community, a commitment to service, and the praxis of justice; and (5) an educational community that is welcoming of all regardless of creed, class, and culture. In short, Catholic schools and universities generally embrace a vision of a holistic and inclusive educational mission that is not narrowly defined but entails many aspects of evangelization, including the promotion of a culture of respect and dialogue with traditions other than Catholicism and Christianity.

How these institutions actually deal with the reality of cultural and religious pluralism, however, remains a challenge. Few models exist as circumstances have not been critical enough to warrant their development. But, by and large, most Catholic educational institutions have been quite accommodating to their students and teachers who come from other cultures and religions in many aspects of school life. For instance, there are accommodations in the area of language (for everyday communication and also the teaching of languages of minority cultures), dress- code (e.g., those who wear the hijab), hairstyle (e.g., Sikh students whose hair must remain uncut), food (menu offered in the school cafeteria or at school functions), celebrations and holidays (to include religious or cultural feasts such as Eid-al-Fitr, Divali, Vesak, Chinese New Year, etc.), school amenities (such as installing taps for Muslim ablution practices), and a host of other day-to-day needs and practices in schools. There are generally few problems in many of these accommodations, though the learning curve may be steep in the initial years when the first students who are not Christians or who come from another culture enroll.

But more needs to be done with regard to the specifically religious or faith dimensions of school life. Given that most Catholic schools are explicit that they are not only open to all, regardless of cultural and religious affiliation, but will also see to the holistic development of all their students, questions need to be asked about how the spiritual development of the students who are not Catholic are attended to. For sure, it would not be appropriate to impose the same religious education or catechetical formation on those who are not Catholic or Christian. Likewise, there needs to be a rethinking on the practice of daily Christian prayers and monthly Masses for all, especially since students who are not Christians will find themselves excluded from such practices. In short, Catholic educational institutions need to explore appropriate models for the expression of the faith life of their students where their student body has become increasingly multicultural and multireligious.

This call has been clearly articulated in the 2013 document by the Vatican Congregation for Catholic Education titled *Educating to Intercultural Dialogue in Catholic Schools: Living in Harmony for a Civilization of Love* (EID).[3] Acknowledging that contemporary society has become multicultural and multireligious and so needs to foster mutually enriching encounters, the introductory paragraph of the document asserts that "schools have a great responsibility in this field, called as they are to develop intercultural dialogue in their pedagogical vision" (EID introduction). It then goes on to state that "education, by its nature, requires both openness to other cultures, without the loss of one's own identity, and an acceptance of the other person, to avoid the risk of a limited culture, closed in on itself" (EID introduction). Addressing directly the criterion of Catholic identity, it states that "the goal of Catholic schools, in all their forms, is to live in fidelity to their educational mission, which has Christ

3. Congregation for Catholic Education, *Educating to Intercultural Dialogue in Catholic Schools: Living in Harmony for a Civilization of Love* (October 28, 2013), http://www.vatican.va/roman_curia/congregations/ccatheduc/documents/rc_con _ccatheduc_doc_20131028_dialogo-interculturale_en.html.

as its foundation" (EID 63). At the same time, the document avers that "the values of other cultures and religions must be respected and understood," advising that "schools must become places of pluralism, where one learns to dialogue about the *meanings* that people of different religions attribute to their respective signs" (EID 63, emphasis in original). In short, *Educating to Intercultural Dialogue in Catholic Schools* challenges Catholic schools to be at once faithful to their educational mission, with Christ at its foundation, and at the same time promote openness to other cultures and facilitate an education for dialogue.

In view of this, the document stresses that Catholic schools "are to be open to encountering other cultures. They have the task of supporting individuals so that each person develops his or her own identity in an awareness of its richness and cultural tradition" (EID 50). In other words, it is the school's responsibility to ensure that its students who are not Christians are equally supported in their religious growth. This is in accordance with the teachings of the Second Vatican Council, especially as taught by the document *Nostra Aetate* (NA), which calls on Catholics to "acknowledge, preserve and encourage the spiritual and moral truths found among non-Christians, together with their social life and culture" (NA 2). This is the challenge that Catholic schools and universities have to deal with in the contemporary context of cultural and religious pluralism, not only of their respective societies, but within the Catholic institutions themselves.

The Church's Evangelizing Mission and Interfaith Dialogue

Aside from questions about the identity and mission of Catholic educational institutions in multireligious contexts, questions have also been raised about the mission of the church itself in religiously plural societies. This is a major challenge to the church, especially in how it understands itself and its mission. In particular, tensions have arisen around the relationship between the evangelizing mission of the church and the ministry of interfaith dialogue. The jury is still out as to whether the church should prioritize mission over dialogue or whether dialogue ought to be the new mode of mission. Also bandied about is that the traditional understanding of *missio ad gentes* (mission to the nations) ought to steer toward *missio inter gentes* (mission among the nations), especially in contexts where the people of the "nations" are richly sustained and nourished by the great religions of the world. While the former considers persons of other religions as objects of the church's mission, the latter regards them as subjects of the one mission of God.

In part to resolve the paradox, the Catholic Church has clearly spelled out what mission means and distinguishes it from the ministry of proclamation. While the former is a holistic activity of the church that encompasses many ministries, the latter is what most people think of as mission understood in the narrower sense, that is, aimed at bringing the other to Christ and baptism into the church. The ministry of proclamation, therefore, is often seen as being in conflict with the ministry of interfaith dialogue. The post–Vatican II church weighed in on the debate and affirmed the importance and necessity of both proclamation and dialogue in the one evangelizing mission of the church. It states unambiguously that the mission of the church cannot be understood narrowly as aimed at only the conversion of the religious other. Instead, according to the 1991 *Dialogue and Proclamation* (DP) document of the Vatican curia, the evangelizing mission of the church is a "single but complex and articulated reality," and "the principal elements of this mission [are] presence and witness; commitment to social development and human liberation; liturgical life, prayer and contemplation; interreligious dialogue; and finally, proclamation and catechesis. Proclamation and dialogue are thus both viewed, each in its own place, as component elements and authentic forms of the one evangelizing mission of the Church. They are both oriented towards the communication of salvific truth" (DP 2).[4]

While the above is what the church teaches, the practical reality on the ground is that proclamation and dialogue continue to be held in a creative tension. To be sure, a lot of thinking and effort is still needed to ensure that they actually become the one evangelizing mission of the church. In view of the lack of resolution on the matter, it would not be helpful here to engage in further debate on the issues. Instead, what follows will be a case study that engages narrative theology to discuss the questions

---

4. Pontifical Council for Interreligious Dialogue, *Dialogue and Proclamation*: *Reflection and Orientations on Interreligious Dialogue and the Proclamation of the Gospel of Jesus Christ* (May 19, 1991), http://www.vatican.va/roman_curia /pontifical_councils/interelg/documents/rc_pc_interelg_doc_19051991_dialogue -and-proclamatio_en.html.

raised about Christian mission in religiously plural contexts. Its aim is to address the related critical and controversial questions by means of the theological method employed by Jesus himself, that is, through the use of parables. As in all parables, its intention is to raise even more questions for further discussion.

Parable of the Chief Buddhist Monk

The Venerable Dhammananda, chief monk of his country's Buddhist community, became seriously ill and was hospitalized. As he was in hospital attire only those who knew him personally would know who he was. One morning a Christian pastor paid him a visit and thought he was approaching no more than an elderly, bald-headed, sick gentleman. The pastor introduced himself as one who had come to bring the Good News of salvation, especially to those at critical junctures of their lives. He invited the elderly gentleman to receive Jesus as Lord and Savior. The Venerable Dhammananda accepted, was prayed over in the name of the Lord Jesus Christ, and received the blessings from the pastor. Later that evening, as the pastor was leaving the hospital, he passed by Dhammananda's room again. Imagine the shock when he saw a group of young Buddhist monks clad in saffron robes kneeling by the old man's bedside. They were receiving some sort of teaching and blessing from him. As the monks were leaving, the pastor asked one of them who the old man was. "He is our chief," came the reply. Troubled, the pastor rushed into the room and asked for forgiveness: "I am sorry, sir. I did not know you are the chief Buddhist monk. I did not mean to insult your religion. Had I known who you are I would not have invited you to receive the Lord Jesus Christ." Surprised, the Venerable Dhammananda said: "Young man, I don't know why you have come to apologize. You offered me something good and I accepted it graciously. I thank you for the wonderful gift and blessing of the Lord Jesus Christ. Go in peace!"

The narrator of this story was the Venerable Dhammananda himself. He related it at a Buddhist-Christian seminar, which means it was meant for both the Buddhist and the Christian communities. It conveyed a message to both parties. The Venerable Dhammananda, however, did not attempt an exegesis of the story. He left it at that. Everyone had a good laugh. It was indeed a parable, a story with a powerful religious lesson, with an unexpected twist, meant to provoke reactions and facilitate discussions. Some reflections on the theological issues and questions raised in such situations, however, might be useful for our purposes here. The first question to be raised would be on the theology of Christian evangelization in multireligious contexts. What guides our mission theology especially vis-à-vis persons of other religions? Many will probably refer to the biblical mandate or the Great Commission: "Go therefore and make disciples of all nations, baptizing them in the name of the Father and of the Son and of the Holy Spirit" (Matt 28:19). This is usually cited as the basis for the door-to-door approach in mission and evangelism. A follow-up question is weather the method of aggressive evangelization is appropriate in multireligious settings. Would Christians be equally welcoming of their children being visited by Muslim or Buddhist or Hindu evangelists at their hospital beds? The Golden Rule or ethic of reciprocity informs this question: "In everything do to others as you would have them do to you; for this is the law and the prophets" (Matt 7:12). To be sure, numerous charges have been made against Christian missionaries for employing less than ethical methods, some of which border on proselytism. The statement *Christian Witness in a Multi-Religious World: Recommendations for Conduct* is instructive here. Issued jointly by the Vatican's Pontifical Council for Interreligious Dialogue (PCID), the World Council of Churches (WCC), and the World Evangelical Alliance (WEA) after deliberations over a period of five years, it advises Christians not to use "inappropriate methods of exercising mission." Instead, it is emphatic that Christians should "build relationships of respect and trust with people of different religions" and "listen in order to learn about and understand others' beliefs and practices."[5]

Returning to the Venerable Dhammananda, while it is probably not a problem for him to be evangelized, one cannot say the same for his flock. The fact that the pastor apologized seems to indicate something was not altogether appropriate in his door-to-door missionary approach. Why did the pastor think it was fine if the "target" was simply an elderly, bald-headed man? This raises the issue of power, which would be obviously asymmetrical if the pastor were encountering a lay Buddhist, and an ill and vulnerable one at that. Questions have often been raised about

---

5. *Christian Witness in a Multi-Religious World: Recommendations for Conduct* (January 2011), http://www.vatican.va/roman_curia/pontifical_councils/interelg /documents/rc_pc_interelg_doc_20111110_testimonianza-cristiana_en.html.

the ethics of targeting the vulnerable and less educated segments of society for conversion, as they are more prone to falling prey to Christian allurement. Why not only convert those who can hold their own and make informed and thoughtful decisions about matters of religious conversion? The chief Buddhist monk would certainly fall into this latter category, enabling him to accept the pastor's gestures graciously since he was already well-grounded in his own faith. For him, grace, blessings and even baptism are transcendental entities, not economic. Accepting one does not necessitate the rejection of another or one's own. There is room for many. That was perhaps the message the chief Buddhist monk was imparting to his own Buddhist disciples: be open to others and to their blessings but, at the same time, be grounded in your own faith, for you don't have to give it up. Theologians may be tempted to see hints of double belonging here. Needless to say, such thoughts probably did not cross the mind of the Christian pastor as he would have viewed the Venerable Dhammananda's reception of the Lord Jesus Christ as an expression of exclusive faith.

Many other theological issues could be interrogated from this narrative of the chief Buddhist monk. Likewise, more discussions can also be engaged on how Christian missionary activity should be expressed in multireligious contexts. Suffice it to say that the implications and challenges of religious pluralism on how the church ministers in the contemporary world need to be taken seriously and given further thought.

Conclusion

How does the church engage in respectful interfaith dialogue while at the same time be in the service of its evangelizing mission? This remains a difficult theological problem that will probably not find a resolution anytime soon. Perhaps it would suffice at this stage to conclude the discussion as well as the book with a quote from Pope Francis on how we should be evangelizing:

> Interreligious dialogue and evangelization are not mutually exclusive, but rather nurture each other. We do not impose anything, we use no

underhand strategies to attract the faithful, but rather evangelize with the joy and the simplicity in which we believe and which we experience.[6]

Suggestions for Further Reading

Goosen, Gideon. *Hyphenated Christians: Towards a Better Understanding of Dual Religious Belonging.* Oxford: Peter Lang, 2011.

Gort, Jerald, Hendrik Vroom, Rein Fernhout, and Anton Wessels, eds. *Dialogue and Syncretism: An Interdisciplinary Approach.* Grand Rapids, MI: Eerdmans, 1989.

Kalu, Ogbu U., Peter Vethanayagamony, and Edmund Kee-Fook Chia, eds. *Mission after Christendom: Emergent Themes in Contemporary Mission.* Louisville, KY: Westminster John Knox, 2010.

Knitter, Paul F. *Without Buddha I Could Not Be a Christian.* Oxford: Oneworld Publications, 2013.

Roozen, David A., and Heidi Hadsell, eds. *Changing the Way Seminaries Teach: Pedagogies for Interfaith Dialogue.* Hartford, CT: Hartford Seminary, 2009.

---

6. "Evangelization and Inter-faith Dialogue Are Compatible, Pope Insists," *Catholic World News* (December 2, 2013), https://www.catholicculture.org/news/headlines/index.cfm?storyid=19832.

Index

CPSIA information can be obtained
at www.ICGtesting.com
Printed in the USA
LVHW020417120523
746755LV00001B/70

9 780814 684221